Dead Men Flying

Dead Men Flying
A Remembrance

Going to War in the A-4
Rolling Thunder Over Hanoi

Mike "Mule" Mullane

OK-3
PUBLISHING
Annapolis, MD

Published by OK-3 Publishing
262C Admirals Dr. #124, Annapolis, MD 21401

Library of Congress Cataloging in Publication Data
Mullane, Michael
Dead Men Flying, A Memoir

COVER DESIGN AND ART BY DON PURDY
BASED ON A PHOTOGRAPH BY CHUCK NELSON

To Beth and Ginger

Ginger who remembered me everyday in 1967 when she read the newspaper, clipped, and sent my favorite comic strips to me.

Beth who made it her business to be my anchor to windward in the twenty-first Century, making sure I did not drift away.

Contents

INTRODUCTION

remembrance . . .
The action of remembering; . . . the act of being remembered.

The Shorter Oxford English Dictionary, Fifth Edition.

This book is a remembrance of war. I wrote it so that I would remember what I tried to forget, and in the hope the men I flew with and what they endured will find a place in your memory.

Many have noted that everyone's war is limited to what they can see from their foxhole. My foxhole was a cockpit, but the point is no less valid. At its most granular, there are as many wars as there are survivors to remember.

It is also true that combatants do not fight for God, mother, or country. They fight for those who share their foxhole. As individual as our memories are, the experiences of threat, exhilaration, fear, brotherhood, and loss are shared by all combat veterans, regardless of their unit, battle, or war. These things are what bind us together and set us apart.

Memories are tricky things. Our brains are not video recorders. Our memories are subject to the distractions, avoidances, and emotional overlays of the moment. Up to a certain point, the more exciting the experience, the more indelible its memory. Past that point, the brain refuses to remember.

Old memories are also subject to the erosion, needs, and accretions of decades. Some of my memories of combat are as vivid today as they were in the 1960s. A few, the "safe stories," the stories I could tell, were inevitably refurbished in the retellings. Most things, however, I could not, would not remember.

I have done my level best to strip away the polish of stories retold, and to unearth the unremembered and suppressed. I have tried to recount as honestly as I can what I and my combat brothers experienced in the moment.

Although *Dead Men Flying* is primarily a memoir of the war from my cockpit, I am privileged to include firsthand accounts by several of my combat brothers. I am, however, solely responsible for the context and connective interpretations in which they are imbedded.

Mike "Mule" Mullane

PROLOGUE

A-4s of Attack Squadron 164 (VA-164), the Ghost Riders refueling from a buddy tanker after a mission.

July 21, 1967

HOW MANY *days has it been? . . . How many have we lost?. . . . We'll all be dead long before this is over.*

Forty minutes ago, I catapulted off the bow of USS Oriskany. Forty minutes ago, I catapulted off the bow of USS *Oriskany*. My A-4 Skyhawk is configured as a buddy tanker. My mission is to go in over the beach to refuel anyone who has a hole punched in his wing and needs fuel to get back to the aircraft carrier. So, for now, I am boring holes in the sky flying a racetrack pattern at 15,000 feet a few miles off North Vietnam.

Over the last week, I've flown my first seven combat missions, dropped more than five tons of bombs, and lost count of the number of times I've been shot at. But, for the moment, I am safe, with lots of time to think. Too much time to think.

I try to reconstruct shards of memory from the kaleidoscope of the last week. I come up with a number. *That can't be right.* I go through the losses again, and this time do the numbers on my kneeboard. Same count. Then I make a mistake: I project those numbers out for the rest of this cruise. I look at the grease pencil numbers on my kneeboard.

I am not going to make it out alive. My replacement's replacement has less than a 50-50 chance of surviving both cruises. If I stay—I die.

I am twenty-four years old.

Part I

GETTING THERE

Recruiting poster, 1953

CHAPTER 1

COURSE CORRECTION

Mother, Wayne, and me, circa *1944.*

WAYNE MULLANE was my father. He was also a Naval Aviator for the first twelve years of my life. Wayne entered the Navy flight training program in 1940, getting his wings just weeks before Pearl Harbor. He stayed in the Navy after the war, and so we were a Navy family.

I always called my father Wayne. My mother called him Wayne and so did all his friends, so I thought I should too. No one ever objected. My younger sisters and brother were more conventional and called him Dad.

I grew up among Naval Aviators. It was only natural that, as a boy, my stock answer to, "What do you want to be when you grow up?" was "A Navy pilot."

Even after Wayne left the Navy in 1956, I thought of us as a Navy family.

Somewhere in college I lose my way and decide I want to work for the State Department. When I graduate in 1964, I apply for graduate school. That summer, I am home basking in the glow of surviving the self-imposed academic brinkmanship of my undergraduate career. One afternoon when I am doing nothing, for no particular reason at all I remember, *I always wanted to be a Naval Aviator—If I don't do it now, I never will. I will never fly those beautiful airplanes that decorated the ceiling of every bedroom and dresser top I ever had. Get a master's in poly sci? What am I thinking?*

I tell my parents, "I want to join the Navy and fly."

"You sure?"

"Yes."

"Well, see if you can get in."

I apply. I am tested, poked, and prodded. While I am going through the process, Wayne tells me, "The government is buying more small-arms ammunition than it needs, a lot more. . ." He pauses. He always pauses. I look at him, waiting for him to go on.

"There will be a major war in Asia in the next two or three years."

"Oh?" My Grandpa Frank served in the cavalry during the first World War; Wayne and my Uncle Ev served during World War II;

Wayne, my Uncle Gene, and my cousin George served during Korea. I just stand there thinking, *This will be my war.*

Wayne has more to tell me, "Pilots who were in the training command when Pearl Harbor happened had it tough—they got a hurry-up version of the peacetime training with none of the benefits of the wartime experience."

This information rolls off me like water off a duck's back. I never get much past, *It's my turn.*

Wayne makes it clear I am not to tell my mother, or anyone else. "Okay."

Author being congratulated upon taking the enlistment oath and being accepted into the Navy Flight Program, July 1964.

I AM ACCEPTED and have an appointment to take the enlistment oath. I raise my right hand and swear:

I do solemnly swear that I will support and defend the Constitution of the United States against all enemies, foreign and domestic; that I will bear true faith and allegiance to the same; and that I will obey the orders of the President of the United States and the orders of the officers appointed over me, according to regulations and the Uniform Code of Military Justice. So help me God.

As I recite the words, I actually listen to what I am saying. I am surprised at the promises I am making. Before that moment, I really hadn't given it much thought.

WAYNE WILL BE RIGHT about the war, but off on the timing. I am twenty-one years old when I am sworn in at Naval Air Station (NAS) Los Alamitos in July 1964. I am ordered to report to NAS Pensacola, Florida, on September 19. Until then, I go home to wait.

On August 2, the news reports that North Vietnamese torpedo boats attacked a United States destroyer in the Tonkin Gulf. On August 4, American destroyers are attacked by North Vietnamese radar ghosts.

On August 5, two carrier aircraft from USS *Constellation* are shot down during the first retaliatory bombing raid on North Vietnam. Lieutenant, Junior Grade (Lt.j.g.) Richard Sather is killed when his propeller-driven A-1 Skyraider is hit by antiaircraft fire during his third dive bombing run against an oil storage depot near Than Hoa. Lt.j.g. Everett Alverez's jet-powered A-4 Skyhawk is hit while attacking torpedo boats in a place called Hon Gay. The newspaper says he ejected safely but was taken prisoner.

Everett Alvarez is still a POW when I get my wings in 1966; still a prisoner when I fly my first combat mission in 1967, and when I leave the Navy in 1969. I will graduate from law school in the spring of 1972—Alvarez will still be in the Hanoi Hilton.

I will be thirty years old, married, and living in Phoenix with my wife and two children on February 12, 1973, the day Everett Alvarez will finally be repatriated.

I will be divorced, remarried, and 42 years old when Richard Sather's body is repatriated in August 1985.

WHEN I GRADUATED from college, my father gave me his '60 Chevy as a graduation present. In September 1964, I plan to drive it from Fullerton, California, to Pensacola, Florida, for Pre-Flight training. During my senior year in college, I had met and dated a young woman from South Bend. I want to see her on my way to Pensacola, so I leave Fullerton on Wednesday, planning to arrive in South Bend Friday afternoon. I will leave South Bend and drive south to Pensacola on Sunday morning.

At the end of the first day of driving, I am not tired, so I press on, thinking any extra miles I make will add to my time in South Bend. I drive through the night and "wake up" in heavy traffic. The sun is shining. I am in a city. My last memory of the night before was of stopping for gas in Shamrock, Texas, on the Oklahoma border. Eventually, I figure out that I am driving through Saint Louis during the morning rush hour. I need gas and a rest room. I stop. When I get back in the car, I am wide awake.

I arrive in South Bend at two o'clock on Thursday afternoon. She is impressed. So am I.

CHAPTER 2

SCHOOL OF PRE-FLIGHT

I REPORT to the U.S. Navy School of Pre-Flight at NAS Pensacola twenty-five years after Wayne. I know the Navy, I know naval aviation, I know Naval Aviators, I know about flying—well, as much as anyone who has never flown anything can know. What I don't know about are Marine Corps gunnery sergeants, especially those who are drill instructors—the most awesome and fearsome creatures on God's green earth. It is into their tender care we are committed upon arrival at NAS Pensacola.

We are assigned a bunk in a "splinterville" temporary wooden barracks built for World War II. The next morning, we are herded outside, put in a formation, instructed to start on our left foot, and told to keep in step with the cadence and the man on our right. The man on the far right of each file keeps in step with the man in front of him.

There are several MarCads (Marine aviation cadets) in our class. They have been to Marine boot camp. Our drill instructor (DI) puts the MarCads in the front rank and starts us off. With the MarCads leading, we must look like a very short military parade followed by a gaggle of street cleaners.

The first few weeks are spent in the indoctrination battalion (Indoc), a condensed version of boot camp. Indoc is up early, calisthenics before dawn, shave, shower, room inspection, then classroom, military training, and physical training (PT) all day. The schedule is figured to the minute, including the time it takes to jog or march to the next event. After dinner, it is one hour of policing (cleaning) the barracks, a one-hour study period, and a half hour of "personal time" to write letters and prepare for the morning personnel and room inspections. Taps and then—reveille.

During the first week, I learn from Rich, the MarCad in our four-man room, that the worst thing that can happen to you is for the gunnery sergeant to learn your name. A day later, Gunny orders us to fall out in PT gear. We have done this every day, wearing our gray sweats to calisthenics on a grass field a block or two from our barracks. I put on my jock, sweatpants, sweatshirt, and gym shoes. Gunny jogs us past the exercise field to a hangar that has been converted to a gymnasium. He marches us inside, halts us, has us face left, and orders us to strip out of our sweats and stow them against the back wall and then fall back in. I am slightly bewildered.

Everyone else is smartly shedding their sweats, revealing their gym shorts and T-shirt. *Shit.* I approach Gunny, brace, and tell him I don't have anything on under my sweats. He locks his gaze on my caged eyeballs, takes a pace forward so the brim of his Smokey Bear hat is two inches from my nose. Without breaking his stare, I feel two fingers in the waistband of my sweatpants. Pull. The hat brim tips down, leaving me staring at the hat crown. The hat tips up. The waistband snaps back.

"What's your name, cadet?"

"Aviation Officer Candidate Mullane, Sir."

"Mullane, are you one of the two percent that never gets the word?"

"No, sir."

"We'll see. Fall in."

I turn to face the class. They are now back in ranks in their shorts and tees. I fall in, a gray lump amongst the blue-and-gold gym clothes.

I become our DI's favorite for a few days. Eventually, Gunny has cause to learn all of our names, so I am no longer the sole object of his attention. Not that he ever stops watching me or ever forgets my name. Gunnery sergeants are miracles of nature and the Marine Corps.

BEHIND THE INDOC BARRACKS there is a large paved area called the Grinder where we practice marching and close-order drill. Across the Grinder from our barracks is the ACRAC, the cadets' version of the officers' club—a bar and restaurant. On Friday evenings, the Grinder becomes a parking lot for the ACRAC. One Friday we arrive behind the barracks standing in something that is now recognizable as a military formation. Gunny gives us our instructions for the rest of the evening, while a small horde of young women stream past in short dresses and high heels. It is not for nothing that Pensacola is called the mother-in-law of naval aviation. A voice from the rear of the formation sings out,

"Give us liberty or give us death!"

Gunny pauses. "Who said that?!"

The same voice answers, "Patrick Henry, sir!"

Gunny continues with his instructions. We are dismissed. As always, we sprint for the barracks. I, and not a few others, glance wistfully over our shoulders at the small clouds of colorful dresses drifting toward the ACRAC.

We have been in the barracks less than five minutes, preparing for yet another room inspection, when the intercom crackles to life. It is the raspy voice of Gunny. "Now hear this. Now hear this. Cadet Patrick Henry will lay down to the sergeant's office on the double." *Click.* A long five seconds of silence. Then, I hear the pounding of boondockers going down the stairs at the double. Cadet "Patrick Henry" is about to introduce himself to Gunny.

During our parachute training in Pre-Flight, someone asks Gunny,

"If we do all the training, why can't we do a practice jump?"

"Because the Navy has already spent too much money on you to let you break your silly leg. Besides, you don't practice parachute jumping. You do it right the first time."

Gunny has a point. Up to now, my approach to education has been more or less planning to figure it out on the fly during classes and cramming for exams when the time comes. It occurs to me: *I have never had to do anything right the first time.*

OUR CLASS STARTS WITH NINETY. Most of us have our hearts set on flying. Those who don't, don't last the first week. They DOR—drop at own request. They don't count. They made a mistake coming here. For the rest of us, the learning curve is fast and steep, and not every lesson is in the syllabus.

During the second week, we are running in formation back from the obstacle course, headed somewhere for something. A kid from New Jersey veers out of formation, hands on knees, head down, mouth open, gasping for breath, pale as stationery. As I jog past, he collapses. "Halt!" Our drill instructor jogs over. A pause. From behind us he calls for two of our Marines by name. A moment later, they jog past, carrying the kid, turning at the corner toward the base hospital.

Gunny takes his place at our right rear with his slow glide walk.

"Forwarrrd—'arch! At the double—'arch!"

And off we go to somewhere for something, picking up the pace to make up for the lost time.

Later we hear they found a hole in the kid's heart. They patch it up, say "You're out of the program and out of the Navy," and send him home.

It breaks his heart.

I complete Pre-Flight and am commissioned as an ensign (equivalent to a second lieutenant) and move from the barracks to the bachelor officers' quarters, or BOQ.

CHAPTER 3

PRIMARY FLIGHT TRAINING

T-34 Mentor, circa *1985.*

AFTER PRE-FLIGHT, we are sent to Training Squadron One (VT-1) for primary flight training at Saufley Field, a few miles from Pensacola. In VT-1, we will actually fly an airplane. In 1965, VT-1 is equipped with the T-34 Mentor, a military version of the Beechcraft Bonanza with a two-place, fore-and-aft cockpit and a conventional "t" tail instead of the Bonanza's side-by-side cockpit and "v"-shaped tail.

Before we fly or even touch an airplane, we attend classes on the T-34's engine, hydraulic, electrical, and other systems. It is one thing to study generic engines as we did in Pre-Flight but entirely another to learn the nuts-and-bolts details of a particular engine.

In our spare time, we commit to tactile memory the location of every one of the hundred or so gauges, dials, levers, switches, and circuit breakers in the cockpit so we can touch each while blindfolded. We practice in mockup cockpits in the back of the ready room. We must also commit to memory large chunks of the *Naval Aviation Tactical and Operational Procedures* (NATOPS, pronounced "nay-tops) manual for the T-34, starting with all of the steps in each of the emergency and routine procedures.

There is a NATOPS manual for every aircraft type and model. It is a telephone-book-size volume, that includes the preflight inspection of an aircraft you intend to fly, and the engine shutdown procedures when you are done. In between are the pre- and post-start, pre-taxi, pre-takeoff, and landing checklists. There are emergency procedure checklists for low-altitude engine failures; high-altitude engine failures; emergency landings; landing gear failures; fire, full, and partial electrical failures; hydraulic failures; procedures for bailing out; ditching (water landings); lost aircraft procedures; and on, and on.

There will be no flying until we can sit in the cockpit and recite the emergency procedures letter perfect, touching each control, switch, and gauge in sequence—while blindfolded.

They take us out to an old T-34 that is chained to the ground. It has a large sheet of canvas suspended like a trampoline over the right wing alongside the fuselage. We are all dressed up in our newly issued flight suits, steel-toed flight boots, gloves, and helmets. There is an instructor in the back seat with the engine running at idle. One by one, we put on a dummy-parachute backpack, climb into the cockpit, strap ourselves in, and hook up the radio leads. When we are in, we close the cockpit. The instructor pilot in the back seat runs the engine up to a high-power setting. On a signal from an instructor standing on the left wing, we open the cockpit, unhook, unstrap, stand on the seat facing right, grab the sides of the canopy with both hands, and dive out of the cockpit through the engine slipstream onto the canvas. Now we know how to bailout should the occasion arise.

After two interminable weeks, ground school is finally behind me. We report to the ready room in the hanger. I pass the blindfold cockpit test. My name appears on the massive flight schedule blackboard with the syllabus painted on it in a horizontal grid. Students' names are chalked in vertically on the left. Your progress or lack thereof is chalked in every day for all to see.

ON MAY 27, 1965, I fly my first instructional flight with Lieutenant (Lt.) Moore, USN, in the backseat. Lt. Moore is taciturn and demanding. He demonstrates every step of everything on the syllabus for the hop, talking me through them as he does them. On the first hop, he demonstrates the preflight inspection, engine start, taxi, and pre-takeoff checklist. I have memorized them all from the NATOPS manual, but doing it is something else.

On the runway ready for takeoff, he tells me to "ghost" him on the controls: left hand on the throttle, right hand on the stick, feet on the rudders with just the lightest touch so I can feel what he is doing. He demonstrates the takeoff and climb out.

While we fly out to the practice area, he points out landmarks that will help me find it and find my way home to Saufley. Once in the practice area, he does a couple of clearing turns to check the airspace around us for other aircraft in our blind spots behind and below us. He returns the aircraft to straight and level. My turn.

In my headset, I hear: "You have the aircraft. Maintain our heading and altitude."

I thumb the mic button on the throttle: "Aye, aye, sir. I have the aircraft."

I feel his presence on the controls disappear. *I am flying this airplane!* My eyes are riveted on the altimeter and radio compass, watching the altitude and heading like a hawk.

"Get your head out of the cockpit."

"Aye, aye, sir."

"Look where we are pointed. Keep it pointed that way. Look where the nose is relative to the horizon. Keep it there."

"Aye, aye, sir."

"Now take a look around."

"Aye, aye, sir."

"Don't forget below us and behind us."

I lean and twist until I can look past his helmeted visage in the back seat and see the tail. Not that I am seeing what is there to see. I have yet to learn the trick of running my focus out to infinity and back in again to see everything from bird to airliner that is out there.

"Check the instruments."

"Aye, aye, sir."

I use the scan pattern I learned sitting in the dummy cockpits in the back of the ready room. Next, I get to try the mysteries of coordinating the stick, rudder, and throttle inputs necessary to produce a level turn—in both directions (different in propeller aircraft because of propeller torque)—and to try a couple of climbs and descents to predetermined altitudes at a constant air speed. Enough for the first hour.

Lt. Moore takes control of the aircraft, and I am back to ghosting on the controls as he talks us through entry into the landing pattern and the landing.

Keeping my head out of the cockpit, maintaining lookout, and still scanning the instruments at a regular interval does not come naturally. I have to work on them constantly until they become habits. Eventually they will constantly play in the back of my head like Muzak in the brain.

On the second hop, I do the takeoff. Lt. Moore is ghosting me on the controls, but I do it. Then I fly us out to the training area for more level flight, turns, climbs, and descents. When we are done, I fly us back to Saufley. He takes over as we approach the downwind end of the runway. I ghost the controls as he does the break, downwind leg, approach turn, final approach, and touch down. I stay on the controls as he brakes and turns off the runway. I am allowed to taxi back to the flight line.

On the third hop, the syllabus says I will land the aircraft. He directs me to an outlying airfield, demos a touch-and-go—a landing followed by full power as soon as the wheels touch down followed by an immediate takeoff. Then, it's my turn. He talks me through my first touch-and-go. Not great, but not too bad. My head is swimming with all the new things I am supposed to remember.

Next on the syllabus are more touch-and-gos and stalls. A stall is when the aircraft stops flying because the angle of attack between the wing and the air moving over it is too high to generate any lift. No lift, and you stop flying and start falling. Just before it stalls, the aircraft gets sloppy on the controls and shudders. The remedy is to add power and push the nose down. I commit these to memory the night before, visualizing each step, over and over. I have already figured out I need to do this stuff right—or else. Navy flight instructors are more demanding than the average college professor. And I am the only student in the cockpit/classroom. There is no place to hide, no one else to distract him. Besides, uncorrected stalls lead to crashes.

Once I learn to recognize an incipient stall and recover promptly, we move on to spins. If you don't correct a stall quickly, the aircraft will enter a spin where the nose falls steeply, and the aircraft literally falls in a corkscrew pattern. In the early days of aviation, spins were known as the "the death spiral." In the mid-1960s, the book says, "The spin is sudden and disorienting."

In the airplane, those are more than just words. The aircraft snaps into the spin. The horizon goes past like you are on a manic merry-go-round in free-fall. The ground rushes up at an increasingly alarming rate. Your instinct is to pull the stick back to go up, but that just makes it worse. To recover, you must push the nose down, increasing your plunge toward the earth, apply full opposite rudder to stop the corkscrew, and level the wings. When the spin stops, you must still hold the nose down, go to full power, and wait until you build back up to flying speed, and only then gently pull the nose back to the horizon. Pull too hard or give it too much rudder, and you risk snapping into a spin in the opposite direction. I am a bit slow mastering spin recovery.

Unlike my former college professors, the flight instructors feel free to yell at me, challenge my manhood, tell me to put my head between my legs so they can bang the joystick off my helmet a few times, or tell me to look left and then roll the plane hard right so my visor bangs off the canopy (I'm pretty sure some of my professors would have loved a few such educational opportunities). I know Moore is doing this to create stress so I will learn to perform under pressure. He certainly achieves the first, and I learn the desired lesson.

ON FLIGHT SEVEN, Lt. Moore is not satisfied with my progress. I get a down (unsatisfactory) and am assigned a new instructor. Enter Captain Cavagnaro, United States Marine Corps (USMC), who is quiet, patient, and demanding. Other than the quiet, patient part, he is all Marine. Although I witnessed the Marine ethos with the MarCads and DIs, Cavagnaro is the first Marine I get to know well. Collectively, they and Al Tripp, who I will be my instructor in Training Squadron Two, give me a lifelong respect for the Corps and all who serve in it.

I have two do-overs of hop seven. Captain Cavagnaro is satisfied. Five more hops, and I am up for the "safe to solo" check ride. Captain Cavagnaro tells me to take him to an auxiliary field. On the way, he gives me a simulated high-altitude engine failure, followed by a spin and approach turn stall recovery, followed by a simulated low-altitude engine failure.

The aux field is a strip of asphalt carved out of the piney woods. Nothing there but a crash truck (a fire engine designed to smother fires at aircraft crash scenes). I enter the pattern and shoot some touch-and-go landings. The captain is as silent as the tomb back there. He tells me to make a full-stop landing and taxi back into place for a takeoff. I am surprised when he unstraps and climbs out of the back seat. Standing on the wing, he tells me to take off, go play for half an hour, then come back, do a touch-and-go and a full stop to pick him up. He steps off the wing. His last words are, "Don't forget to come back and get me."

I take off, do some stalls and a couple of spins, all without scaring myself. The half hour flies by. I enter the pattern at the field, do a touch-and-go, and land to pick up Captain Cavagnaro. Life is good. I fly him back to Saufley. *I made it!* As I stride across the apron to the hangar, I feel ten feet tall.

That night, I meet Captain Cavagnaro in the officers' club, treat one and all to a round while he cuts my tie with a giant pair of scissors kept behind the bar. I tack the tail of the tie on the wall with all the others. I present Captain Cavagnaro with a bottle of Chivas Regal for risking his life with me. The proprieties have been observed.

Author after first solo

The rest of the syllabus includes basic aerobatics. Every night, I mentally rehearse each step of the next day's maneuvers while sitting in my chair with my eyes closed, miming the control movements, and imagining the horizon sliding about my canopy. The next day, we brief, and he quizzes me on the prescribed maneuvers for the hop, testing me on the checks and criteria for each step. I routinely handle the takeoff and flight to the practice area, where he takes control of the aircraft and demonstrates the day's maneuvers, talking himself through it as he does it. For example, a simple loop might go:

check your altitude—three-thousand feet minimum

line up on a road

check the area for other aircraft—don't forget to look up and behind

check the prop at full pitch

full power

scan the instruments

dive until your airspeed is above the required minimum

level off

check for aircraft

note your heading

smoothly apply full back stick

hold your heading

check the ball—rudder as necessary

ease the stick as the aircraft slows

when the horizon disappears behind and below you, watch the artificial horizon

when it tumbles, look up and back for the real horizon

check for aircraft

find your road

keep the nose coming down to line up with the road

check for aircraft

more stick in as you come down, easing the throttle as the speed builds

check your altimeter

gauge the recovery to end exactly on heading, level at three thousand feet directly over the road

check for aircraft

scan your instruments

The chair and I quickly get better at translating words in the book into what actually happens in the airplane. I learn to do all the basic aerobatic maneuvers, each with its own recipe—each more exciting than the previous:

aileron roll—rolling the aircraft to the left or right, through inverted and back to upright, losing no altitude in the process, keeping the aircraft on the same heading;

wingover—a graceful climbing-rolling turn timed so the aircraft has turned forty-five degrees when the wings are at ninety-degree angle of bank and then descending as you rollout of the turn with the aircraft on the opposite course as it returns to wings-level at your original altitude;

barrel roll—a rolling turn with a roll rate twice that of the wingover, so the aircraft is pointing ninety degrees off the original heading when it is inverted, and then returns to the original heading when the roll is completed;

Immelmann turn—a half loop with a half roll from the inverted position at the top of the loop so the aircraft has climbed and reversed direction;

hammerhead stall—the aircraft is pulled into a vertical climb, and, as the airspeed falls to zero, full rudder is applied so that, when it begins to fall tail first, the nose will flop off on its side and point straight down in the opposite direction, regain flying speed and pull out on the reciprocal of your original heading;

Cuban eight—starts as a loop, but when the aircraft is at forty-five degrees nose down on the back side of the loop, the pilot rolls to right side up, pulls out of the forty-five-degree dive, and immediately pulls back into a second loop, then repeats the process, thereby flying a figure-eight lying on its side;

half Cuban eight—starts as a Cuban eight but ends when the pilot dives back to the original altitude flying in the opposite direction.

THESE MANEUVERS are great fun, especially when choreographed together. We continue to practice simulated engine failures, and recoveries from stalls and spins. Spins are now great fun. Cavagnaro teaches me the snap roll, a maneuver not in the syllabus. The snap roll requires you to cross-control the aircraft with a hard, rolling turn in one direction and full opposite rudder. The result is to completely stall the down wing, while increasing the lift on the rising wing. With lift on only one side, the airplane rolls—*very* quickly. A violent and very sudden few seconds. The snap roll is hard to control precisely but a real thrill.

I learn things called the S-1 and S-2 patterns, which I will be required to fly blind while "under the hood" during instrument flight training in the Basic Training Command—assuming I make it through Primary. Instrument flying is flying without visual cues from outside the cockpit, necessary when flying inside clouds or on dark nights.

We cover the aerobatics, stalls, spins, and the S-1 and S-2 in less than two weeks. Every so often in the syllabus, I am scheduled with a different instructor for a check ride to see how I am progressing. The check ride instructors are, inevitably, *screamers*—men who yell at you for anything and everything you do or don't do—a far cry from the church-quiet enforced during academic examinations. Screamers are not a problem. Thanks to Lt. Moore, I have already learned to ignore the commotion in the back seat and focus on what I am doing.

I find out later, they only allow instructors to be screamers for about six months. After that, they are told to go back to trying to help us. It seems that, after six months, the cost to the instructors is too much. Longer, and the instructors begin to have problems.

AFTER EVERY HOP, there is a debriefing. The student turns in his parachute, signs the maintenance gripe-sheet on the aircraft, then waits in the ready room for the instructor to come and catalog his sins. Meanwhile, the instructor hits the head (Navy jargon for "toilet") and refills his giant plastic glass with iced tea.

When I get to VT-1, I hear the story of the missing student pilot. After one less-than-stellar hop with a screamer *par excellence*, the student pilot does not answer up when called for the debrief. They search, but he is gone. Meanwhile, the flight schedule rolls on without a ripple. The next morning during colors outside the VT-1 ready room, someone notices the missing pilot as they play the national anthem and raise the flag. He is sitting in a tree, still in his flight suit. The formation is dismissed, and the area cleared. An ambulance arrives. He is never seen again.

CHAPTER 4

BASIC FLIGHT TRAINING

T-28B Trojan

WITHIN the Basic Training Command there are squadrons for jets, props, and helicopters. Which type you are sent to is determined by the needs of the Navy, then by student preference in order of class ranking at VT-1. Jets are the most glamorous and therefore the most popular and so require the highest-class rank. Perversely, I want props because I am in love with the World War II aircraft. The Navy still flies the propeller driven A-1 Douglas Sky-raider, a carrier-based light-attack aircraft. The A-1 is powered by a huge Wright Cyclone engine producing 2,800 horsepower swinging a thirteen-foot, four-bladed propeller. The Skyraider was developed during World War II, but it became operational too late for combat. The planes did yeoman service as attack aircraft during the Korean War in the early 1950s, but, even then, the advent of the Soviet MiG-15 and MiG-17 jet fighters rendered them obsolescent.

When I arrive in the training command in 1964, I learn the A-1 Skyraiders are nicknamed "Spads," after the World War I biplane, to signify that they are hopelessly old-fashioned and obsolete. But there are still some attack squadrons equipped with A-1s. To my eyes, the A-1 is the last of the glory airplanes, and I want to fly them. Therefore, "props" are my first choice, and I am happy when I receive orders to VT-2 at Whiting Field up near the Alabama border to fly the T-28 Trojan. The T-28 was designed as a high-performance prop trainer intended to prepare pilots for the likes of the Hellcat, Corsair, and Bearcat. The T-28 is as close as I will ever get to flying one of those magnificent aircraft. It and the Skyraider are all that are left of my childhood dreams.

The Navy versions of the T-28 are the B and C models. Both are powered by 1,425-hp Wright R-1820-86B radial engine, with a three-blade propeller, and a belly-mounted speed-brake. The C model also has a tailhook for carrier operations. They are wonderful airplanes with lots of power. They can do anything except go jet-fast, but after the T-34, it seems plenty quick to me. At VT-2 we learn formation flying (including how to rendezvous with other aircraft and fly aerobatics while in formation), instrument flying, cross-country navigation, and night flying (and landings). I love formation flying. Looking at the other aircraft in the formation, you can see just how cool you look. I get goose bumps as I come sliding into a rendezvous with other aircraft.

Instrument flying is difficult and disorienting—literally. Having learned to keep my head out of the cockpit and fly with visual cues, I now must learn to fly without them. We start by "flying" Link Trainers, a single-place cockpit mounted on a pedestal. It will bank, spin, and nod up and down as the flight controls are moved, thereby stirring up the inner ear, which in turn disorients the brain and stomach. This is decades before computers and electronics become widely available, and the simulators are a hodge-podge of electrical motors and mechanical linkages. The simulators "fly" like no aircraft ever built.

Once we have learned not to crash the Link, we move into the back seat of a T-28 equipped with a hood so we can experience actual flying on instruments. The "hood" is a collapsible canvas device like the hood on a baby carriage fitted in the rear cockpit of the training aircraft. An instructor pilot enjoys the view up front and keeps us from running into something.

The author and the T-28C, fully aerobatic and carrier capable.

(Picture taken at the Pima Air & Space Museum, Tucson, Arizona, circa 1976).

Like everything else, instrument flying is stressful until mastered. Then, it becomes exciting stuff, although I admit that instrument flying never becomes a favorite of mine. I discover that I am more susceptible than most to vertigo. Or, maybe, I just hate it more.

Vertigo is a condition that occurs when your sense of balance, inner ear, and muscle sense tell you up is someplace other than up, or that your body is moving when it isn't—or isn't when it is. Worse, there are moments when these three all disagree. During flight that can mean your brain is telling you the aircraft is in a bank, climb, or dive when it is doing something else, or that it has no idea what you are doing. It is profoundly unsettling, not to mention dangerous. While I was waiting to report to Pensacola, Wayne told me about vertigo, "You must trust your instruments, no matter what your ears, stomach, and brain are telling you." If he told me once, he told me a dozen times. I think he may also have had a propensity for vertigo.

Night flying on a clear night overpopulated areas is cool. I like the lights of the towns and highways of the Florida panhandle. Besides, they only let us fly on beautiful, clear nights, preferably with a full moon. This is not instrument flying. There is not only a visible horizon, but you also have all those wonderful straight lines pricked out by city streetlights, and the cars on the interstate to lead you back home. When you get there, the airfield is lit up like Main Street at Christmas. Not much chance of vertigo.

WHITING FIELD has two separate airfields: North Whiting, where VT-2 is based, and South Whiting, which hosts VT-3, the other T-28 basic training squadron. Both squadrons have about a hundred aircraft and send up six or so launches a day. That's more than two-thousand takeoffs or landings. The main access road to the airfields runs east-west between the runways. VT-2 aircraft never go south of the road. VT-3 planes never come north.

Every strip of concrete is two runways, one in each direction. Whichever runway is more closely pointed into the wind is designated as the duty runway. You need a minimum airspeed to take off and land. In still air, airspeed equals ground speed. With a headwind, the air speed is the ground speed plus the speed of the wind. To take advantage of this simple fact, all takeoffs and landings are done into the wind to lower the amount of time and distance it takes to attain minimum flying speed on takeoff and to reduce the stopping distance on landing. Aircraft carriers have the advantage of being able to point their "runway" directly into the wind and to add the wind generated by the ship's speed to the available natural wind.

At both North and South Whiting, everyone must approach the field by flying over the IP (initial point) for that field's "duty runway" at a given speed, altitude, and heading. That means that, every ninety minutes, there is an aerial rush hour over the IPs. When approaching the IP, it is important that I check up, down, and all around for other aircraft, using S turns to check behind and below, and, if necessary, maneuvering to get a safe interval behind the aircraft ahead of me. From the IP, everyone flies the prescribed pattern route, airspeed, and altitude to the downwind end of the duty runway. Because the T-28 does not have an ejection seat, we fly with the canopy open when taking off or in the landing pattern just in case a quick exit is needed.

When over the downwind end of the duty runway, I check my interval and then break left. The "break" is a sharp roll to 60 degrees angle of bank, followed by a hard, descending turn through 180 degrees (a U-turn), so the aircraft ends up flying downwind alongside the duty runway.

While in the turn, I chop the power to idle, push the prop up to fine pitch, and drop the flaps and landing gear. I slow the aircraft to approach-speed, keep an eye on the airspeed to avoid a stall, and descend to two hundred feet. When I am headed downwind on speed and altitude, I check to make sure the flaps are down, and three-landing gear are down and locked. As I pull abeam the upwind end of the runway, I check the interval again and begin the descending approach turn, timing it to rollout wings level on final approach a couple hundred yards short of the upwind end of the runway, leaving a short straight descent onto the landing area. Through it all I must monitor my airspeed carefully. A stall during an approach turn leaves no time to recover or bail out before crashing. Except for the arrival call at the IP, all of this is done with never a word spoken on the radio.

Bailout practice at VT 25.

When I am at Whiting, two VT-3 aircraft enter the break at five hundred feet over South Field at the same time. Both are duals— instructor and student. One is slightly below and to the left of the other, hidden under the other's left wing. The aircraft on the right breaks left—directly into the second.

The aircraft on the left is an instrument flight with the student pilot in the rear seat. Out from under the bag while the instructor lands the aircraft, the student sees the aircraft on his right a moment before impact. He watches its propeller slice into the front cockpit, killing his instructor. As his aircraft plummets toward the ground, the student manages to:

unstrap his seatbelt and shoulder harness
unhook his radio leads
stand on the seat
dive down and out through the open canopy
pause to clear the aircraft
and pull the rip cord on his parachute,

all in about the same time it takes to read this sentence. His chute opens; he swings past vertical once and hits the ground hard. He survives. Hurt but alive. Both pilots in the other aircraft are killed.

I learn something. Three men died because none of the four pilots saw the other aircraft until it was too late. The student pilot survived because he saw the other aircraft a split second before impact. His adrenaline and awareness of what was happening gave him a sliver of a head-start—just enough to save himself. A moment later, and he would have hit the ground before the chute opened. I begin to understand the importance of keeping your head on a swivel *every* moment you are in the air and of the need to see—comprehend—decide—act in one fluid sequence. Lots of second looks before, but no second-guessing after. Within eighteen months, I will experience just how hard edged a lesson this can be.

MY TIME AT WHITING is wonderful. It is challenging, stressful, and exhilarating. I realize I made exactly the right decision when I chose to forego more college and enter the flight program.

I think, *I am a pilot.* I know I have a long way to go before I become a Naval Aviator, but my competence grows with every hop. I get to fly almost every day, some days twice. On my solos I have time to play. I fly low alongside the interstate, with the gear and flaps down, slowing to highway speed, blipping the prop—the equivalent of gunning the car engine at a stoplight—inviting the truck drivers to a drag. When the soot-black smoke pours from their exhaust stacks, the race is on. I stay with them for a bit and then pull the gear and flaps up, accelerating in front, raise the nose, and do a roll.

I eat, live, and sleep flying—and I love it.

Nevertheless, I find time to think about other things. My girlfriend and I manage to see each other three times during Pre-Flight, Primary, and while at VT-2. I fly down to Miami to join her and her family for Easter Sunday. I drive up and down the Dixie Highway to spend forty-eight of the seventy-two-hour Fourth of July weekend with her and her family at their lake cottage in southern Michigan. She flies down to Pensacola for a long weekend, staying with a married friend from Pre-Flight and his wife, who rent a little place off-base. I decide I want to marry her. I have my commission, a regular salary, and flight pay—not a lot, but more than many. I save up a thousand dollars, buy a ring, and mail it off to her father. A week later, I call her and propose over the phone.

She says, "Yes."

"Great. Go see your father. I'll hold."

She likes the ring. The next subject is when we can get married. I tell her the Advanced Training Squadrons are all in Texas. When I finish Basic in Pensacola, I will get ten days leave and travel time. I am scheduled to finish Basic training on a Wednesday. If we get married on the Saturday, we will have a week for a honeymoon—and to get to Texas. After that, my next time off will be at the end of Advanced training. We opt for sooner.

WHEN I LEAVE VT-2, I am engaged, and the wedding date is set. All I have to do is finish Basic on schedule, something I am sure I can do. At this point, I am a pilot in every civilian sense of the word. The last hurdle in Basic is learning to take off and land on an aircraft carrier—the one thing that sets Naval Aviators apart from our land-based peers.

Teaching carrier landings in the T-28 is the mission of VT-5 based at Saufley Field. After my last hop in VT-2, I put all my earthly possessions in the trunk of the car and drive back to Saufley.

LANDING SIGNAL OFFICERS (LSOs) supervise every carrier landing from a small platform on the port side of the flight deck abeam the landing area. They spend hours watching hundreds of landings and are able to detect trends in the landing approach before they become apparent to the pilot. The LSO is in radio contact with the pilot and provides him with corrections and information about the deck movement in heavy seas. If the landing becomes unsafe, he waves the pilot off to go around for another try. The instructor pilots in VT-5 are all LSOs.

As a student pilot, my goal is to get an entry in my flight logbook saying I am "carrier qualified" in the T-28. Getting "CarQual'd" will be the end point of every phase of our training from this point on.

Aircraft carriers are expensive to operate, hard to land on, and dangerous to crew and foe alike. Therefore, we will spend weeks practicing carrier landings on a runway at Barron Field, an old auxiliary airfield in the woods of the Florida panhandle near Pensacola.

VT-5 operates a fleet of tired T-28s, which we fly from Saufley to Barron Field every morning. There's not much there. An old wooden hangar, a rusty water tower, a crash truck, fuel truck, a bunch of ratty, overstuffed chairs under a shade roof, a flight line, and an old brown dog. Flying yourself to work at this re-creation of an RAF field during the Battle of Britain is cool. The dog is a great touch. He ignores the airplanes and student pilots with polite disdain, unless the latter bring treats.

On the first day at Barron Field, we gather to hear the safety brief by a Marine major. He begins by reviewing the low altitude bailout procedures for the T-28. He says, "While here, you will never be higher than 200 feet in the landing pattern. You need at least a hundred feet after you pull the rip cord for the parachute to open. The pine trees surrounding this field are forty feet tall. It is impossible to bailout while you are still a hundred feet above the treetops."

What he says next become words I will live and almost die by.

"If you have an engine failure in this squadron, it will happen when you are in an approach turn over the piney woods, low, slow, flaps and gear down. You are going to run out of flying speed and altitude in seconds. No time to restart. No time to bail out. Your only chance is to level the wings and push the nose down to maintain flying speed.

"You will do this because you have been trained to do this. *But* then you'll look over the nose and see the trees rushing up at you. In that moment you will have an overwhelming urge to close your eyes, say, 'God, save me. You fly the airplane.'

"*But*, if you do, you will die! God fucks it up every time. While you wait for God to take over, you will subconsciously pull the nose up to stay out of the trees. You *will* run out of flying speed—you will *stop flying* and *start falling*. The plane always falls off on a wing. The down wing catches a treetop, and you cartwheel into the trees in a ball of flames.

"When we notice the smoke, we'll send the crash truck to put out the fire. We will look around for some bits we think were you and put them in a box. That night we will send a telegram to your mom saying, 'Sorry, ma'am. Where would you like us to send the box?'

"*But*, you have far more time in the T-28 than God. *If* you stay with it, *if* you don't quit, *if* you fly the airplane all the way to the ground, you will probably survive. That big engine in front will go through the treetops like they are toothpicks. As you get deeper into the trees, the trunks get thicker, trees to either side take off the wings with all that av-gas, while you and that big engine keep right on going—leaving the fireball behind. Pretty soon that big engine will hit the ground and grind to a stop. When it does, unstrap; climb out over the nose; and run straight ahead. When you can't run any farther, stop, sit down, lean back against a tree, light a cigarette, watch the fire, and wait. We'll come get you, say 'Good job,' and buy you drink at the officers' club.

"That night you can call Mom and say, 'You'll never guess what I did today.'"

The major's message is clear: You quit; you die. I learn the lesson. I learn to stay with it until it's over. Staying in the moment saves my life countless times during the next two years. But it will also nearly kill me at least once. I still apply it to all sorts of problems other than engine failures in a T-28 at two hundred feet over Barron Field.

At age seventy-plus, I will realize I may have overlearned the major's lesson. Because I "know" coping is up to me, I never admit there are things that I can't deal with, solve, or cure on my own. So, I never ask for help. I will also realize that staying alive by staying in the moment has emotional costs for me and those around me.

Immediately after his safety briefing, the major puts on a parachute, climbs into a T-28, and shoots three touch-and-go landings—on the top of the field's old water tower, each accompanied by a loud-hollow *GONG!*

Later, when I take off and look down at the water tower, the top is flattened and covered in skid marks. "Landing" on the top of that tower with no visual references to guide you is mind-bogglingly hard, especially when you realize that the tower disappears under the nose when the aircraft gets in close. Inches off in any direction and the major dies. To this day I cannot figure out how he managed the water tower trick, other than having a preternatural spatial awareness.

After that trick, another LSO, who is watching with us, tells us that if we all go stand out on the apron, the major will do a few high-speed, low passes for us.

He says, "The major is willing to bet a case of beer that you will duck or flinch."

We instantly take the bet. We are not afraid. We stand in a gaggle on the apron away from the parked planes. The major is climbing to three or four thousand feet, turns, and dives at full power for the treetops. As he clears the trees at the field boundary, he drops again until his propeller is clearing the ground by less than five feet, lower than the minimum height requirement for the flight program. He is coming right at us. Ducking is not a matter of courage but of self-preservation. I duck and turn my head to watch as he flies over, getting an open mouth full of sand and gravel from his prop blast. The major wins the bet. We buy him a case of beer. He is what we learn to call a "cowboy"—an undisciplined pilot who takes unnecessary risks—but the major is also one shit-hot pilot.

CARRIER LANDINGS require precision. To help the pilot, carriers have an optical landing system called the mirror. Originally it was a mirror that reflected a light source back up the glide slope. Although still called the "mirror," by the 1960s the mirror has become a stack of five Fresnel lenses, each projecting a narrow beam of light behind the carrier. The middle light shows the glide slope necessary to bring the aircraft to the exact spot on the deck for an optimum landing. There is a row of horizontal "datum lights" on either side of the middle lens. The light, as seen by the pilot, is called the "meatball" or "ball." If the aircraft is on glide slope, the pilot will see the ball between the datum lights. If the ball is above the datum, the aircraft is above glide slope and will land long. If it is below, the aircraft is below the glide slope and will land short. The bottom lens projects a red light—a reminder that if you go any lower you will crash into the back of the ship. Either way it tells the pilot what correction is needed.

We learn to land on the carrier by practicing on long, forgiving runways using a portable mirror system. The practice carrier landings are called FMLPs (field mirror landing practice). We use the same procedures for FMLPs as we will on the ship. As I rollout on final approach, I "call the ball" to tell the LSO I see it. If I am so high or low the ball is off the mirror, I call "clara." I also give our fuel state in thousand-pound increments, so the LSO will know how many passes I can make, and, aboard ship, so the arresting gear can be set to my aircraft's gross weight.

Ashore or on the carrier, the mirror and ball are the same from the pilots' perspective, with one exception: Ashore, the glide slope is adjusted to a shallower angle for FMLPs to account for the fact that the runway is stationary, as opposed to the carrier deck, which is moving away from the pilot during the approach. This small detail fails to register with me.

A portable mirror optical landing system

Other than coming and going to Saufley, every hop at Barron is the same. It is a day filled with FMLPs, one after the other. We take off:

leave the gear and flaps down,

climb to two hundred feet,

turn downwind,

fly the approach turn,

acquire the ball,

start our landing scan:

airspeed–lineup–ball,

make positive corrections to each as needed,

full power on touch down,

take off without stopping (a touch-and-go)

climb to two-hundred feet.

Repeat eleven to fourteen times. When low on fuel, we turn on our landing lights and do a full-stop landing. We climb out and report to the LSO for his debrief while the aircraft are refueled. The LSO reads his shorthand account of each deviation from perfection and an overall grade for each of our landings.

Debrief over, there's time to hit the head, pet the dog, mount up, and repeat the above (times two). At the end of a long day of tense, exacting flying we go back to Saufley.

WHILE I AM in VT-5, they close the A-1 Skyraider (Spad) pipeline. The Spad squadrons are taking unsustainable losses flying against targets over North Vietnam. The last of the glorious airplanes of my childhood has reached the end of its road. Spad squadrons will be reequipped with A-4s as the aircraft become available, or, worse, de-commissioned. Those squadrons waiting to be re-equipped will be used to escort the helos on search and rescue (SAR) missions and maritime patrols offshore.

Although "Spad" may have originated as a derogatory term, the Skyraiders performance as helicopter escorts and close air support for downed pilots will cause "Spad pilot" to become a term of respect, affection, and deep gratitude by all the combat pilots. But that is in the future. As of 1965, the Navy does not need to train any more pilots to fly the A-1 Skyraider. That means all the combat roles are now allocated to jets. I am trapped in the prop pipeline and doomed to chauffeur a crew of techies around in the twin-engine S-2 Grumman Tracker or, God forbid, the four-engine, land-based P-3 Orion on interminable antisubmarine patrols in the Atlantic and Mediterranean, while a shooting war is going on in the Pacific.

A Douglas A-1 Skyraider of VA-152.
A single place, single engine aircraft, it can carry a maximum bomb load
greater than the four engine B-17 Flying Fortress and its crew of ten.

The only way out is to jump from the Basic prop pipeline to the Advanced jet pipeline. I don't know if it is possible to do this. But I know I have to ask. In my naiveté, I think I should ask the Chief of Naval Air Training (CNATRA, pronounced "Sinatra"), the admiral commanding the entire flight training command. If anybody can make it happen, he is the one. CNATRA's headquarters is at NAS Corpus

Christi, Texas, where the Advanced prop squadrons are based. The Advanced jet training squadrons are at NAS Kingsville and NAS Beeville, both also in Texas.

About a month before the wedding, I begin to wonder if I will finish on time. I call South Bend and say, "We may have to slide the wedding a week." I am astounded at the consternation and panic this sentence causes.

AT THE END of the VT-5 syllabus, we fly out to USS *Lexington* (CV-16) cruising offshore south of Pensacola. The *Lexington* services the training command for all CarQuals. The "*Lady Lex*" is an Essex class carrier, named for the previous USS *Lexington* (CV-2)[1], which was lost in the battle of the Coral Sea during World War II, nine months before my birth. She is a direct connection to everything I love about naval aviation.

When we take off to go to the carrier for the first time, there is no one in the rear cockpit. No use losing a trained, experienced instructor pilot to a student who might close his eyes and pray when he should be saving himself. Besides, doing it alone is a character-builder. We go out in groups of four or five student pilots, with an instructor tagging along in his own aircraft just to make sure we find the ship.

By the 1960s, all attack carriers have an angled flight deck. The back half of the deck, the landing area, is angled off to the left so that, if the airplane's tailhook does not catch one of the four arresting cables, it is possible to take off without crashing into the aircraft parked on the front end. It also lets you shoot touch-and-go practice landings on the carrier.

To CarQual we must do two touch-and-go landings and six arrested landings and takeoffs.

EVERY CARRIER LANDING is exhilarating, to say the least. It must be precise in speed and placement. Too slow you stall. Too fast you will rip the hook out of the aircraft and fall off the angled deck. You must belexing within two feet of the centerline or risk careening over the deck edge or into the carrier's island superstructure. If you land long, your tailhook will miss the last arresting cable, and you must fly it off the angle to try again—a "bolter." If you land short, you risk crashing into the back edge of the flight deck—a ramp strike. The ramp is armored. Aircraft are not. Ramp strikes tend to kill aircraft and pilot alike. These facts are attention-getters. The tension builds as you fly down the glide slope, closer and closer, the mirror giving you glide slope information that is more and more accurate, more and more demanding, narrower and narrower.

When landing on a runway, most pilots flare the aircraft to break the rate of descent, so the aircraft just caresses the runway as it lands. This saves wear and tear on the landing gear and airframe, but makes it difficult to touch down on a precise spot. Navy pilots are taught to keep descending at seven hundred feet per minute until we hit something hard. The aircraft literally collides with the flight deck, but it does so at the precise spot where the glide slope intersects the flight deck.

CarQuals
T-28 in the landing pattern for USS Lexington with landing gear, flaps, and hook down. Canopy open just in case.

At impact, we push the throttle to full power. If the hook catches, we are stopped, full power or no. If it doesn't catch, we pull the nose up slightly and fly off the angled deck for another try.

On my first pass at the carrier, I start my final approach with a centered ball, but seem impossibly high. I fly the ball, but the angle of descent is much steeper than I am used to from the FMLPs. My anxiety grows. I stay with it and do the touch-and-go. As I circle around for the next pass, I watch another student on his final approach. He, too, looks high but appears to be coming down slowly. The penny drops: the glide slope seems steeper because it is. The mirror is set at a higher angle to compensate for the ship's movement away from us.

One more touch-and-go, and it is time for my first arrested landing.

In the groove and okay with the steep approach, I fly a decent pass. My aircraft impacts the deck–full power–WHAM–I am slammed forward against my lap and shoulder harness. The aircraft has come to a dead stop with the engine roaring at full power.

I did it!

I landed on an aircraft carrier.

A successful carrier landing is a moment like no other. It is as if you made love for the first time and had your first serious car accident simultaneously. Hot shit! Hook up, taxi clear of the landing area to make room for the guy behind me.

The T-28's slow takeoff speed and powerful engine means it does not require a catapult to launch off the carrier. We do take-offs the old-fashioned way—a deck launch. With no ejection seat, we leave the canopy open and lock our shoulder harness against the impact of hitting the water if we have to ditch.

They line me up with the nose wheel on the launch line. Then I must hold the brakes for all I am worth, run the engine up to 80 percent power, check the gauges, salute the launch officer standing to my right, going to full power when he circles a little flag over his head. Just as the bird starts crow hopping down the deck, the launch officer points the flag at the bow. Feet off the brakes and enough right rudder to counteract the prop wash on the tail. The T-28 literally leaps forward, racing for the impossibly close bow—roaring down the deck just as they did when launching to engage the enemy fleets at Coral Sea and Midway, and then, aided by the wind and the speed of the ship, I fly![2]

On my second or third landing, I get a bolter. Not from landing too long, but because my tailhook skipped over the arresting cable(s). I finish the required six arrested landings without further misadventure. I am carrier qualified. I am a Naval Aviator—Well, not quite, but I can do something no Air Force pilot does.

Dead on schedule, that Wednesday, I get orders to report to Corpus Christi in ten days to start training in multiengine props. The wedding is on for Saturday.

No problem. I have a plan: tonight, I will drive from Pensacola to Dallas. Thursday morning, I fly to Chicago, rent a car, drive to Indiana. The rehearsal and dinner are on Friday. On Saturday morning, I will do a touch-and-go down the church aisle, reception at noon, drive to Chicago with my bride that evening. Sunday we will fly to Dallas, pick up the '60 Chevy with everything I own in the trunk and plenty of room left for my bride's two suitcases. Her hope chest will have to catch up later. We will drive to Corpus Christi, find a motel. Monday morning, I will put on my service dress blues, kiss my wife good-bye at the motel, and go to the base to find CNATRA's office, where I will ask for a few minutes of his time. All of which goes to prove the Navy has already taught me to see past the end of my nose.

CHAPTER 5

ADVANCED FLIGHT TRAINING

F-9 Cougar of VT-25.

THE LOGISTICS work. We are married on Saturday. Fly to Dallas and drive to Corpus Christi on Sunday. Zero eight hundred Monday finds me in the admiral's outer office speaking with his very pleasant, very in-charge secretary. I politely explain what I want and ask if I can wait in her office on the off-chance the admiral might have an unexpected five-minute gap in his schedule. She explains to the very junior ensign that the admiral is a busy man and has no openings in his schedule. I ask if I can wait—just in case. She smiles and tells me I can wait, but it is unlikely that such an event will occur. I wait.

About 1720, she tells me the admiral has left for the day. He apparently has a back door.

I drive back to the motel to find my slightly bewildered and thoroughly bored bride. We eat dinner in a Texas road tavern across the street. She asks me what I did during the day.

"Waited for the admiral. What did you do?"

"Waited for you."

For the rest of the evening, we act like newlyweds, while trying our best not to look like newlyweds.

Next morning, I am in the passageway outside the admiral's office at 0730, hoping I might get a few minutes before his schedule kicks in. The secretary arrives about 0740. She laughs when she sees me. After she gets settled in and takes the cover off her typewriter, she offers me a cup of coffee. The admiral's first appointment is off base. He isn't expected until 0900. She asks how long I am going to keep this up. I tell her I don't have to report to my new (*and unwanted*) training squadron until Monday, so I have the rest of the week. She shakes her head with a patient smile, puts a sheet of paper in her typewriter, opens a steno pad, and starts typing. When the coffee is ready, she pours a cup for both of us. I thank her for the coffee and sit.

Tuesday is a repeat of Monday, right through the dinner conversation. Wednesday goes the same—all day. About 1700, the admiral buzzes her on the internal phone line as he does a dozen or so times a day. When she hangs up the phone, she looks up at me and says, "The admiral will see you now, ensign."

I go in. Stand at attention, front and center between the two hardwood chairs facing his large mahogany desk with my bridge cover (hat) tucked under my left arm. The admiral is reading some papers. He has manufacturer's models of the F-6F Hellcat and F-8F Bearcat on the back bar behind his desk. I am able to read my upside-down name on the top edge of a file sitting on the desk to his right.

He puts down the papers, reaches for my file, looks up at me, and says, "At ease. Sit down," nodding at the chair on my right. I sit on the edge of the chair, back straight, an unnatural posture for me. I am not at ease. I am concentrating on not hyperventilating.

He asks, "Why didn't you request jets at the end of Primary?"

I tell him.

He asks, "What do you want to fly now?"

"A-4 Skyhawks, sir."

He shakes his head. He tells me that most who try to transition from props to jets at this point in the program wash out. I tell him I will be the exception.

He says, "If you flunk out, do not come back to me and ask for another chance."

"Aye, aye, sir."

I stand, put my cover under my arm, sidestep to between the chairs, do a smart about face, and leave his office. I wait while his secretary types my orders to Advance Jet Training Squadron 25 (VT-25) stationed at NAS Beeville, Texas.

That was easier than I thought.

My feet touch the ground about every third stride.

I drive back to the motel. Pumped. I am not going to be stuck in the Atlantic playing tag with Russian subs. I am going to fly light-attack aircraft in the Pacific Fleet.

My wife and I have what I at least think of as a celebratory dinner. I call Wayne to tell him what I have done. I'm pretty sure my bride must call her family to say we would be in someplace called Beeville, Texas, instead of Corpus Christi, but I don't remember that part. I am too excited. She is still a little shell-shocked.

THE NEXT MORNING, we drive sixty miles north to NAS Beeville. We drive around the town until we find an "Apartment for Rent" sign. It is outside what once was a largish family home, with four mail slots next to the front door. We call the number on the sign from a gas station. The owner says he has a one-bedroom-furnished apartment that's available. The rent is something like ninety dollars a month. My housing allowance will cover it. He drives over to show us the place. The two rooms are tiny. The kitchen and bathroom are smaller. I write a check for the first and last month. We set up housekeeping on the spot. I unload the car; she unpacks the suitcases. We go to the grocery store together for the first time. Our first act of domesticity. Like my mom said, "Life is an adventure marked by little milestones."

I have time left over to drive out to the base to watch the two-place old TF-9Js and older single-place F-9F Cougars taking off and landing. Once the frontline carrier fighter, the F-9Fs became obsolete hand-me-downs from the fleet to the training squadrons sometime in the late fifties.

Meanwhile, my bride stays in the apartment. I wonder now if she cried or called her mother and they both cried. Probably the latter.

STANDING OUTSIDE the car at the approach-end of the duty runway, I remember Dave Pollack. When I was four, we lived on Allendale Road in Washington, DC. One night, Wayne woke me up in the middle of the night. "Mike, get up! A man from Mars has come to visit Earth, and he is sitting in our living room." I wasn't sure what he was talking about, but I got up and came downstairs in my jammies to meet the man from Mars. When I turned the corner into the living room there was a man-thing sitting in my father's chair. It was wearing what I recognized as a khaki flight suit, but it had a big shiny gold head, no hair, two huge dark-shiny eyes, and no ears. The bottom of his face below the eyes had no mouth. Instead of a nose, he had a green crinkly trunk like an elephant hanging down. The man thing reached up pulled his eyes up onto his head—it was Dave Pollack.[3]

In 1945 my father was one of forty-five Naval Aviators selected to go to the California Institute of Technology (Caltech) to earn the wartime equivalent of a PhD in aeronautics. The families became a close-knit group and were busy getting a head-start on the baby boom. My earliest memories were of those days.

Dave Pollack was one of the Caltech crowd. He had just flown into DC from somewhere and is wearing his state-of-the-art flight gear for jet pilots. I was not scared or even too confused, but the grownups enjoyed my expression as I stood there trying to piece it all together. It might have scared me if I had known what or where Mars was.

In 1950, my parents wanted Dave to be my second sister's godfather, but he couldn't come to the baptism because he was in Korea flying F9F Panthers from an aircraft carrier off Korea. Mom told me I would get to be Dave's proxy. "Proxy" was a new word to me, so Mom explained it. I remember thinking,

I am just a little boy, but today I get to be Dave Pollack, a grown man, a fighter pilot, my father's friend.

Heady stuff for a seven-year-old. Soon after, Dave gave me a manufacturer's model of the swept-wing Cougar, one of the treasured possessions from my childhood.

WHEN I WAS ten years old, we lived on Sacramento Street in Altadena, California. We were at dinner one night when the phone rang. My father answered. I could tell from Wayne's voice that something was wrong. When he hung up, he said Dave Pollack had been killed. Dave was then a test pilot at NAS Patuxent River, east of Washington, DC. He was flying a F9-F Cougar at low altitude over the base housing area. The engine failed. Dave stayed with the aircraft, banking it toward an uninhabited area before he ejected. Because of his extreme low altitude, the chute did not open before he hit the ground.

I had only a catechism understanding of death, but I remember feeling sorry he was dead, and that both my mom and dad were upset. Mom tried not to cry in front of us, but she left the table and went into their bedroom for a while. Dad sat down with my sisters and me and said, "Mom will be all right. She just needs a few minutes."

Dave's wife wanted to move back to California with their two young daughters. No one wanted her driving their car across the country alone with the little girls. Ed Monteath, another of the Caltech crowd, was stationed on the East Coast. He took leave and drove them as far as St. Louis. Wayne took leave and flew to St. Louis. They met at the airport, and Wayne drove Dave's wife and children the rest of the way. It was all just part of being a naval aviation family.

The movie *The Bridges at Toko-Ri* was released in 1954, but I was "too little" to go see it. I eventually got to watch it on the family TV when I was about thirteen or fourteen. The movie was based on James Michener's book of the same name and is about carrier pilots during the Korean War. Dave Pollack is in the movie flying the F9F-2 Panther, an earlier, straight-winged version of the swept-wing Cougar I am watching at Beeville. His squadron did some of the flying for the aerial scenes in the movie. In one scene, Dave is sitting in the ready room during a mission briefing. My mother said, "Look Wayne, there's Dave." Wayne just nodded.

In the book and movie, Michener has the narrator ask while watching landing operations, "Where do we find men such as these?"

All these memories come flooding back that afternoon at Beeville. The airplanes are no longer painted the beautiful navy blue of the Korea era. Now they are white with a lot of orange on them, the standard training-command paint scheme. Orange is kind of like a "student driver" sign warning off other pilots. It also makes the wreckage easier to spot.

ABOUT THE FIRST THING we do at VT-25 is go through the ejection-seat training. The finale is a ride on a seat attached to a near-vertical rail.

> Back straight, head up against the headrest
> feet flat on the deck
> eyes on the horizon
> elbows in tight against the ribs
> reach up for the face-curtain handle above my head
> pull down smartly
> BLAM!

I am at the top of the rail wondering how I got there.

The ejection trainer is incredibly violent. When you pull the curtain, a blank 40mm cannon cartridge with a half charge fires under your butt. The F-9 ejection seat is powered by a 40mm blank with a *full charge*. I wonder what the real thing must be like.

Ejection seats are rated by the minimum altitude, airspeed, maximum rate of descent, and the angle of bank at which you can expect to eject and have the parachute open before you hit the ground. The faster and higher the seat fires you out, the lower these minimums are. Therefore, ejection seat accelerations are designed right at the maximum limits the human body can withstand. The result is that the odds are about 50-50 that, if you "successfully" eject, you will come away with a compression fracture in your spine or some other injury. We will repeat the ejection seat training every time we change aircraft type and once a year after that. In the years since my training, I learn the Navy restricts pilots to no more than one ejection trainer ride *per career* to avoid cumulative injury to the spine. *Now they tell us!*

THE ADMIRAL knew what he was talking about. Learning to fly the F9F after flying the T-28 is difficult. The first thing I notice is that I cannot see the swept-back wings in my peripheral vision. In the straight-winged T-34 and T-28 I could, and that had become an autonomic visual cue to the aircraft's attitude. In the F-9, I feel like I am riding on the tip of a telephone pole. I have to recalibrate my brain to use the canopy frame against the horizon to judge my angle of bank, and the pitch or angle of the nose relative to the horizon.

I also have a problem with the rudder. Having flown props until now, adding rudder when I add power and taking it out when power is reduced has become second nature. But jets don't have propeller torque. My instructor finally tells me, "Trim to center the ball when you get the flaps and gear up after takeoff. Then take your damn feet off the rudder pedals."

"Aye, aye, sir."

On the plus side, the F-9 allows us to pull more than a few Gs. Gs are a measure of the apparent weight generated by the centrifugal forces in a turn, climb, or pullout from a dive. Higher Gs mean tighter turns and quicker pullouts, both of which can save your life when divebombing or trying to turn tighter than enemy fighters or missiles.

One-G is what we all experience while standing on the ground or sitting upright. We hardly notice. It's what our bodies are designed for and what we are used to. But, as the Gs increase, so does your weight. If you weigh 170 pounds at one-G, at six-Gs you weigh 1020 pounds. The weight of every part of your body and everything in it increases proportionally. Your arms and head become heavier. So does your blood.

A pint of blood weighs about 1.1 pounds. At six-Gs, it weighs 6.6 pounds. At just four or five Gs, your heart can no longer pump it uphill to the head. No blood equals no oxygen to the brain. First you lose your peripheral vision, then you black out, then you are unconscious. It takes some time after you return to one-G to revive. With training and physical conditioning, I will become able to tolerate six or even seven-Gs without blacking out.

We are taught when pulling Gs to tense our muscles, strain as if constipated, and grunt—all in an effort to keep our blood from rushing below the waist. We are issued G-suits. They look like a pair of tight leggings suspended from a cummerbund. It has bladders over the abdomen, thighs, and calves. When you pull Gs, the bladders inflate with high-pressure air, squeezing the lower half of your body to trap as much blood as possible in your upper body.

Push the stick forward and you nose down, creating negative Gs. One negative G is like standing on your head; multiple negative Gs cause too much blood to go into the head and let none out. Your eyes fill with blood, and you lose vision—a redout. For the next few days, your eyeballs look like maraschino cherries. The food in your gut also reverses direction. Unpleasant.

For me, the biggest challenge in switching to the F-9 from T-28s is the engine. The T-28 has power to spare, and the engine response is like a hot rod. Push the throttle up and you get the power—now. The throttle response of all jets is slower than that of reciprocating engines. For that reason, all jets fly the landing approach with the speed-brakes deployed. This requires a higher power setting. For a wave off, bolter, or touch and go, the speed-brakes are retracted at the same time as the throttle is advanced. The result is that the power needed to climb is instantly reduced and the engine gets to full power quicker.

If all jet engines are slow to accelerate, the F9F's engine is slower. It is an old-fashioned centrifugal engine that is so laboriously slow, someone once said, "When you push the throttle up in the F-9, it sends a postcard to the engine requesting more power."

Speed-brakes or no, the F-9's slow engine response means I have to add power seconds before I need it. That makes landings difficult. I have maybe a dozen "arrivals" with the instructor demanding in my headset, "**Power. Power. POWER!**" before I finally achieve something approaching an acceptable landing. Nevertheless, I manage to get an up on the "safe to solo" check ride and go on learning to fly the single-place F9F and do all the things I did in T-28s as well as learning the rudiments of strafing, dive bombing, and air combat maneuvering (ACM or dogfighting).

A COUPLE of months into the VT-25 syllabus, my bride is having stomach problems. Our downstairs neighbors are a young flight surgeon and his wife. My wife goes down, knocks on their door, and talks to him.

He says, "Come see me at the hospital on Monday."

She does.

Diagnosis: "You have indigestion, maybe an ulcer from all the stress."

The antacids don't help. A couple of weeks later, there is a return visit to the doc. The diagnosis changes.

"You are pregnant."

THE WEEK I finish all but the CarQual part of the syllabus, there are only two others who also finish. We are told the *Lexington* is not going to be available to us for several weeks. The three of us are sent to VT-26 for advanced air combat training in the Grumman F-11 Tiger. We will come back to VT-25 for CarQual in the F-9 after we finish at VT-26. We carry our gear across to the VT-26 hangar, are assigned a locker, have a class picture taken, handed the F-11 NATOPS manual, and sat down for an orientation lecture.

The Tiger is the smallest, most streamlined airframe the Grumman engineers could wrap around a late-1950s engine. The engine has an axial flow design, and the throttle response time is much faster than the F9F. I love it. The Tiger's engine is also equipped with an afterburner (the equivalent of a turbo charger for a jet engine) and is supersonic. It is the aircraft the Blue Angels are flying.

There is no two-seat trainer version of the F-11, so my first takeoff will be solo, albeit with an instructor in a chase plane. My first landing will also be solo. (Hard swallow.) When I taxi out for my first flight in the F-11, it rumbles and rattles down the taxiway like an old dump truck. I think:

This thing is falling apart. What have I gotten myself into?

The instant the wheels leave the ground, it all changes like the moment Dorothy wakes up in Oz. In the air it is the smoothest aircraft I will ever fly. You put it someplace, it stays there. It is so stable we can fly in parade formation with 36 inches of separation between our canopy and the other's wingtip—just like the Blue Angels. Well, maybe not *just* like them, but we do it. What a gun platform. Like shooting from a rest.

Grumman F-11 Tiger and author at Pima Air & Space Museum, Tucson, Arizona, circa 1976. The F-11 is painted in Blue Angels' colors

I, however, fail to score a single hit on the target banner towed by another aircraft on the air-to-air gunnery range. That means I am not going to a fighter squadron in the fleet. That's okay, I want a light-attack squadron flying the A-4 Skyhawk. Single seat, small, agile, and in combat, it delivers the punch. The fighters just come along to protect them. But I would have liked at least one or two hits.

NOW IT'S BACK TO VT-25 to CarQual in the F-9. I have problems with the FMLPs. Seconds are an eternity in a carrier approach. I am not anticipating power changes soon enough. I get a "down" on my check ride, and my class goes to the boat without me. I have a Student Pilot Disposition Board (a.k.a., a Speedy Board) before the senior instructor pilots in the squadron. They give me another two weeks of FMLPs, a fairly routine outcome of a Speedy Board under these circumstances. After the extra two weeks—another down.

Arghh!

The Speedy Board can grant me no more extra FMLPs. Only CNATRA can do that. Back to the admiral's office; this time I have an appointment, but I am not invited to sit.

"I told you, young man."

"Yes, sir, you did."

"So, why should I send you back?"

Time for my over-rehearsed, one-breath argument.

"Sir, I can do this. If you look at my record in Primary and Basic, and even making field landings in the F9F, you will see I was a little slow getting the picture on landings, but, once I get it, I do as well as anyone. Sir, I've completed the entire program and done everything except CarQual in the F9F. I completed the advanced air-to-air program in the F-11, soloing on my first flight without a problem. It would seem a shame to throw away all the time and money the Navy has invested in me, when another two weeks will solve the problem."

The admiral literally sighs, "Ensign, our studies show that even if you manage to get your wings, you will always be a weak sister—one of the worst Naval Aviators in the Navy. Is that what you want to be?"

Oh shit. I didn't expect this question. Pause. *Think!*

"Sir, if my choice is to be the worst Naval Aviator in the Navy, or not be a Naval Aviator, I would rather be a Naval Aviator. *But* I don't believe that I will be the worst or anything like the worst. Other than my problem with FMLPs in the F9F, I have done everything else and done it well."

Pause. "Okay. Two more weeks—*but* no more."

He scribbles a signature on something in my file and tosses it in the outbox. "Dismissed."

"Thank you, sir." About-face and get out.

When I leave the admiral's office this time, I am not euphoric, but I am determined not to fail.

If all the other guys can learn to land the F-9 on a carrier, so can I.

As I drive back to Beeville, I am sure my arguments convinced the admiral.

About 18 months later, it will occur to me that the losses being incurred by the light-attack and fighter squadrons over North Vietnam may have had something to do with his decision. Junior pilots are expendable, but cannon fodder is a necessary commodity in every war.

HIGH Gs DON'T just make the body heavy. They multiply the weight of the airplane. While I am struggling in the FMLP pattern at VT-25, a student manages to pull both wings off his F-11, leaving only a two- or three-foot stub on either side. He regains control and finds he can turn the aircraft using only the rudder. He also discovers he cannot fly slower than 300 knots (345 miles per hour) without stalling.

That is way too fast to land, so they vector him out over the Gulf of Mexico for a controlled ejection where his falling aircraft will do no damage. He is recovered by a helo, but that is the end of the F-11 in the training command. I am glad to have had a chance to fly that gorgeous aircraft. It is the only chance I have to break the sound barrier and fly supersonic for a few minutes.

HAVING BEEN an ensign for eighteen-months, I am promoted to Lieutenant junior grade. It is automatic, but still nice. I'm off the first rung of the ladder.

AT THE END of the extra-extra two weeks, I get an "up." On August 23, 1966, I go to the carrier and come back alive. In between, I make three arrested landings and three catapult launches. I love the catapult. Ninety feet from a dead stop to flying sixty feet off the water. What a ride. I am carrier qualified and done with the training command.

THE NEXT DAY, the entry is made in my flight log. It is official: I am a Naval Aviator. My mom and Wayne fly out for the ceremony. Mom brings Wayne's wings of gold. She had a jeweler engrave "LWM 1940 – 1956" on the back of one wing and "MWM 1964 –" on the back of the other. At the graduation, she pins them on my chest. I am so full of myself. *Look out, world. Here I com*

At last!.

You cannot imagine how proud I am. I am a Naval Aviator. I am married. My wife is pregnant. I am twenty-three years old. I think, *I am all grown up*. I have no idea. We have no idea.

CHAPTER 6

Replacement Air Group

Welcome to NAS Lemoore, circa 1966.
An A-4C with two AGM 45 "Shrike" air-to-ground missiles.

I RECEIVE ORDERS to report to VA-125, at NAS Lemoore in central California in September 1966.

VA-125 is the A-4 Replacement Air Group (RAG) for the West Coast. For those just out of the training command, the RAG is like the anteroom we must pass through to join the fleet. The mission of all RAGs is to train pilots to fly and fight the type of aircraft they will fly in the fleet. There is one RAG on each coast for each type of aircraft the Navy flies operationally. I am headed for the Pacific Fleet. Just where I want to be.

*A newly minted nugget naval
aviator, wearing my father's and
now my wings of gold.*

On October 14, 1966, I fly the A-4 for the first time. It is a single-place A-4C. Once again, my first takeoff, flight, and landing are solo, but, *What the hell? I am a Naval Aviator. Give me the book and show me the airplane. I can fly it.*

I know the A-4E with its more powerful engine and other upgrades out performs the C model, but all the Es are going to the fleet squadrons. The Cs may be old and tired—but *wow!* The controls are more sensitive than those of anything I have flown, especially the roll rate. It is like trying to keep the aircraft balanced on the head of a pin. At first, I overcontrol. I feel ham-fisted. Clumsy. I lighten my grip on the stick, and my reflexes quickly adapt. I get four familiarization rides, then go across the street to VA-127 for instrument training.

VA-127 is equipped with TA-4Fs, the two-seat trainer version of the Skyhawk. I make my first flight in the TA-4F on October 21. On October 27, I am about halfway through the instrument syllabus. That evening, I walk into the VA-127 ready room to brief for a night hop. There is a lot of animated discussion going on. I wander over to find out what's up. USS *Oriskany* (The *O Boat*), an Essex class aircraft carrier, has had a major fire while on Yankee Station off the coast of North Vietnam. I don't have time to listen, and go back to preparing for my next hop.

In the mid-1960s, there is no such thing as night vision equipment for pilots. If you want to bomb something in the dark, you need to turn on the lights. To do this, A-4s carry Mark 24 illumination flares on an out-board wing-station. When and if the prowling section leader finds something of interest in the dark, one aircraft flies over it at twenty-five hundred feet and drops a flare. The flares are aluminum tubes about three feet long and five inches in diameter. The tube is stuffed full of powdered magnesium, an igniter, a five to ten second fuze, a small parachute, and an arming lanyard. One end of the lanyard is connected to the aircraft. When the flare is dropped, the lanyard is pulled out of the cannister, lighting the fuze. Seconds later, a little parachute is ejected and the powdered magnesium that fills most of the tube is ignited.

Powdered magnesium burns fiercely, producing a very bright, hot flame that is almost inextinguishable. The flare illuminates a large circle on the ground below. The flare's parachute captures a bubble of heated air created by the burning magnesium and the flare floats in the night air like a hot air balloon. Unused flares are brought back on board, unloaded from the aircraft, and taken down to the hangar deck on little carts for storage until needed.

The carrier conducts flight operations for twelve hours and then shuts down for twelve hours to do necessary maintenance on the aircraft and rest the aircrew and flight deck personnel. When the ship is conducting daytime flight operations, we maintain flare-equipped strike A-4s on alert during the night in case the North Vietnamese send out PT boats.

At dawn on October 26, 1966, flares on *Oriskany*'s alert A-4s are downloaded to be replaced with bombs for daylight missions. The flares are taken below to be stored in the flare locker, a compartment on the hanger deck, forward of the hanger bay. The task of unloading the carts is assigned to two sleep-deprived young men. Both are new on board. Neither is a trained ordnance man. They start with one man taking a flare off the nearest cart and handing the flare to the other man who stows it in the locker.

After they empty the first cart, the first sailor steps back to the next and starts tossing each flare to the other who is standing inside the locker. One of the flares was not put on safe when downloaded. The arming lanyard on that flare catches on something as it is tossed. The flare starts to hiss. The fuze is lit.

The young sailor in the locker, steps out, picks the flare up, tosses it in the locker, slams and dogs the hatch shut behind him. They both run back to the hanger deck to report the incident. The duty fire party is called out.

Inside the locker, the parachute pops out, and the flare ignites.[4] The powdered magnesium in the flare burns at 5,610-degrees Fahrenheit. Aluminum melts at 1221-degrees Fahrenheit, carbon steel at between 2600 and 2800 degrees. The flares are hot enough to ignite anything that will burn. All the flares stowed in the locker ignite. The locker is surrounded by officers' quarters, most assigned to pilots.

There are 2.75-inch rockets with live warheads stored in the locker with the flares. Within minutes they begin to explode. Things get rapidly worse. The fire burns through the bulkhead separating it from the hanger bay. Aircraft and bombs become involved in the fire. The fire also burns through the bulkhead separating it from the staterooms. An explosion sends a fireball down a passageway filled with pilots trying to get to safety. It fills the passageways and staterooms with acrid-toxic smoke that kills others, some in their bunks. In the hanger bay, a five-hundred-pound bomb explodes killing men fighting the fire.

The fire alarm is changed to a call for general quarters (all hands man your battle stations).

When the fire is finally put out, there are forty-four dead and more than a hundred and fifty injured, most from burns and smoke inhalation. Three dozen of the dead are pilots who were sleeping in their staterooms near the flare locker.

Oriskany returns to the United States for major repairs. I am not to know it that night in Lemoore, but that fire will become a part of my life in more ways than one.

WHEN I FINISH at VA-127, I am instrument qualified in the A-4. I walk back across the street to VA-125 where I will learn do everything else the A-4 can do.

The A-4 was designed as a throwaway nuclear bomber in the 1950s. I am told that, in the early 1950s, the Air Force argued that aircraft carriers were irrelevant because the strategic air command would win the next war. Naval aviation needed chips in the nuclear deterrent game or it might go out of business. To solve this problem, the A-4 was specifically designed as the smallest, cheapest jet that could operate from an aircraft carrier, make a low-level trip flying under the radar to a target at least eight hundred miles away, and deliver a nuclear weapon. A return trip was *not* a design requirement.

Many of the A-4s are assigned targets beyond our point of no return for a round-trip. No problem. After delivering the weapon, the pilots were to fly away from the target until they ran out of gas, eject, dig a hole in the ground, lie down in the hole, pull the dirt on top of themselves, and wait a week for the radiation to cool down a bit, then climb out of their hole. If our side "won" the war, someone would come get the pilot. If we lost, the pilot would have to negotiate a separate peace.

That is still a pretty accurate description of the mission when I step up in the mid-1960s. It is a sobering prospect in every respect. By then, however, the A-4 has also evolved into the Navy's primary light-attack weapon, tasked with dropping conventional bombs when and where our political masters decree. In 1967, that means both Vietnams (not to mention a couple of their neighbors to the west).

The A-4 is so small that, unlike other carrier aircraft, it does not need folding wings to fit a reasonable number aboard the aircraft carrier's flight and hangar decks. The Skyhawk is so small and crammed with redundant systems that the largest critical components are the head and torso of the pilot. In 1965, the A-4 may be the backbone of the carriers' conventional strike capability, but it still has a mission in the United States' nuclear triad strategy.[5]

For the nuclear mission, we are trained to penetrate enemy defenses by flying to the target at low altitude. This puts us under the radar coverage, and, hopefully, will get across any antiaircraft gunners' local horizons before they have time to react. At the target, we use a toss delivery to give enough hang time for us to gain a "safe" separation from the bomb before it detonates. At a predetermined distance from the target, we pull-up and fly a half Cuban Eight—three quarters of a loop where the pilot rolls upright from a forty-five-degree inverted dive to race away in the opposite direction. During the pull-up on the front side of the loop, the bomb is released at a set angle, "tossing" the bomb at the target.

One release, called an over-the-shoulder delivery, throws the bomb straight up. This is the most accurate of the toss deliveries but requires the aircraft to fly directly over the target and its flak defenses. It also provides the shortest escape distance. Other deliveries release the bomb at lower angles that send the bomb further downrange, allowing the aircraft to avoid flying over the target, and increasing the escape distance from the blast. However, the longer the lob, the more difficult it is to be accurate. On the other hand, nuclear weapons don't need to hit the target on the head.

Whichever toss delivery is used, the computers say we will get far enough away to escape the nuclear blast. Computers are wonderful, but no one at that time had ever actually tried it with a live atomic bomb. So far as I know, the mission still exists today.[6]

The mission is grim if not macabre, but the training is great fun. The A-4 is a wonderful bird to fly, a highly maneuverable aircraft with no nasty surprises or vicious quirks. At high speeds, the bird can bend around a turn at more Gs than you can stay conscious for. The rate of roll is incredible. At full deflection of the stick, you complete *two* 360-degree rolls in one second. Think about that. It takes only one-eighth of a second to go from straight and level to a ninety-degree bank. That is one-fourth of your nominal half-second reaction time. You can't fall off a barstool that fast. The A-4 climbs off the runway at 8,400 feet-per-minute. It can carry a maximum bomb load of 8,000 pounds.

Navigating while flying at 360 knots or better at low altitude is difficult. We get to practice doing it on what we call sand-blower routes, which snake across the west where a low-flying jet is unlikely to cause too much annoyance.

There is nothing more exhilarating than booming along at six miles a minute as low as I dare. Up mountains, down the other side, winding down canyons, booming across the flats, everything zipping past, my mind out a mile and more in front of the aircraft, my handmade strip chart with one-minute time ticks every six nautical miles and five-minute "on time" notations on my kneeboard. After several hundred miles scaring the jackrabbits, antelope, and an occasional bunch of wild horses, I arrive at the target dead on time. I pull up and execute a toss delivery of a two-thousand-pound practice bomb in the shape of a nuclear weapon onto the target. Accuracy is measured in feet and direction from the bull's-eye. I can't remember them ever calculating the escape distance. They may have done it and just not told us.

Of more immediate concern, we also learn to dive bomb—mostly with little-blue-bomb surrogates for the Mark 80 series of conventional bombs, but sometimes with actual bombs (live or water-sand filled). We have a simple reflecting bombsight with an inverted "V" we call the "pipper" to mark the aim point. The pipper can be adjusted up and down to account for the distance the bomb will fall behind the aircraft while falling from the release point to the ground.

The A-4's bomb-sight is reflected onto a glass shield in front of the cockpit. The trick is to have the pipper sweep the target in the same instant that we pass through five thousand feet at 450 knots, wings level, in a forty-five-degree dive, with the correct windage. Get all that right and the bomb should hit the target. About as easy as juggling six running chainsaws in a wind tunnel.

So, with all that in mind, I roll in past vertical, just like on *Victory at Sea*:

pull the nose down to a forty-five-degree dive

roll upright

wings level

check the altimeter

accelerating down the pipe

throttle back to 85 percent

put the top of the bombsight center line on the target

rollout

offset for the predicted winds

check the altimeter

speed-brakes out to hold the speed at 450 knots

check the dive angle

check the speed

check wings level

check the pipper tracking up to the target

adjusting the dive so the pipper will sweep the target as I pass through five thousand feet

dive angle

speed

wings level

altimeter

pipper track

altimeter

pipper

altimeter

pipper sweeps the target–five thousand feet–bombs away

a six- or seven-G pullout

speed-brakes in

full power

bottom at thirty-five hundred feet (above the effective range of small arms)

the nose breaks the horizon

off the Gs

snap roll to sixty-degrees angle of bank

put the Gs back on in a climbing turn

to spoil the gunners' aim

at six thousand feet

Gs off

quick roll in the opposite direction

put the Gs back on

All of this in the ten seconds it takes to plunge from ten to five thousand feet. The forty-five-degree dive is our primary weapon delivery; all the other weapon deliveries are just variations on this theme. We also practice fifteen-, thirty-, and sixty-degree dives and low-altitude deliveries with snake-eye fins on the bomb. With snake-eyes, we fly directly at the target at low altitude, releasing the bomb just before we pass over it. The snake-eye fins pop open on release and slow the bomb so we can race ahead, getting out of its blast effect and shrapnel pattern before it hits the ground.

We spend time learning to strafe and use air-to-ground rockets. We also practice delivering the Bullpup, a glide bomb the pilot guides onto the target with a little joystick in the cockpit, something much more difficult than it sounds—even when no one is shooting at you. The little joystick is on the right console, so you have to take the left hand off the throttle to fly the aircraft, and use your right hand to fly the Bullpup. Even for a left hander like me, this is like trying to rub your stomach and pat your head at the same time.

Finally, we get to practice dogfighting. Great fun.

AS I GAIN experience and skill, the A-4 becomes an extension of my mind in the same sense that my body is doing my bidding without conscious manipulation. Just as when I think "run," my body takes off with no conscious thought about all the muscles and balancing problems involved, when I think "left," the aircraft banks left.

Functionally my body and the aircraft merge into one. I am in love with the A-4.

The autonomic bonding with the aircraft does more than just let me manipulate the machine without conscious thought; it gives me super-powers. When I think "up," I soar, climbing more than a mile and a half a minute. Think "down" and I am rushing at the ground, impossibly steep, impossibly fast, and when my mind says *"pull out,"* I make the bend, six- or seven-Gs turning, blood becoming mercury, my hands, arms, and head become leaden. Think *"roll"* and the earth and sky spin about my navel. It is a transforming state of being. Flooded with adrenaline, time slows to a crawl, I am aware of everything about me, thoughts flash faster than you can imagine. I am addicted.

In my dotage, I will miss it terribly, knowing that my mind is no longer quick enough nor my body strong enough to exercise the superpowers granted me in those few, short years of my youth.

AS ALWAYS, CarQuals are last on the syllabus. We are dispatched to NAS Fallon, an airbase in the desert outside Reno, Nevada, to conduct FMLPs. For the first time, we will be required to land on the carrier at night as well as during the day. The deployment coincides with my wife's predicted due date.

We go up to Fallon two weeks before Christmas. They let us fly back to Lemoore after some FMLPs the night of December 23 to spend Christmas at home. The next afternoon, my wife starts labor. We drive to the base hospital. At about 2100 hours, they move her from the labor room to the delivery room. The nurses tell me to go to the officers' club and wait. They will call me when I am needed. (I know, I know, but that is what they did then. No fathers in the delivery room.)

It is Christmas Eve. I am the only one at the bar. About an hour later, somebody else wanders in and sits a few seats away. I offer to buy him a beer. He declines and asks for a tonic water.

"What are you doing here?" he asks.

"My wife is in labor, and I am waiting until they need me."

"Me, too." He laughs. "I'm the doctor."

My daughter is born a few minutes after 2300. My wife is tired but okay. My daughter is beautiful. I remember my mother saying the first thing she did when they brought her newborns to her was to start counting. "I just wanted to make sure they had five of the things they are supposed to have five of, two of everything they are supposed to have two of, one of everything else, and three of nothing."

I start counting. *All present and correct.*

When I get back to the apartment at about 0200 Christmas morning, I call my parents. Before I hang up, Mom tells me, "Wait a bit before you call her parents. Phone calls at two in the morning scare parents." I wait to call the in-laws.

About dawn I lay down for a nap. As I fall asleep, I think, *Maybe I should get some more life insurance.*

The next morning, my mother drives up from Southern California, leaving Wayne to hold down the fort with my sisters and brother. While she makes the drive up to Lemoore, I drive my wife home from the base hospital, making sure she has what she needs until Mom arrives. A hug and a kiss, and I have to leave for the base. I fly back to Fallon to finish the FMLPs. I celebrate the stroke of midnight on New Year's Eve in the FMLP pattern. I have no problem learning to land the A-4 on the carrier, but night landings up the challenges by several orders of magnitude.

ON JANUARY 10, we fly out to USS *Yorktown*, another Essex-class World War II veteran, to do our day qualifications. I do four touch-and-go landings, then six arrested landings, each followed by a ride on the catapult. At the end of the day, we fly home to Lemoore.

The next day, I fly back to the *Yorktown* and get four more arrested landings. After the fourth trap, we are parked. We shut down, are told to dismount, shepherded off the flight deck, and directed to the wardroom for dinner while we wait for dark.

That night, I get five-night cat shots and four-night landings. In some ways, I find night catapult shots more difficult than the landings. The instant transition from being slammed back by the catapult to flying with no horizon, dependent on instruments that are momentarily discombobulated, is a real heart-stopper. "Trust your instruments" doesn't work well when they are all bouncing around.

Eventually, I will become comfortable with the momentary uncertainty, and night cat shots become more thrilling than anxious.

I am done about midnight and launch for the return flight to our home base at Lemoore. My landing gear does not fully retract. I put the gear handle down. All three gear go fully down and locked. Okay, I can land and I can fly—but not very fast. Rather than spend the night on the carrier while they fix the aircraft, I elect to fly (slowly) home to wife and infant daughter. The adrenaline wears off, and I become very sleepy.

Lemoore tower calls and asks where the hell I am. It has obviously been a long day for them, too. I explain I will be there in about an hour and a half. I ask them to give me a call in an hour, turn on the autopilot, and take a nap. It is the only time I ever use the A-4 autopilot. It is also the only time I ever sleep in a plane I am flying.

I am through the RAG. I receive orders sending me down the street to the Ghost Riders of Light Attack Squadron 164 (VA-164). I am a "nugget" headed for his first operational carrier deployment and a combat virgin headed for war. I am green as grass.

Part II

THE GHOST RIDERS

Squadron patch of Attack Squadron (VA) 164, the Ghost Riders.

CHAPTER 7

WELCOME ABOARD

A4-E Skyhawks of VA-164,
flying over the Sierra Nevada Mountains of California, 1965.

DURING its third consecutive combat cruise as part of Carrier Air Wing (CVW 16) embarked on USS *Oriskany*, the Ghost Riders had lost four pilots when the cruise was cut short on October, 16 1966 by the fire. Two had been killed in action, one was shot down and captured, and one was killed in an operational accident. They lost four more to the fire. A total of eight losses out of the twenty-one they started with. CVW-16's other squadrons fared no better.

When *Oriskany* returned stateside for repairs, the air wing's attack squadrons came home to NAS Lemoore. The two fighter squadrons return to NAS Miramar just north of San Diego. The other detachments in the air wing return to their home squadrons.

The Ghost Riders moved into hangar space down the street from the Replacement Air Group's squadrons. The surviving pilots and crew went on thirty days' post-combat leaving only a skeleton crew behind to man the phones and open the mail. When their leave ends, the squadron will receive an influx of new pilots, including me, to replace the losses and those transferred out as "combat limited." The squadron will have a four-month period of intensive workup before sailing west for its fourth consecutive combat cruise.

On January 20, 1967, I walk with orders in hand to the Ghost Riders hangar and climb the stairs to their ready room on the mezzanine deck. The only officer present is an ensign. His name tag reads "Barry Wood." He is a handsome young man who carries the self-assurance of a combat veteran.

Barry sits at the squadron duty officer's desk in the ready room. From that humble station he is apparently in charge of everything. All the other surviving pilots who will carry over for the upcoming cruise are on leave. Roger Duter, one of my compatriot JOs (junior officers) in the new-guy group, dubs Barry "The World's Most Powerful Ensign." He certainly is all that and more to us.

Barry takes my orders, putting them directly into the out-basket on his desk.

I hold out my hand, "I'm Mike Mullane."

He shakes my hand. "I'm Barry Wood. Welcome aboard."

I stand there not sure what to do.

Barry seems reluctantly busy. He is welcoming, friendly, and apparently harassed by lots of people more important than me.

Having been through variations of the new kid theme for most of my life, I sense he is holding back. I figure he will be friendly but not a friend. I will be right.

I learn later that he was shot down and rescued before the fire. During the fire, he was the last survivor out of the JO bunkroom. Before the year is out, I will understand why he holds back, and will consciously emulate his social distancing from new arrivals.

Meanwhile, Barry has rummaged around on the desk and comes up with a list. "You'll be the aircraft division officer and first lieutenant."

"Okay, thanks."

"There's no one here but me. Come back at 0700 Monday. Most will be back by then."

"Thanks. See you then."

I walk away. I at least know that all Navy pilots have "collateral duties" in addition to flying, jobs that in the Air Force are assigned to nonflying officers. The shipboard limits on space and resources make this a necessity. I know the aircraft division is in the squadron's maintenance department (as opposed to the operations or administration departments). But, "aircraft" is an overly broad and generic term, and I can't guess what they actually do. I feel a pang of apprehension because I am not mechanically inclined. My knowledge about the mechanical details of airplanes comes from my various Pre-Flight and familiarization courses. Apparently, the Navy assumes that will be enough. I have my doubts.

My other collateral duty is a complete mystery. I have no idea what the first lieutenant does. I don't even know what department it is in. I will have to find some subtle, non-embarrassing way of finding out. Eventually, I discover that the air wing and squadrons are treated as tenants by the hosting ship and are responsible for all nonstructural maintenance of their assigned spaces in the ship. The first lieutenant is in the admin department and is responsible for custodial services in the squadron spaces. I am to be the chief janitor. During my short time in the Navy, I have learned how to clean a space, swab a deck, and run a buffer. *Okay. I'm ready.*

Outside on the apron is the squadron flight line with a dozen or so beautiful A-4Es, the latest and best version of the Skyhawk. They have the long, straight, lance-like refueling probe that extends some two feet beyond the nose on the right side of the aircraft. They have also sprouted little cone-shaped antennae under the nose and tail, gear I don't recognize. I will learn they are part of our electronic countermeasures, or ECM gear, which we rely on to warn us of and jam or deceive the radars and computers the North Vietnamese use to control their surface-to-air guided missiles and antiaircraft artillery.

They lack the disfiguring hump that will grow like tumors on their backs when we return from the '67 cruise to accommodate the state-of-the-art electronic gear crammed into an already crowded airframe.

There is an ugly-looking honeycomb of several dozen two-inch diameter holes that mars the smooth curve of the fuselage near the tailpipe. It is a chaff dispenser. "Chaff" is a bundle of aluminum foil strips cut to a length that matches a multiple of a radar's wavelength. When scattered in the air, it creates a large radar return that can confuse and distract the radar operators. It also screens any aircraft on the far side of the chaff. The chaff is deployed by thumbing a button on the end of the throttle-holdfast. Each push ejects one chaff bundle. I will become a heavy consumer of chaff.

I walk to the nearest A-4. In the moment, I just want to touch the aircraft and explore it, climb up and sit in a cockpit, but I am afraid that I might be breaking some rule or other. So, I just stroke its nose and cheek like Grandpa Frank taught me to do when I met his horses.

I use the down time to try and buy more life insurance. No deal. In the last few months all the life insurers have added aviation and war exclusions to their policies. If the insurance won't cover me when I am flying or being shot at, it isn't much use to me. We are stuck with the $15,000 government soldier and sailor policy.

I AM ONE of five JO replacement pilots. The combat losses, the fire, promotion, and normal rotation, have left only two combat experienced JOs in the squadron. Barry Wood is one. The other is Larry Duthie, who is off enjoying his postcombat leave.

Even more unusual and problematic for the squadron, the four senior pilots—the commanding officer (CO), executive officer (XO), operations officer (Ops), and maintenance officer—have no combat experience.

It is the middle of the squadron community that has the experience so vital to surviving the first few weeks of combat. Fortunately, this group is led by five lieutenant commanders (Lt.Cmdr.) who are all exceptional combat leaders: Leon "Bud" Edney (dubbed "Budney" by the JOs), Deny "Wuff" Weichman, Dick Hartman, W.D. "Gus" Jones, and Dick "Batman" Perry. Of these five, two will die. Two others will live to command their own squadrons and air wings, one will become a four-star admiral. Following the lieutenant commanders in our chain of command is a solid core of lieutenants who survived the last cruise as JOs: Tom Lamay, John Davis, Russ Decker, Gary Kirk, and Chuck Nelson. It is the head and tail of our squadron that are all untested in combat. I am blissfully unaware of most of this.

At the end of the next week, the outgoing squadron CO, Commander (Cmdr.) Paul Engel, and all of the pilots holding over for the next cruise are back, including Larry Duthie.

Larry Duthie 1966 cruise after 2 missions

79

Duthie is an affable guy, very intelligent, and something of a free spirit who has issues with authority figures. The last two attributes create a certain tension for him in and with the Navy. He has a dark streak and clearly worries about things more important than what the first lieutenant does. Duthie also has an irreverent sense of humor and is not wound as tight as Barry Wood.

Duthie has already led an interesting life. He went to high school in Saigon, where his father was a communications engineer designing a modern microwave phone system for South Vietnam. A few years later, Duthie joined the Navy flight program. He proved to be a good pilot and was selected for the "must pump" program. The program was created to provide a stream of pilots that can be sent to replace losses in mid-cruise. Must pumps were pushed through the flight training program and RAG and then sent straight from the RAG to combat. Duthie finished the RAG and was flown across the Pacific to join the Ghost Riders on Yankee Station as a replacement pilot during the '66 cruise. On arrival, he was assigned to be Skipper Paul Engel's wingman.

Paul Engel, the Ghost Riders' Commanding Officer during the 1966 cruise.

Duthie soon learned that his two predecessors as Skipper Engel's wingman had both been lost.

Must pumps were at a serious disadvantage. They missed the four months of pre-cruise workup with the squadron—a time dedicated to developing teamwork and immersion in the squadron's operational practices and culture, all critical to survival in combat.

Duthie had not been with the squadron long when the fire occurred.

The ready room is the pilots' battle station. When general quarters sounded, Duthie was already in the ready room, waiting to launch, but many of his friends were still in the JO bunkroom, cheek by jowl with the flare locker.

USS Oriskany *fire, October 1966.*
The Ghost Rider ready room was located midships, just below the flight deck, and aft of the island, about where the smoke is darkest in the picture. The ship is listing due to all the water pumped into the starboard side.

Lieutenant Commander Dick Perry was also in the ready room. When it started to fill with smoke, Dick said, "It's time we get out of here. Follow me, I know a way out." He tells everyone to get a grip on the belt of the man in front of him, hang on, and stay low because the smoke is not as thick down close to the deck.

Navigating by touch, Dick Perry led them out, duck-walking through pitch-black smoke-filled passageways to a hatch he knew that led to a weather deck and fresh air. When he gets there, the hatch is dogged (the mechanical locking levers around the heavy steel door have been thrown and pulled tight), rendering the hatch air and watertight. Dick passed the word to the man behind him and stood up into the smoke to un-dog the hatch. As the word was passed down the line, it became garbled. Those at the end of the line thought Dick couldn't get the hatch open. They turned around and headed off to find another way out. The decision to turn around was passed up the line. The result was that the whole line turned around—except Dick, who was still standing up in the smoke trying to open the hatch. The hatch had expanded from the heat of the fire and is wedged tight in its frame. Drawing on his last reserves of adrenaline, Dick finally managed to get the hatch open. He stepped out into fresh air. He was astounded when no one followed him out. He yelled down the smoke-filled passageway. No answer.

Meanwhile, the line behind Dick, Larry Duthie included, had duck-walked back down the passageway. They found another route out, emerging on the hangar deck aft of the fire. When they discovered that Dick was not with them, Duthie and some others went forward on the hangar deck toward the fire to find some oxygen breathing apparatus (OBAs, each letter pronounced), so they could go back into the smoke-filled passageways and find Dick. As they went forward, they bumped into Dick, who had found an OBA and was just about to go back in to look for them.

Duthie's account tells me volumes about the squadron.

THE NEW Commanding Officer (CO or Skipper), Cmdr. Douglas Mow, has a week left at the RAG. He was originally scheduled to be the executive officer (XO) on the upcoming cruise and, all things being equal, would assume command of the squadron for the cruise after that. But, Cmdr. Clyde Welch, the XO on the 1966 cruise and slated to be CO during the '67 cruise, was killed in the fire. Doug Mow was bumped directly to commanding officer of the '67 cruise without having been the squadron executive officer during a combat cruise. The best the Navy can do, is hold Paul Engel over for six weeks, to help Doug with the transition to CO during the first weeks of the workup at Lemoore. Back in Washington, the Bureau of Personnel (BuPers) rummaged about and found someone to take Mow's place as XO.

Sometime during the week, I meet Larry Cunningham. He, too, is a newly minted Lieutenant junior grade straight out of the training command. Nicknamed "C-10" by his Pre-Flight DI who thought "Cunningham" was too many syllables, C-10 looks like he is 17 or 18. Blond hair, round face with a small nose, flanked by blue eyes, and all underlined by an infectious smile. C-10 is irrepressible and full of beans. He is single, determined to enjoy life, and more than happy to have you come along for the ride. He is always ready for a laugh. Men like him. Women like him even better, and he returns the feeling. He is a charmer. What's not to like?

C-10 takes to calling me "Mule." The name sticks.

Larry "C-10" Cunningham.

We will share a four-man stateroom with Barry Wood and George "S-10" Schindelar on the '67 cruise. We become more than friends. We become brothers who always have each other's six [short for "six o'clock," the blind spot directly behind your aircraft]. C-10 and I will share a two-man stateroom during the second cruise. I will spend more time bunking with C-10 over the next two years than I will spend with my wife and child—or anyone else for that matter.

C-10'S SECTION LEADER is Deny "Wuff" Weichman. Wuff was with the squadron on the '66 cruise. Before joining the Ghost Riders, he was sent to South Vietnam where he flew a militarized version of my beloved T-28 as an "advisor/flight instructor" to the South Vietnamese Air Force. While in South Vietnam he was co-opt by the CIA to fly A-1 Skyraiders on combat missions both north and south of the Demilitarized Zone (DMZ) that, in theory, was the fence that would make North and South Vietnam good neighbors.

At some point, Wuff was asked if he would fly C-123B Providers, a twin-engine cargo aircraft with short-field takeoff and landing capabilities. It was being used to deliver people and contraband to places north and west of South Vietnam.

Wuff agreed and was scheduled for a familiarization (fam) flight to check him out in the C-123. Most fam flights involve an experienced pilot walking and talking the new guy through the aircraft's routines and rituals. After takeoff, the new pilot flies around for a while getting the feel of the airplane, followed by several touch and go landings.

Wuff's fam flight is as copilot on a night mission. They will fly to an abandoned French runway in North Vietnam. There they will extract some South Vietnamese paratroopers who had been dropped in earlier to create some havoc.

The lead pilot and Wuff find the abandoned runway and land. Rolling out to the upwind end of the runway, they spin the aircraft about and pause to load the troops. Mortar fire erupts all around them. Near misses pepper the aircraft with shrapnel. One mortar shell makes a direct hit. It plunges through the top of the fuselage and explodes in the cargo bay just aft of the bulkhead separating it from the cockpit.

Shrapnel pierces the bulkhead. The flight engineer is killed outright. The shrapnel continues through the backs of the pilots' seats. The pilot is mortally wounded. Wuff is hit by multiple frags, one will leave a scar from his spine around to his navel. Others will leave a handful of jagged holes in his back.

Wuff jams the throttles against the stops. Taking off downwind, he manages to get airborne, just clearing the tree tops at the end of the runway. He heads south nursing the wounded bird along. He makes it across the DMZ and heads for the nearest runway. As he approaches the field, both of his engines are on fire. They last long enough for Wuff to get the bird on the ground. He shuts down, levers himself out the copilot's seat and steps past the flight engineer's body into the cargo bay. Everyone, in the back of the aircraft is dead.

Wuff is the sole survivor.

This was only his first flight in the C-123. Including the seventy or so missions he flew on the '66 cruise before the fire, Wuff has flown almost three hundred combat missions when I meet him in January 1967. He is the coolest man in a fight I ever saw, and I saw some of the best. He was also a dedicated and gifted practical joker.

ACCORDING to Navy tradition, all officers newly assigned to a command are invited to pay a formal social call on the commanding officer in his quarters at the earliest possible opportunity. Commander Paul Engel is still CO of the squadron and issues the invitations. The tradition includes strict rules of etiquette. The rules require us to RSVP, appear at the appointed time accompanied by spouses, leave our printed calling card on a silver salver on the entryway table, introduce ourselves and spouses (if any), be polite, and leave after no more than twenty minutes.

In the Ghost Riders, the formal visit becomes a squadron party at Paul Engel and his wife Tan's quarters. They both are genuinely warm and friendly people. It is Skipper Engel's proud boast that he joined the Navy as an Aviation Midshipman.

At the end of World War II, experienced pilots left the Navy in droves to return to their civilian lives. To fill the shortage, the navy created the Naval Aviation College Program. It offered to pay for four years of college and flight training with a commission upon graduation. While in college the participants held the rank of Aviation Midshipmen. The program was cancelled after four years due to budgetary problems. As a result, Aviation Midshipmen were rare birds indeed.

In his early years, Paul Engel got to fly all the glory aircraft of my childhood dreams and the first generation of jet carrier aircraft. Prior to joining the Ghost Riders', Paul was Carrier Air Wing 16's operations (Ops) officer the 1965 combat cruise. The Air Wing Commander (CAG) was Jim Stockdale.[7]

After leaving the Ghost Riders, Paul Engel will rise to the rank of rear admiral during his thirty-two years of active duty in service to our country. He will die in his sleep in May 2020, and the world will become a smaller place.

In 1967, Paul Engel is already an uncommonly gifted and generous leader. One of the enduring legacies he leaves with the squadron, is his personal motto: "Press On!" Paul Engel is what my father describes as a "good man," Wayne's highest accolade. Paul is exactly what I hope to become.

Doug Mow, the incoming CO, and his wife, Rosalie, are also at the party. Doug is quiet, reserved, polite, and unflappable. He is, above all, a gentleman. Don Purdy remarks, "Cmdr. Mow is old-school Navy." Don is right.

When my wife and I arrive at the party, all the holdover pilots are wearing name tags with their collateral duty jobs. I set about memorizing faces, names, ranks, and jobs of the old hands. An hour into the party, they all switch name tags, this time wearing, they say, their own tag. *Shit. I have enough problems remembering names.* The name tag switch was Wuff's idea.

Later, the JOs and Skipper Engel crowd into the kitchen while the wives stay in the living room. Skipper Engel is telling us what we can expect. It is one of those nights when every drink goes straight to my head. By the time we get to the kitchen, I am drunker than I realize, and a lot drunker than I should be.

While standing there trying not to sway or stagger, I drop my cigarette. I bend down to fetch it. I can't find it.

Where is it? . . .

It has to be down here someplace.

I see a curl of smoke—coming from the cuff of the skipper's trousers.

I retrieve the cigarette and extinguish the skipper's smoldering pant leg. I rise, survey the astonished and embarrassed expressions on the other JOs faces, and apologize to an equally astonished Paul Engel. I excuse myself, go to the guest bathroom, where I violently and loudly vomit.

That done, I find my wife and suggest we take our leave. We are the first to leave by a wide margin.

A glorious start to my naval career.

AT THE PARTY, I learn that I am assigned to fly as Lt.Cmdr. Dick Perry's wingman. I already know that Dick is one of the heroes from the fire that ended the '66 cruise. It turns out that is just the tip of the iceberg.

Early on during the '66 cruise, Dick was on a twilight armed reconnaissance when he took a direct hit by a 37mm anti-aircraft gun. The cannon shell blew large chunks of the nose off his aircraft and a piece of shrapnel through his flight boot. Gone with the nose were all of his electronic and static-air flight instruments. He also lost the radio, lights, and alternate generator. This was not the worst of it.

The A-4's engine air intakes are located on both sides of the fuselage, just behind the cockpit—perfectly positioned to swallow most of the debris that used to be the nose of Dick's aircraft.

Jet engines find hard objects indigestible. Behind the intakes, our engine had ten compressor stages, each a wheel lined with blades that rotated at high speeds. Behind each rotating compressor, there are fixed stator rings, each with its own blades. The intakes suck in large volumes of air, compressing it and passing the now high-pressure air into the combustion section where jet fuel is sprayed in and ignited. The heat of the fire creates even higher pressures. The hot gases then pass through a two-stage turbine that powers the compressors and continue out the tailpipe to thrust the aircraft forward.

Hard objects knock blades out of the first compressor stage, then the hard object and broken blades knock blades out of the fixed stator before moving on to the second compressor, and so on. After passing through all ten compressor stages, the entire mess passes through the combustion chamber too wreak more havoc in the turbine section. Every lost compressor and turbine blade reduces the engine's thrust, until at some point the engine quits. At best, you are left with an underpowered engine that is tearing itself apart. If the debris pokes a hole in the combustion or turbine sections, it will leak hot gases into the fuselage. If this happens—*Boom!*

KNOWING ALL THIS, Dick was not surprised that his engine lost a lot of power. The surprise was that he had enough to keep the aircraft in the air—barely. He turned his badly wounded bird east, into the growing darkness toward the water and Yankee Station. He had to find a carrier. Any carrier would do.

Dick and his wingman flew with no running lights over the beach. They became separated in the darkening twilight. Alone, without a radio, he could not call for a radar vector, he had no electronic navigation, lights, or artificial horizon. Dick would have to find his own way back to the ship.

He was left with the magnetic compass and clock mounted on top of the windscreen frame. He had only the goose-necked flashlight hooked on his survival vest to see them in the darkened cockpit. His only hope was dead-reckoning—the crudest form of navigation.

He estimated a course and distance from where he was when hit to the predicted location of the carrier. Without an airspeed indicator, he had to estimate the speed his wounded engine was producing so he could calculate the estimated time it would take him to travel the estimated distance to the carriers. Any errors in this cascade of estimates would compound each other and reduce his chances of success to near zero.

He focused the flashlight on the wet compass and headed off into the night. With no altimeter, Dick strained to see the eastern horizon so he could maintain altitude, keep his wings level, and avoid vertigo. In the meantime, he did the calculations for his dead reckoning in his head. When he thought he should be in the neighborhood of the carriers, he started an ever-widening box search, looking for a deck ready to recover aircraft.

Dick finds a carrier. Great. But, it has all the aircraft pulled aft in readiness for a launch. It was then full dark. He had no way to tell the carrier he was there and needed to land. He began flying low passes along the port side of the ship with his hook down. Someone saw the blacked-out, noseless A-4 flying by in the dark.

The air boss ordered an emergency pull forward to clear the landing area. He ordered a signalman to flash signal "Delta" (wait) to Dick with an Aldis lamp. After what seemed an interminable wait, they flashed signal "Charlie" (land) to Dick.

Dick started his approach. He had only one shot at a landing. His engine could not give him power if he needed it to correct for being low, much less take off after a bolter or wave off if his landing became hopeless. The pass had to be perfect, but he has no airspeed indicator or angle of attack indicator, at least one of which is critical to a successful carrier landing.

With no radio, the landing signal officers could not help him by giving corrections for airspeed, glide slope, and lineup. Worse, in the dark, Dick's visual cues and depth perception were gone. He landed the bird. It is a stunning piece of airmanship.

Dick's flying that night makes shooting touch-and-goes on a water tank look like child's play.

BEYOND HIS AIRMANSHIP and coolness under pressure, Dick is also an acknowledged leader within the squadron. He is known to be skilled and steady at everything he does. He extends trust to his subordinates and is trusted by them. He is an officer with a bright future in the Navy. The best flight leader and role model I could ask for.

My Irish luck is holding. I am so damn lucky to fly on Dick Perry's wing.

When I start flying with him, he also turns out to be a nice guy. He is genuinely interested in helping me become a better pilot and officer. I like him and want nothing more than to earn his respect and trust. Dick also has a reputation as a superb poker player. Given his emphasis in our talks about making "smart plays" in combat, I am not surprised.

The Ghost Rider pilots are individually and collectively competitive. We bet on everything, even if only for bragging rights: who can park their nose wheel on a quarter (there's a trick), bombing scores, rockets, strafing, first to see this or that, mock dogfights, you name it. When someone wins, we compliment them while trying to figure out how to beat them next time. It is all about getting better. On the bombing range, I am average at best. Most bombing errors are long or short; oddly, I miss more to the left and right. I work at it but can't seem to improve the left/right problem.

Dick is a patient and constant teacher. We compete to spot wild horses in the high desert of Nevada and call all airborne traffic from airliners down to buzzards and hawks. He talks to me about how to improve my bombing skills. Through it all, his focus is on helping me become a professional, diligent wingman. In the air, we become a bonded team. I come to know what he will do and how he will do it. I know what he expects of me, and he knows I will be there with him, whatever he does.

His call sign is Batman. When we fly together, I am Robin, not Batman 2. This is when the TV *Batman* with Adam West is popular, not the later *Dark Knight* special-effects extravaganzas. The TV show is very camp, with comic balloons of "WHAM!" and "POW!" I don't fancy myself as a teenage boy in tights, but the bottom line is, I know I can follow Dick Perry anywhere and trust him to lead me out again. So, what the hell, Robin it is.

During the workup period, the squadron becomes a cohesive team, regaining its combat edge.

WHEN WE JOIN the Ghost Riders, we are told to plan on going to Reno, Nevada, for a party hosted by Dick Perry's good friend Jessie Beck. Wives are welcome.

When I meet Jessie in 1967, she is well into middle age, at least from my twenty-three-year-old perspective. She is open, friendly, and comfortable talking to someone at the other end of the age, economic, social, and education spectra. I soon hear her backstory. Jessie came to

Reno as a single mom for a job at Harold's Club. While there, Jessie met Fred Beck, Pappy Smith's partner in Harold's Club. Jessie and Fred fell in love and married. They worked together managing Fred's gaming concessions in the casino. Unfortunately, Fred died in a car accident. Jessie inherited the keno, horse racing, and several other gambling concessions within Harold's Club. She actively managed her interests.

Dick grew up in Carlin, Nevada, a small railroad town in the northern Nevada desert. Dick worked at Harold's Cub during college. There he met Jessie. They developed a work mother/son relationship. Even though he was a part-time employee, Jessie helped nurture his professional growth in the casino. Dick worked hard and became the youngest pit boss in Reno, if not Nevada. He also learned to play poker.

Jessie and Dick's relationship endured after Dick graduated from college and entered the Navy flight program. During the '66 cruise, Jessie found out that playing cards were in short supply on Yankee Station, where cards were used until the spots wore off. With no fanfare, the squadron began receiving big boxes filled with decks of cards. If you've been to a casino, you know they don't use cards past a few deals, retiring the deck before individual cards become recognizable to sharp-eyed gamblers. The casinos usually cut the retired decks in half to prevent someone doctoring cards and slipping them into play. Jessie managed to convince the casinos to let her ship them to the Ghost Riders on Yankee Station. It was not long before the air wing, then the ship's crew, were awash in cards, so they began passing them on to all the ships on Yankee Station.

Jessie also found out that books were read and passed on until the covers were gone and whole chapters missing before they were deep-sixed (i.e., thrown overboard in deep water). Jessie organized the telephone operators, first in Reno and then statewide, to collect used paperbacks "for our boys on the Tonkin Gulf." Boxes of books began arriving on *Oriskany*. Once again, Jessie's powers of persuasion and procurement swamped the local demand. Boxes of books filtered their way through the fleet.

The boxes were packed with bags of popcorn, a welcome treat, and packets of corn starch. The corn starch baffled everyone. Dick wrote Jesse. She said she heard the troops used it instead of aftershave so the enemy could not smell them coming in the jungle. Dick explained, we didn't use aftershave. Alcohol and oxygen could turn our face masks into blow torches.

My wife and I drive to Reno for the party. Dick introduces us to Jesse. I am impressed to learn that Jessie is on the floor from evening until the small hours, then working through the rest of the night on the business details, going to bed in mid-morning, only to rise again late in the day. The casino does not close for weekends or holidays. Every night, she is on her feet managing her staff, watching the action, and taking care of the customers. I am impressed by the way she treats her employees, gently correcting any deviation from her standards and expectations; and by how patient she is with the public, no matter how drunk, demanding, or unreasonable.

Jessie has arranged dinners and private tutoring sessions by the casino staff on the rudiments of all the gambling games at Harold's Club. She even gives each of us a five-dollar stake in chips to try our luck. Jessie is there every minute, making sure we are having a good time and want for nothing.

On Saturday night, she hosts a sit-down banquet. Afterward, Jessie finds me. She knows I am Dick's wingman for the upcoming cruise, and she wants to get to know me. Because of Dick, Jessie knows quite a bit about naval aviation. She knows my job as wingman is to alert Dick to every threat. As we talk, she tells me she knows Dick and I will make a good team and take care of each other. I recognize her look and tone of voice. They are the same as my mom's when she thinks about what is coming. I tell Jessie, with all the heartfelt conviction I can muster, "Jessie, I will bring Dick back safe."

I am not much for gambling. I am certainly competitive and winning feels good, but, for me, losing money hurts more. Jessie tells me, "Look at it like going to a movie. Just set aside how much you are willing to spend for the entertainment. Make your money last and quit when it's gone. If you are up and had enough fun for one night, quit and take your winnings to bed with you."

I use Jessie's five dollars to play "pass" or "don't pass" on the craps table because they told us that is the closest to even odds a bettor can get in a casino. Over several hours, betting one-dollar at a time I parlay Jessie's five dollars into thirty-five dollars. No skill, just dumb luck. In 1967, thirty-five dollars is a chunk of change for a married ensign with a new daughter.

Sometime after midnight, my wife has gone through her five dollars playing the slots. She is tired and so am I. As I pick up my chips to leave, I think, *Just once in my life I'd like to place a really big bet.* Of course, I have already placed a bigger bet, but ignorance and denial go well together—kind of like butter and honey for the brain. *What the hell.* I plunk all thirty-five dollars down on one more bet. My wife never says a word.

I get my money's worth. My bet sits there through seven rolls of the dice without a bust or a win. On the eighth roll—I lose. My wife laughs. She enjoys the drama and walks away without a regret that I ever know about. Telling this story in the next century, I will think: *I should have been paying more attention.*

THE WAR in Vietnam grows progressively less popular among the people of the United States then progressively more unpopular. The political and social antipathy for the war spills over onto those fighting it for the United States. It's to the point that people in uniform are accosted, chastised, and insulted on the streets. Some family members feel compelled to cut off their serving relatives. But—the books and cards never stop coming. Jessie and her volunteers never abandon us.

It is hard for someone who didn't live through the late 1960s and early 1970s to understand the disdain and open hostility the public had for those in active military service during those days. By 1969, no one would wear their uniform in public unless they had to. It was just asking for trouble.

At the end of our second cruise, my wife, daughter, and I will fly back to South Bend to visit her family during my post-combat leave. I buy tickets for my wife and daughter. To save money, I will fly "military standby," which means I have to wear my uniform. While waiting for the flight at the Los Angeles airport, I am accosted by a pair of "hippies." They call me all sorts of names in front of my wife and child. I try to defuse the situation, but they aren't having it. I stop saying anything and get very still. Inside I am getting angry, very angry. Two police officers appear at my side and ask if they are bothering me. "Yes." The police escort the two young men away. I calm down somewhere over Iowa. It is impossible to express what Jessie meant to us in that atmosphere.

It wasn't just us. Jessie will also adopt army and Air Force units, mothering us all—and it all grew out of her love for Dick Perry.

THERE IS a longstanding custom of painting pilots' names and the number of missions flown under the canopy rail on an aircraft. It has survived, even though pilots are no longer "assigned" a particular airplane. We fly whichever aircraft is available. Because there are more pilots in the squadron than aircraft, some planes have two pilots' names, senior on the left side, junior on the right.

At the end of the '66 cruise, Dick wanted to paint "*Lady Jessie*" on the nose of his aircraft to recognize all she had done. Naming and painting nose art on an aircraft was also a longstanding custom. It survived both world wars—but not the 1950s. By the 1960s, there is no more naming aircraft and no more nose art in the Navy.

Dick knew this but thought there ought to be an exception for Jessie Beck. He asked Paul Engel, the squadron skipper, if he could submit a formal request up the chain of command. Skipper Engel thought that such a request was unlikely to make it up more than one or two levels before being denied. So, he said, "Let's just do it and see what happens." It was done. They painted "*Lady Jessie*" in large letters diagonally across the nose of Dick's aircraft and invited Jessie to come down to Lemoore for the unveiling with appropriate press releases. She was wowed.

You have to keep in mind that Paul Engel was a career naval officer who had hopes of being selected for command of an air wing and, who knows, might even become an admiral. Silly as it may sound, doing this for Jessie without the approval of the powers that be put his professional future at risk. But we also have to remember, Paul Engel had led his squadron through a brutal cruise and lost eight pilots out of his ready room. My guess is he no longer gave a shit about the small stuff. This speaks volumes about the man. It also tells you how important he thought Jessie was to his squadron, the air wing, and the ship.

"Lady Jessie" flown by Dick Perry over the Sierra Nevada Mountains, 1967.

Whatever the chain of command might have thought about Paul Engel's decision, they apparently agreed that Jessie Beck deserved the honor of being the exception to the rule. *Lady Jessie* became the only Navy aircraft to be named for someone during the Vietnam War. It became the most famous Navy aircraft of the Vietnam era—a fitting tribute to both Jessie Beck and Dick Perry.

THE PRE-CRUISE workup is intense, hard, and focused. It is also a great time. The old hands are enthusiastic, supportive, rigorous, and having a lot of fun. They are all professional naval officers and pilots. I work hard to be good enough to become one of them. I am also having the time of my life. Everything we do is exciting and just flat-out cool. The stuff of my childhood daydreams. The old hands treat us with respect, even though we are entitled to little by rank, experience, or proven ability.

THE GHOST RIDERS are the designated Iron Hand squadron shooters in CVW-16. We are trained to use the AGM-45 Shrike anti-radar missile. It is designed to take out the guidance radars of the Soviets' SA-2 guided missiles used by the North Vietnamese. The Shrike is shot high in the air much like a nuclear weapon toss delivery to increase its standoff range and hang time. More fun.

While we train on the Shrike, our sister squadron, the VA-163 Saints, are trained to deliver the AGM-62 Walleye. The Walleye is the first drop-and-forget precision bomb. It glides to the target guided by a television camera in the nose the pilot focusses on the target.

Initially, we fly between Lemoore and the bombing ranges at NAS Fallon near Reno for section and division bombing practices. About halfway through the workup, the air wing gathers at NAS Fallon for a week of mock Alfa Strikes (a mission where the entire air wing flies against a single high-value target).[8] We also practice mounting search-and-rescue (SAR) operations for a downed pilot. For these, a pilot who is not flying the mission is deposited by helicopter somewhere just outside the bombing range. A pilot who *is* on the strike is taken aside and told to leave the formation and fly back to base when they get to where they have put the pilot on the ground. When the strike group passes overhead, the pilot on the ground turns on his survival radio's emergency beeper. He uses the call sign of the pilot who has "disappeared," saying he has been shot down. The strike commander details an on-scene SAR commander and additional aircraft to find the downed pilot, provide close-air support, and fighter protection until the helo flies in, escorted by the A-1 Spads. All very exciting.

On one such occasion, we are using actual weapons with inert warheads. A rancher is out driving on *his* land that abuts the bombing range. His dog is along for the ride in the bed of the pickup. He sees the "shot-down" pilot standing on top of a small hill. He drives over to see what is going on.

An F-8 pilot detailed to defend the downed pilot spots the rancher's pickup, keys his mic, and says, "Simulated enemy truck, approaching from the south."

His F-8 is armed with Zuni (five-inch, high-velocity) rockets. As the pickup stops beneath the hill, the F-8 pilot calls, "Rolling in on simulated rocket run."

He dives, takes aim, and, as the pipper moves across the truck, squeezes the trigger. A Zuni screams off the F-8. *Oh, shit!* The pilot forgot he had turned his master-arm switch on as they approached the bombing range.

From the air, the pilots see the truck disappear in a cloud of dust. To the pilots, it looks like a direct hit.

Sitting in his truck cab, the rancher watches a rocket come directly for him at supersonic speed. Fortunately, the rocket hits a few feet short of the pickup with a loud bang and cloud of dust. From the rancher's point of view, it sounds and looks like he has been shot at by a rocket with a live warhead. He jumps to a not unreasonable conclusion, *Somebody up there is trying to kill me.*

Back in the cockpits, there is a long second's pause and held breaths—then the dog emerges from the cloud of dust, running flat out back up the road. An adrenaline-fueled heartbeat later, the truck roars out of the dust cloud going the opposite direction. Our clearly agitated SAR commander punches his transmit button and orders no one in particular to "Stop that truck!"

The truck driver completely misunderstands the intended message of a series of low passes over his truck by various jet aircraft. The helicopter arrives and is ordered to abandon the downed pilot and pursue the truck. The rancher has the bit in his teeth and is going flat out down the road. He ignores the helicopter crew's gesticulations, as it flies alongside his truck only a rotor's length from the driver's window.

Finally, the helicopter pilot flies ahead and lands on the road in front of the truck. The crew chief and door gunner dismount and run toward the oncoming truck waving their arms, trying their best to look friendly and harmless.

The rancher comes to a cautious halt, keeping the engine running. He hunches down behind the wheel, as men wearing flight suits, helmets, and sidearms run at him.

Through the open window of the running truck they explain, "It is all just a big mistake." They tell him the air wing commander wants to meet him to apologize and explain. The rancher says he will be home later and gives them directions, but, right now, if it is safe, he is going back to look for his dog. He is assured there will be no more pyrotechnics. He declines their offer to help look for his dog.

That evening, the Air Wing Commander (known as the CAG), accompanied by the unhappy fighter pilot, the pilot's unhappy squadron CO, and the ever-cheerful air wing public affairs officer, arrives at the rancher's home in a black Navy sedan bearing a case of beer. They sit on the porch and begin to work on the beer and the rancher. They apologize. Happily, the dog made it home on his own. They explain what and why. The rancher understands. He supports, "Our boys." Besides, it is the most exciting damn thing that has happened to him in a long time.

"Uhh—please don't tell anyone what happened. We wouldn't want the North Vietnamese knowing about how we rescue pilots."

The rancher gives a disappointed sigh, "Okay, I won't tell anyone."

After the dust settled, I remember thinking, probably for the first time:

What we do is dangerous to people other than ourselves.

It was the first incident of what is known as "collateral damage" that I witness. It won't be the last.

WE LEARN to refuel from a tanker aircraft while flying. Unlike the Air Force, the navy uses a probe and drogue system where the tanker streams a hose behind it with a drogue (a small-conical basket) on the end. The aircraft seeking fuel is equipped with a refueling probe that will pop into a fitting in the center of the drogue. The refueling aircraft pushes the drogue forward a foot or two putting slack in the fuel hose. This gives the tanker pilot a green light in his cockpit, and he turns on a fuel pump transferring fuel to the thirsty bird behind.

We have two kinds of tankers: the KA-3, affectionately known as the Whale, and the A-4 buddy tanker with two drop tanks and a tanker pack on the centerline. The tanker pack is a drop tank with the hose, pump, and drogue mechanisms in its tail.

It is easier to refuel from the whale because the drogue is streamed in a clean airstream between the two wing-mounted engines. On the A-4, your tail sticks up into the engine exhaust of the buddy tanker, which bounces you around a bit.

The A-4's refueling probe is on the right side of the fuselage and extends about two feet beyond the nose. Getting the probe in the basket requires some very precise flying. Because of the parallax caused by the offset probe, I have a hard time getting it in the basket. Dick Perry tells me,

"There is a trick. Just fly your right foot into the basket."

I try it. It works. Cool.

Refueling from an A-4 Buddy Tanker.
The picture is taken by the co-pilot of a KA-3 Whale. The A-4 is about to land and is giving all its extra fuel to the Whale to keep as much fuel as possible available in the air. A-3 refueling probe is on the left.

LATER IN THE WORKUP, the air wing gathers again, this time at Marine Corps Air Station (MCAS) Yuma, on the Arizona border with California and Mexico, to use its live-fire bombing ranges.

Wars are won on the ground, but winning on the ground is difficult if the other side has command of the air. Since World War II, the accepted tactics have been to strike the enemy's air bases first and hard at the beginning of a campaign to ensure air supremacy. However, at the beginning of the air campaign against North Vietnam, its air bases were off the White House's target list. When we get to Yuma, we practice cutting runways. *Hmmm.* Obviously, something new is blowing in the wind, and we have been chosen to be an agent of change.

To cut a runway, we will run sticks of bombs across it in three places, so the craters cut the runway into four portions, each too short to be usable. To minimize risk to the strike group, we want to swamp the defenses by making all three cuts simultaneously. This requires that the strike group approach normally, splitting at the last moment into three subgroups, each with its own roll-in and aim points. This requires tight choreography, so no one flies into another aircraft, its bomb-fall, bomb-blast, or exit route.

Those who keep the Yuma bombing ranges find a virgin patch of desert somewhere off on the edges of the range where it is safe to use a road grader. The "runway" is scraped on the desert. The day comes when we will have a dress rehearsal, complete with live ordnance. *Yippee Ki-yay!* After all the little blue practice bombs, dropping live ordnance is still a special treat.

There is another change. Some F-8 fighters will also carry bombs. The idea is that, because the A-4 attack squadrons will not always be at full strength, a division of F-8s will be a welcome addition to the strike group. It will also give the senior officers in the fighter squadrons a chance to earn career-enhancing experience (and medals) as strike commanders.

The F-8 can carry two Mark 83 thousand-pound bombs on the side of the fuselage instead of their normal Sidewinder air-to-air missiles. The fighter jocks are given a crash course in dive bombing, and the game is on. If MiGs show up, the F-8s will jettison the bombs and engage with their 20mm cannons.

A fighter CO is picked to lead the dress rehearsal against the faux runway. Off we go. The strike leader calls the target in sight and leads us all to the roll-in. Glancing down, I see a runway plowed on the desert floor. Dick and I are in the group tasked to make the middle cut on the runway. The flight leader calls in; I can see the bomb-laden F-8s begin their runs. I concentrate on setting myself up to follow Dick Perry down the pipe.

"Abort! Abort! Abort! There's a plane on the runway!"

Holy shit! Looking down to my four o'clock, I see a little blue private aircraft turning onto the runway for takeoff. At about that moment, the F-8s' thousand-pound bombs begin to explode across the runway in front of the little blue airplane. Strike lead has apparently found a rancher's private airfield. *Oops.*

Once again, we luck out. No one is hurt. Once again, our CAG and his supporting cast, with a case of beer and sincere apologies, are out explaining away a slight navigation error. A Navy road grader and crew are dispatched to repair the runway, and, once again, a patriotic citizen is persuaded to keep the incident to himself. We particularly do not want the North Vietnamese to hear that we are practicing bombing runways.

I remember thinking: *Well, we did a pretty good job cutting the runway. That's encouraging.* I also conclude, *Thank God the ranchers are on our side.* Their willingness to forgive us and help us is a sincere affirmation that they are with us. That feels good—but we really need to be more careful, especially with live ordnance.

MCAS YUMA SHARES the airfield with the Yuma International Airport. The Marines use the long northeast-southwest runway, while the city uses the shorter east-west runway. The two runways intersect. The Marine tower is on the east side of the airfield. The city tower is on the west. The towers use different radio frequencies.

One day, I taxi out to the south end of the long runway headed for one of the bombing ranges. I stop and do my pre-takeoff check list. The Marine tower clears me for takeoff. I acknowledge, take the runway, push the power up, and begin my takeoff roll. As I approach the intersection with the east-west runway I am accelerating through 100 knots.

The tower calls, "Alpha Hotel 403, Tower, can you stop short of the inter-section?"

What the hell? "Negative."

"Alpha Hotel 403, can you get airborne before the intersection!?"

Oh shit!

I scan the short runway. At my one o'clock, there is a twin-engine prop airliner, nose down with blue smoke from both main landing gear as he tries to stop before crossing in front of me.

I flash through the intersection ahead of it with fifty feet to spare.

Airborne, I raise the gear and flaps, thinking: *That was close to being really ugly.*

When I land, I am met by Doug Mow, Bob Arnold (our Ops officer), the CAG, some Marine officers and civilians from the FAA. Doug speaks first.

"Mike, we've listened to the tapes. We know you were cleared to takeoff, but these gentlemen will need a statement from you."

WHEN WE FINISH the Yuma deployment, we go back to Lemoore before redeploying to NAS Fallon for FMLPs leading to day and night CarQuals.

While at Lemoore the word spreads: there is an insurance agent at the Base Exchange who is selling life insurance policies from CUNA Mutual, a Wisconsin insurer, that have no aviation or war exclusions. I stand in line and buy a $30,000 policy. Problem solved. I figure that will give my wife $15,000 to live on for a year while she gets back on her feet; fifteen thousand buy a house or save for a rainy day; and will leave the $15,000 government policy for our daughter's college.

Two days later, the agent moves on to the next military air base.

THE FIRE aboard *Oriskany* casts long shadows. Before we move on board, every man in the air wing is sent to a one-day firefighting course. If you are in a burning building, you get out of the building and watch the firefighters attack the fire from the outside. Shipboard fires are different in two respects: First, you can't run out of the building. The fire must be fought from inside. Second, there are no spectators. During a fire on the ship, everyone but the dead are firefighters.

After a morning of lectures, we put on OBAs so we can breathe during a trip through a windowless maze filled with smoke. Inside I can see nothing. When we get out, they tell us that aboard ship we must know two routes to fresh air from our berthing and working spaces and know them in such detail that we can travel them blindfolded on our hands and knees.

That afternoon, we go to the fire pan, a shallow square dish forty feet on a side, filled with two inches of diesel and jet fuel. In the middle of the pan is the hulk of an airplane. They light a match. I spend a long half hour on the nozzle of a two-inch fire hose, where I am followed by one guy drenching me in a shower spray and another helping drag the fire hose as I try to put the fire out. It's hot, exhausting work. The smoke is acrid, filled with unburned droplets of oil, burning my eyes, mouth, and throat. The serpent's head of the nozzle constantly fights me, powered by the equal and opposite reaction to the gushing water. The hose itself is heavy and stiff with the pressurized water. I suppress the flame on one side of the aircraft, then turn to the flame under it. Moments later, the flames work around behind me, reigniting the part I just put out. I shuffle quickly back and start again. I have to move more quickly. I try again and again but can't beat the fire. I am tiring fast.

I am not going to be able to do this.

Maybe not, but *I am not going to quit.*

I put it out—but barely.

Oriskany was launched in 1945, before many of her crew were born. The ship is a giant steel box steeped in salt brine and stuffed full with aviation gasoline, fuel oil, jet fuel, rockets, bombs, flares, ammo, paper, wood, decades of paint, superheated steam, high-voltage electricity, and thirty-five-hundred sleep-deprived young men—all things that make uneasy neighbors. The result is three or four fires a week. Not fire drills—fires. Some small, some not. Fires at night are the worst. Hard-won sleep shattered and scattered.

In our four-man stateroom, I have the bunk above Barry Wood. During the '66 cruise, Barry's berth was in the JO bunkroom. Because of the pilots, aircraft carriers have more officers than stateroom berths. The thirty or so most junior are relegated to the JO bunkroom, a barrack-style space located in the fo'c'sle (pronounced "folk-sill.") It is located in the bow of the ship below the flight deck.

A year before, when the fire broke out aboard *Oriskany*, Barry was in the JO bunkroom. He was the last man to get out alive; close friends who were behind him died.

Now, when the fire alarm sounds in the night, Barry has his flight suit and boots on and is out of the state room sprinting up the ladder and out of our cul-de-sac before I can bail out of the upper bunk. I decide:

I'm going to beat him.

I never do. But Barry makes a believer out of me. Get out now! Seconds matter.

WE FLY aboard *Oriskany* for CarQuals and a short workup cruise. The Ghost Riders are assigned Ready Room 2, filled with faux-leather cushioned chairs, each with a pop-up steno arm—just like in the *Bridges of Toko Ri*. And now, *I am in the ready room aboard Oriskany, looking at the same chairs and probably the same duty officer's desk.* I think again of Dave Pollack.

Our parachute riggers have made covers to slip over the headrests on the chairs with a pilot's name on each, just like those in the movie. The seats are assigned by seniority. Skipper sits on the front left side of the middle aisle, XO is on the right side, because traditionally the pilot sits on the left and the copilot on the right. I am in the back on the right side.

This deployment is my first time to live aboard ship. The ship is fresh from six months in the yard repairing damage from the fire.

CarQuals go well. I finally figure out how to handle the "burble." In 1967, all carriers except the nuclear-powered *Enterprise* are powered by oil-fired boilers. That means they trail a hot, turbulent stream of gases from the smokestack in the island superstructure on the starboard (right) side of the ship. Because of the angled deck, we start our landing approaches to the starboard of the ship's wake. As we get in close, we fly through the stack gases. We call this bump in the road the "burble." The disturbed air in the burble causes a loss of lift, which makes the aircraft sink below the glide slope.

During a carrier approach, power controls the rate of descent, and the nose attitude of the aircraft controls the airspeed. If you are low, you add power but do not raise your nose. If you are fast, you raise the nose but do not decrease the power. In the burble, you must add power to avoid sinking below the glide path and risking a "ramp strike." The saying is, "A ramp strike will ruin your whole day." But, add too much throttle and you go high. Being high-in close means you land past the last wire, bolter, and go around again. When you fly out of the burble, the power you added will take you high, above the flight path, and you have the high-in close problem all over again

The A-4 has just caught the arresting cable. The LSO is on the left.
The stack gas that causes the burble is visible behind the island.

Just to make it more interesting, the burble is invisible, and it moves to the left or right depending on the angle of the ship's course to the wind. You must "feel it." All of this happens in the last six or seven seconds of the approach. It is part of what makes every carrier landing interesting. Initially, I had problems handling the burble. Dealing with the burble is not something we can learn to deal with during FMLPs. Airfields do not have stack gas. During CarQuals aboard *Oriskany*, I get the burble down-pat. My landings are less adventurous.

THEY TEACH AND PREACH "lookout doctrine" from day one in the training command. Keep your head on a swivel—always. A sphere has an infinite number of points on its surface. Threats can come at very high speeds from any one of them. Seeing is survival. We all have excellent to preternatural vision, but keeping a constant scan while holding your focus on infinity, catching the smallest spot as your eyes sweep by, is a skill and a discipline.

We go aboard *Oriskany* for the WeapTraEx (pronounced "wepp-tray-ex," an acronym for weapons training exercise). The WeapTraEx is a dress rehearsal for combat operations. The ship and air wing put it all together and practice making strikes against inland targets and defending the carrier from attacks by enemy aircraft or ships. It is observed and graded by outsiders. For the JOs, it is a chance to have some fun and do a lot of cool stuff. For the senior officers, it is just another grand opportunity to ruin a promising career.

The climax of the WeapTraEx is a mock Alfa Strike from the carrier operating west of San Diego. We will cross the beach going feet-dry just north of the city and "penetrate" to the target, a bombing range near Yuma, where we will (hopefully) strike the designated target with irresistible élan and devastating accuracy.

The big day arrives. We brief, launch, and join up as if it is the real thing. As we approach the coast, the air wing shakes itself out and begins to jink about in anticipation of the (hypothetical) flak. Think of thirty fluttering moths doing their best to imitate a cavalry charge. Dick and I are on the right side of the strike group. I am a nugget and concentrate on staying with my leader and not becoming half of a midair collision.

"Airliner! Ten o'clock level!"

I look left. There is a commercial airliner bigger than life surrounded by a gaggle of A-4s scattering like gnats. It's headed south to Lindbergh Field in San Diego. In the snapshot memory I take away, I can see little round spots of faces looking out several windows as I follow Dick, who is pitching down and left.

I remember no official repercussions from the near miss, actually near miss*es*. None of the heavies (i.e., Lieutenant commanders and up) are dismissed. We pass the WeapTraEx. We are sent to Yankee Station. My guess is that there is enough blame to go around. Why didn't those who planned the mission take a look at the published approach routes into San Diego's Lindberg Field? Why does the airline crew miss thirty-plus aircraft on a collision course? Why does the FAA Approach Control for Lindbergh Field miss the convergence of one of its charges with a flock of thirty aircraft? And why, oh why, do all those superb and highly trained eyes in the strike group fail to see an *airliner* until it is among us? Maybe no one wants to throw the first stone.

There is a private repercussion. Dick sits me down. He makes it clear he expects me to notice things substantially smaller and faster moving than a Boeing 727 on a collision course. "Aye, aye, sir." Staying with Dick and avoiding a midair while jinking consumed all my attention. I had no time to maintain lookout. Clearly, I must get my eyes and brain moving faster if I am to not lose my leader (the mortal sin for any wingman), avoid the dreaded midair, *and* see the threats—*all* the threats. Another off-syllabus learning opportunity.

CHAPTER 8

WAITING

Betwixt and between.
USS Oriskany *off Midway Island en route to Yankee Station, 1967*

The legions of soldiers had time on their hands, if not on their side.

—William Manchester,
Paul Reid

THE WEEK after the WeapTraEx, we are back at Lemoore, and the squadron packs to move aboard *Oriskany*. The ship is alongside the carrier pier at NAS Alameda on the Oakland side of San Francisco Bay. The ship leaves port for another brief shakedown cruise, so we can fly the aircraft on board, and ride the ship back to Alameda.

My wife meets the ship, and we drive back down to Lemoore for about ten days of downtime. It is an odd hiatus. Our aircraft are on the ship. We are in Lemoore. I am done training. Now it will be for real. I don't have any fear or anxiety. I just float along in the river of excitement and adrenaline. We are ready. I am ready. I am a good pilot. I know what to do and how to do it. I am a professional. Still have a lot to learn, but I know I can handle whatever comes. The waiting is worse than the week before Christmas when I was little.

My wife is worried, but she hides it well. I feel a little guilty and try to hide how excited and impatient I am to get on with it. I keep telling her, "I am going to miss you," but I am thinking, *I can't wait*. She has to know. I keep rubbing my nose between the sides of my thumbs, something I have done all my life when I am excited. Some doctor once told me it has a name: vaso-something. My wife thinks it makes me look like a squirrel.

She and I find ordinary things to fill the time. I spend a morning getting the oil changed in our '67 Camaro. I go through my books and pick forty of my favorites. I will want familiar places and old friends to visit when I have the time to read. Things like that. I am amazed at how normal we keep things right up until we kiss good-bye on the quay and I walk up the gangway to board *Oriskany*.

I will get better at not thinking about what is coming.

MOST AMERICANS who go to Vietnam in 1967 get there on chartered airliners. We go the old-fashioned way—by ship, sailing out under the Golden Gate Bridge.

USS *Oriskany* is scheduled to depart Alameda for Yankee Station off the coast of North Vietnam on Friday, June 16, 1967. My wife and I leave our daughter with my parents and drive to San Francisco two days early. Wednesday and Thursday become a legendary lost, last weekend. The Ghost Rider JOs are inseparable. We drink, make love to our wives and girlfriends, laugh at not much, and at pretty much everything. Not thinking past the moment.

We go to 39 Main, a bar across the Golden Gate bridge in Sausalito. We all sit outside on the deck over the water. The surrounding decks of other bars are filled with quieter crowds enjoying a sunny day just because it is sunny—not because it is their last day in the land of normal.

C-10, drunk, climbs up on the deck railing, fifteen feet above rocks exposed by low tide. Standing upright, he declaims the poem Old Nell:

"Old Nell was a schoolteacher way out west, who came to know that humping was the best. . . ."

There is no ignoring this blond young man with a perpetual smile in his voice and a willingness to like almost everyone, even you, especially you. Even the staff stand in awe and laugh as he prances on the narrow rails, arms open, hips gyrating, pounding out the relentless cadence of Old Nell enjoying sex as openly and good-heartedly as I can only dream of.

I am aware it is my last grasp at the normalcy of peace-time but am so wrapped up in the romance of the moment that I don't think past today. A successful, if inverted, exercise in avoidance behavior.

The next morning, I kiss my wife good-bye on the carrier pier at NAS Alameda, among a horde of others, ship's company and air wing alike.

I climb the gangway, feeling surreal, detached. Is it happening? Not sure how I should feel, but pretty sure I should be feeling something. When I get to the top of the gangway, I face aft to salute the colors on the fantail, hidden from sight behind the gray bulk of the flight deck, turning back to salute the officer of the deck. "Request permission to come aboard, sir." A last ritual act, asking, "Let me be part of this."

The officer of the deck returns my salute, "Permission granted." I go up to stand on the shore side of the flight deck and watch.

Sailors cast off lines as thick as my calf muscle from bollards on the quay. The Boatswain's deck crew fish them on board. I can hear invisible tugboats growling against the ship's mass. Then, with no sense of motion, there are a few more feet of space between ship and shore; only by looking away and looking back can I measure the movement.

Looking back to the quay, I see her go, walking with the other squadron wives, some holding the hands of children old enough to walk. They walk quickly down the quay, many, especially the children, looking back over their shoulders. They are headed for their cars a half mile away, to race over the Oakland Bay Bridge, through San Francisco to the south end of the Golden Gate Bridge. They will park and walk quickly to the center of the bridge on the bay side, to wave one last time as we sail underneath.

The *O Boat* sails across the bay at a stately pace, on its own, no tugs in attendance. San Francisco slips by on the port side as we duck under the Oakland Bay Bridge. I pick out the Buena Vista Café where we all got together for Irish coffee last night.

We curve left, toward the Golden Gate, the city slipping by behind us. As the bow passes under the bridge, I can hear the voices of the wives calling down, whipped away in the wind, indecipherable. She is there. I raise my arm and wave. The ship's captain orders a single blast on the ship's God Almighty horn, which can be heard over the sound of forty jet engines, a sound so deep and loud you feel it in your chest more than hear it. One long horn blast signifying, "We are going—we are coming."

We emerge on the ocean side. Turning, I look up and back at the ocean side of the bridge. No one there. I am looking at the other side of a door that has closed behind us. We are pointed due west into the vast empty room of the Pacific, headed to war. Finally.

Looking at the western horizon, I remember both of my uncles, one a Marine, the other a Navy Sea Bee, who sailed west on troopships to their wars on the far side of this ocean, and of Jerry Hatchel, my first remembered friend, whose father sailed west on a troopship in 1943 and never came home. It is my turn now. I am where I belong.

Before the week is out, the ship sails into the incredibly blue sea that surrounds the Hawaiian Islands. Two days later, we sail into Pearl Harbor, gliding past USS *Arizona*, the battleship that died on December 7, 1941. The ship whose death I have seen countless times on film. The tomb of 1,102 Sailors and Marines who died with her. It seems odd to see this relic of my father's war wrapped in peace-time tourism while on my way to another war, a smaller war where the stakes are less obviously existential for the country, but no less existential for those of us who make this journey. After a thirty-six-hour stay, we reboard and sail out of Pearl and past Diamond Head.

Somewhere past mid-ocean, the Russians send a Bear, the Soviet's TU 95 long-range prop bomber, out of Vladivostok to overfly us. They just want to remind us the cold war is still on, and prove they can find us. We send F-8s out to intercept and escort it all the way to the carrier to prove we can shoot it down long before it gets close enough to launch its weapons against the ship.

Larry "C-10" Cunningham & Jim "YDK" Waldron

WE SPEND a lot of time in the air intelligence spaces getting briefed. There is an air intelligence officer (AI) attached to the air wing and one to each squadron. The Ghost Riders AI is Jim Waldron, an impossibly young-looking nugget. He quickly earns the sobriquet of

"Young Dumb Kid," YDK for short. Jim was good at his job and enjoyed his status as the one who knew what we needed to know.

ROLLING THUNDER is the name given to the air campaign striking targets in North Vietnam. Designed and directed by the political and military hierarchy in Washington, it encompasses strikes launched from Yankee Station, Thailand, and South Vietnam. As originally conceived, the strategic purpose of Rolling Thunder was to interdict men, weapons, and supplies moving from North Vietnam to South Vietnam. The primary targets were military bases, tank farms, bridges, ferries, railroads, transshipment facilities, and other infrastructure used to move troops and supplies. Although the interdiction effort never stops, by 1967 the campaign begins to shift toward an attempt to persuade the North Vietnamese to give up its efforts to conquer South Vietnam. Washington gradually ramps up the pressure, adding other infrastructure targets: headquarters, power plants, factories, and so on.

The Pentagon partitioned North Vietnam into seven geographic "route packages" for targeting purposes; they are numbered 1 through 5, 6a, and 6b. Each is assigned to the Navy or Air Force. The northeast rail line to China is in Route Package 6a and is an Air Force responsibility. The Navy has Route Package 6b, which includes Hanoi and Haiphong. At some point the Air Force is allowed to poach in Route Package 6b. I don't know how the Navy brass feels about it, but we are glad to have their help.Strategic goals change slowly if at all. Tactics, however, can be changed overnight. Every day of combat is a learning experience. As a result, the war constantly morphs as both sides react to each other. Even the veterans in our squadron have been away from combat for months and their experience is now out of date. As we sail across the Pacific, we attend a series of briefings about the current tactical environment.

THE DEFENSES—By mid-1967, the air defenses of the North Vietnamese included early warning radars, MiG fighters, surface-to-air guided missiles (SAMs), radar directed anti-aircraft artillery (AAA or flak), and small arms, woven into a network of layers. They are not only "sophisticated and effective,"[9] they are the densest, most experienced, and most skilled in the world. Although we have practiced Alfa Strikes against imaginary defenses during the workup, no one who hasn't experienced them can conjure up a realistic sense of what the North Vietnamese air defenses have become. The Soviets and Chinese pour in the equipment, down the rail link through China directly into North Vietnam, and on "neutral" merchant ships that come in through the Tonkin Gulf into Haiphong, protected by international law and White House decree.

SMALL ARMS—The bottom layer of their defense cake are small arms: everything from fifty-caliber machine guns down to pistols. They are ubiquitous throughout North Vietnam, they shoot bullets, not explosive and shrapnel filled cannon shells. Nevertheless, their numbers and high rates of fire make them very dangerous. The good news is they are effective only below thirty-five-hundred feet. We generally stay above that altitude to eliminate them from our risk package.

ANTI-AIRCRAFT ARTILLERY—Flak is the generic name for fire from anti-aircraft cannon. The North Vietnamese have a full arsenal of Soviet equipment: 37mm, 57mm, 85mm, and 100mm cannons. Each has a progressively longer range and bigger bang at the nasty end. The flak batteries are so dense on the ground that we are told to assume we are always in range of several flak sites.

Our ECM (electronic countermeasures) equipment is fairly effective at deceiving the radar-directed flak. It fools the enemy radar systems by giving them a ghost image that is more "real" to it than my aircraft's return. Then, by some sort of electronic trickery, the little black box will move the ghost image away from my aircraft. When it has lured the fire control radar far enough away, it turns the ghost off, leaving the tracking radar to wonder where the hell I went. The North Vietnamese soon turn the gullible computers off and go back to pointing and shooting the old-fashioned way.

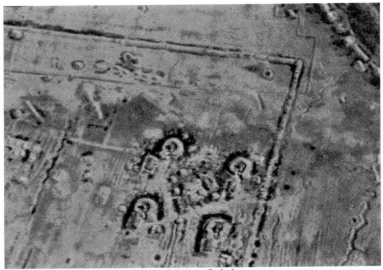

Four-gun 85mm flak battery.
The Fire Can fire control radar is in the center.

We do our best to make it harder to hit us by always "jinking" while flying over the beach. Jinking is the constant and random change of direction and altitude. Because of the ranges involved, it takes seconds for the flak projectile to reach the aircraft. The gunners have to aim where they think I will be when their round arrives. Done right, jinking makes that impossible to predict. They have to guess and hope they get lucky.

The trick is to change direction a moment before a shell fired just after your last change will reach you. Up about ten-thousand to thirteen-thousand feet, that's about every three seconds. Down at thirty-five-hundred feet, it's more like once every second. If you change too soon, you may fly back into the path of the shell just in time for it to arrive. Like most things in life: Timing is everything.

However, AAA systems are cheap and pump out a lot of rounds. Sooner or later, they are going to hit something. But there are things more dangerous than the omnipresent flak.

SURFACE-TO-AIR MISSILES—In the next century will have a friend in Maine who walks everywhere. One day, his wife sends him to get groceries. He takes a short cut through a patch of woods between the grocery store and his house. On his way back, burdened with bags

116

of groceries, he meets a bear. The bear is *not*, as he had been told, "more afraid of him than he is of it." He tosses the groceries at the bear. Spins about and thinks,

Feets, don't fail me now.

He runs back to the store and uses the city streets to walk the long way home.

The bears in our woods are the SA-2 Guideline surface-to-air missiles. Our mission is to get past the bears and deliver the groceries.

Originally the Navy planned to defeat the SAM by flying in at low level where its radar cannot track you due to "ground clutter" (the interference caused by trees, buildings, wires, etc.). However, small arms and flak, supplemented by people throwing rocks, are very effective against aircraft flying so low. It is safer to dance with the missiles at altitudes that rule out small arms and decrease the effectiveness of flak by increasing the lag time between when the gunner pulls the trigger and when the cannon shell reaches the aircraft. So, we fly high, jink like mad, and keep our eyes out for missile launches.

The mere idea of the SA-2 scares the shit out of me. There is just something malevolent and personal about a missile that will "chase" you. The fact the missile is computer-guided makes it seem even more implacable. It rings of John Henry's battle with the steam drill. Heroic but ultimately fatal.

When designed in the mid-1950s, the SA-2 system was state of the art. In the mid-1960s it will prove to have some weaknesses.

It has a search radar that gives them a big picture. The Fan Song acquisition and guidance system has two antennas. One fixes the elevation of the target and provides up-down commands to the missile. The second fixes the bearing and provides left-right guidance. There are three operators, one for the search radar, and one for each of the acquisition antennas. There is a computer that coordinates the two guidance radars and gives guidance commands to the missiles once the booster rocket falls away.

Soviet-made SA-2 surface to air missile; NATO code-named "Guideline."

Our ECM is a life saver. It does two things. First, it gives audio warnings that the aircraft is being painted by radars, and, second, it has active counter-measures to confuse and defeat the Fan Song computer guidance system.

I learn to identify the cricket like pulse-rate signature of the SA-2 search radar when it paints my aircraft. When the ECM gear detects the signal of one of the acquisition antennas, it generates a slow electronic bird song we call the "warbler." If the aircraft is painted by both the acquisition antennas, it generates a fast warbler, signaling that the Fan Song has locked on my aircraft and a missile is targeting me. That warning alone can be a life saver.

The fast warbler also tells me that the ECM gear has started active countermeasures. It uses the same wandering ghost trick it uses on the flak radars. In 1967, our ECM gear is so effective it forces the missile operators to turn off the computer and guide the missiles manually.

Without the computer, the Fan Song is clunky, complicated, and clumsy, requiring a high degree of split-second coordination by the operators. But they have had lots of practice and are good at it. Nevertheless, now it is a human *versus* human contest, pitting my reactions and skill against those of the missile operators.

Here's our problem: Imagine you are riding a bicycle on the Bonneville Salt Flats, and a guy in a powerful sports car with the throttle jammed wide-open is coming at you from a mile or so away. His sole purpose in life is to crash into you. He tops out at about 180 miles per hour. You can do about twenty miles per hour on the bike. As he gets close, there is a moment when you can turn and pedal far enough to the right or left that the guy in the sports car cannot react and turn sharply enough to hit you before he shoots past. The good news is he only gets one pass at you, and, even better, his car blows up shortly after he misses.

The metaphor has its limits. Remember that, on my bike, I must change direction quickly and pedal fast enough to get out of the way. To change direction quickly in my aircraft, I need to pull maximum Gs, but the G-loading greatly increases the drag generated by the airplane's wings. The extra drag slows the A-4 quickly, even at full power. But, while the car and bike can only go left or right, the aircraft and missile can go left-right *and* up-down. Therefore, to counter the extra drag, I can dive steeply, using gravity to help maintain and then build speed as soon as I stop turning and take the Gs off. Although this puts me moving slightly left or right of the missile's flight path, the missile is also rising to me. A steep dive puts my vertical direction almost ninety degrees off that of the climbing missile.

So, our standard evasion tactic is to turn enough to put and keep the missile at our two or ten o'clock position. That gets us moving a little to the side and keeps the missile in view. Then, at the critical moment, we use the A-4's rapid roll rate to go well past vertical and put heavy Gs on to get the nose down to a sixty-degree dive that will displace me both laterally and vertically. Timed right, that will put me inside the SAM's vertical and lateral turn radii, and, with the help of gravity, I can move far-enough fast-enough to get out of its kill zone. If I run out of altitude or there is a second missile, I can put the Gs back on, make a sharp pullout into a zoom climb to get on the other side of its turn radius.

The bottom line is that if I see the missile soon enough and time my evasion maneuver just right, I can dodge it.

But, saying is easier than seeing. The demonic sports car is a lot easier to see and travels a lot slower than the missile. The missile starts from ten to twelve miles away and, head on, is only about twenty-inches in diameter (about the size of a small trash barrel lid). I have very good eyesight, but I am not sure it is that good. Worse, the SAM travels at three times the speed of sound. That is faster than anything you have ever seen short of a lightning bolt.

Compared with most surface-to-air missiles, the SA-2 is huge. Weighing two and half tons, it is thirty-five fee long including the booster rocket that kicks it off the rails, riding on a hundred-foot exhaust. After five seconds the booster is done and falls away. At this point the missile has reached its top speed and is traveling three times the speed of sound. The second-stage motor burns for another twenty-two seconds but has a much smaller, less visible exhaust—especially if it is pointed at you and is mostly hidden behind the trash lid.

There is a bit of good news: the missile has fuzzy vision and is only accurate to within about 250 feet. The bad news is that the SA-2 compensates for this problem by having a proximity detonator that explodes if it gets close to something, and an immense 430-pound fragmentation warhead that is lethal out to more than 210 feet at the altitudes we are flying.

The North Vietnamese have taken to launching two or even three missiles in quick succession, all guiding on the same aircraft. So, there isn't just one sports car. There are two or three. If the first one don't get you, the second will—and if it don't get you, . . .

For our part, we fly in a combat formation that spreads us out leaving them lots of room to miss when they fire SAMs through our formations and to make sure the big warhead does not get two of us. During the work-up we practice maintaining five hundred feet between aircraft. In combat, we soon increase that to between eight hundred and a thousand feet.

NORTH VIETNAMESE AIR FORCE—The frosting on their defense cake are their MiG 17 and MiG 21 fighter aircraft. Both are more than a match for the A-4 in air-to-air combat. However, our airwing includes two squadrons of F-8 Crusaders. The F-8 were designed as air superiority fighters and are flown by pilots whose sole goal in life is to shoot down MiGs. They escort and shield us from the MiGs and the ship from the few bombers in their inventory.

Except for one or two occasions which will be recounted in due course, the MiG's tend to stay well clear of our air wing.

By the time we approach the Philippines, I have a theoretical understanding of these problems and what I must do to avoid becoming a statistic in the far-right column.

ON THE FAR SIDE of the Pacific, we head for the United States naval base at Subic Bay on Luzon Island in the Philippines. There we will stop to load ordinance and provisions for the first line period. On the way in, Dick Perry takes me on flying tours of the Philippine archipelago. Beautiful, verdant islands scattered about a blue cloth. One day he says, "You are going to see something special today." He takes me to a part of Luzon where there is a lake. In the lake is an extinct volcano. In the crater there is a lake, with a little island in it. From ten-thousand feet you can see an island, in a lake, on an island, in a lake, on an island, in the ocean. It is wonderful flying, just the two of us out for some fun.

The sightseeing trips are daily distractions, but even so, my curiosity and anxiety leak through. *How will I react when someone shoots at me?* Thanks to my Marine drill instructors in Pre-Flight and the screamers in the training command, I am pretty much bulletproof when it comes to performing under stress. But I have yet to learn if my composure is *bullet* proof. I think—I hope I know the answer. I am in a hurry to get myself shot at for the first time and get it over with.

On July 2, we tie up at the carrier pier next to NAS Cubi Point in Subic Bay Navy Base. We will depart Cubi on July 12 and commence combat operations on July 14.

Meanwhile, those of us who will be flying over hostile places are sent off to a remote mountainous area near Clark Air Force Base for more training in survival, evasion, resistance, escape (SERE). This time it is the jungle survival course. The instructors are U.S. Navy, but the teachers are Negrito tribesmen. The Negritos are small and wiry. The average man is less than five feet tall.[10]

121

Following them through the jungle, I feel like a clumsy giant. They don't talk much to us, but they can do almost anything with their machetes and a piece of bamboo. Impressed, I hire their village blacksmith fabricate a machete from the leaf spring of a car, and a wooden sheath. It is small enough to fit on my calf between ankle and knee. I ask the parachute riggers to sew a pocket for it on the outside of my G-suit leg.

I hear rumors that the Negritos also deploy with Navy Seals and Force Recon Marines on covert missions into North Vietnam and Laos. The war is getting closer, and the closer it gets the more the anxiety leaks into my thoughts. (Decades later, I will meet a short ex-Marine who spent time in North Vietnam with a team of Negritos.)

Back from SERE, I check the squadron duty officer (SDO) roster. I have the duty on July 14. *I can't fucking believe it.* July 14 will be our first day of combat operations. The last place I want to be on July 14th is flying the SDO desk in the ready room for twenty-four hours.

ON JULY 12, we depart for Yankee Station. We fly to knock the dust off our skills. Lt. D. M. Wood from the Saints, our sister A-4 squadron, gets a "cold cat"—a catapult launch that, for one reason or another, does not give him flying speed. As his aircraft goes over the bow, he ejects. Wood is rescued in good condition by our Angel. I don't believe in omens, but, if they do exist, I can't figure out if this one is good or bad.

WE ARRIVE on Yankee Station during the night of July 13. We are on the line—at the leading edge of battle. At 2400 hours, I relieve the SDO and begin my twenty-four-hour desk marathon. Flight ops don't begin until 0700, so it will be quiet until about 0500. That gives me lots of time to think about what I will not be doing today.

The air wing will be flying cyclic combat operations. That means we will have six-launches at two-hour intervals, each with about half our available aircraft. Each section of two aircraft is assigned a single target. After taking out the target, they will conduct armed reconnaissance ("armed recce" or "recce," pronounced "wrecky") in designated areas near their targets.

122

The targets are scattered across the southern half of North Vietnam, away from the heavily defended targets in the north. The powers that be are trying to ease us into the maelstrom. But anything we think is worth bombing, the North Vietnamese think is worth defending.

Part III

BAPTISM

Flight Deck at dawn.

Well, if I live through this battle, I think I shall have seen war at its worst. Hell must have some bottom.
—Major Harry Dillon,

CHAPTER 9

DAY ONE

Bombed up and headed feet dry

July 14, 1967

DAWN FINDS me sitting at the SDO desk, in my starched, washed khakis, name tag on the right breast of my shirt, wings and my national service ribbon on my left, with a little silver bar on each collar. A combat virgin lieutenant (junior grade) standing watch sitting at a desk.

About 0445, the ready room comes to life. The maintenance desk in the back gears up, and the pilots start wandering in from breakfast. Everyone (but me) is dressed in steel-toed flight boots, intended to save toes during an ejection, and the jungle camouflage fatigues our squadron elects to use rather than the standard flight suits. Unlike the flight suits, the fatigues are not fireproof, but they beat the standard flight suit if we have to eject and find ourselves trying to hide in the jungle until help arrives. Besides, if there is a fire in the cockpit, we'll be reaching for the ejection seat handles, fireproof suit or not. At least those are the arguments we use to justify our deviation from the standard. Besides, we look cool in jungle camouflage.

Energy, excitement, and tension crackle through the room. I can smell it. Feel it in the air. Hear it in the pilot's voices. See it in their strictly controlled nonchalance. The pilots on the first launch ebb out for the air intelligence (AI) briefing. I sit smartly at my desk.

Above me on the flight deck, with no aircraft engines turning, it is almost quiet, broken only by the noise of an occasional piece of yellow gear moving about. The red-shirted ordnance men are pushing the last five-hundred-pound bombs down the flight deck, loaded two on each of the low, teeter-totter carts with two small wheels in the middle, running like hell to bounce them over the arresting cables.

On other days, they will push 750-pound, 1,000-pound, or even 2,000-pound bombs down the deck and over the cables, along with an assortment of rockets, missiles, CBUs (cluster bombs), 20mm ammo cans, and, at night, the illumination flares.

The ordnance men push the carts under a wing then screw the "hernia bars," inch-thick, four-feet-long steel bars, into the threaded fuse housings in the nose and tail of the bombs. Squatting on their heels, backs straight, they lift each bomb up to the underwing racks. One man to each bar for a five-hundred-pounder, two on each end for a seventy-fifty, and three for thousand-pounders. The eighteen men of our ordnance crew are all rangy and zero-fat lean. They will load over a five million pounds of bombs during the cruise. That averages more than a ton and quarter per-man a day. The fuze guys follow behind, screwing the fuses in, dialing in the delays, feeding arming wires through the safety clips, and then tying them off to the bomb racks.

A Red shirt humping two Mark 82 five hundred pound bombs

The blue shirts are "plane pushers," tasked with manhandling the planes by brute force when it is necessary to move them short distances, shoving each into its designated spot with inches to spare on either side, while the brown shirt plane captains sit in the cockpits riding the brakes. As soon as it is parked, they chock the wheels and bind it in place with tie-down chains. One chain for each wing tip, two for both of the main landing gear and the nose gear. More in rough seas. When the bird has to be moved, they unchain it, pull the chocks, and follow along, plodding under the weight of the tie-down chains draped over their shoulders while they carry the chocks. But now, with everything in place for the launch, they stand or squat, chainless for the moment, waiting for it to begin. Teenage kids doing hard, dirty jobs for a fourteen-hour day in the most dangerous working environment imaginable.

The yellow-shirt flight-deck directors stand talking to each other or through their lip mics to the little shack in the island, where their ubergods dwell, or listening to the air boss, Zeus, over all on that deck, whose iron authority extends out to planes in the landing pattern during recoveries, watching everyone and everything from above in his glass-house throne room high over the flight deck, ordering, scolding, complaining, warning about something he wants, doesn't like, or worries him. An Old Testament god, ruling over layered worlds of lesser gods.

Back from the briefing, the pilots gear up: G-suit, harness, survival vest, pistol(s), and the rest. Each with his own ritual. The squawk box at the SDO's desk comes to life: **"Pilots, man your aircraft."**

They grab their helmet bags off the hooks on the ready room wall. Stuffed inside are their helmets, gloves, and oxygen masks, with the kneeboards in a side pocket. They head out the back door.

An hour later and the pilots on the second launch are back from their own AI briefing and going through the same rituals. Among them is my friend and bunky C-10.

Wuff Flight: C-10 and Lt.Cmdr. Deny "Wuff" Weichman.

Wuff and C-10 have been assigned a small bridge in what the old hands call Happy Valley. It is in the North Vietnam panhandle, up against the border with Laos. C-10 is pumped. I sit at the SDO desk—still wondering how I will react when I get shot at. C-10 will have no trouble finding the answer to that question.

Half an hour later, they have launched, and the first cycle is recovering. Pilots start filtering back, sky high on adrenaline, buzzing about their first missions. I am grumpy but listening closely.

Wuff leads C-10 to their bridge. It is defended by a 37mm flak battery. Little gray puffs dot the sky around them. Wuff makes the first run. The flak follows him down. C-10 stays on the perch at ten thousand feet, waiting.

Wuff has a good hit and tells C-10, "Bomb on my smoke." C-10 rolls in, drops two bombs, and pulls up. As the nose rises above the horizon, he unloads the Gs and rolls to start a climbing turn—*BAM*—his aircraft is hit.

C-10 will later tell his story this way:

Things happen pretty quickly for the next few seconds, probably a lot shorter time than it takes me to describe . . . . I have full power on and the engine starts banging. I pull the "T" handle by my right knee, which cleans everything off the underside of the aircraft and pull the power back. I look to my left and see the mountains that divide Vietnam and Laos then look to the right and see the coastline. I am closer to the mountains. I run the throttle up and back a couple of times . . . . I have an engine. Because I have an engine, and I can see the water, I decide to turn right toward the coast . . . .

What C-10 doesn't know is that his aircraft was hit in the nose. The engine intakes swallowed his shattered nose. C-10 has lost his radio and all of his instruments except the wet compass, the barometric altimeter, and the EGT (exhaust gas temperature), which we call the "nickel gauge."

In that moment, C-10 stays low as he turns toward the coast. Wuff is climbing back for another run and doesn't see him go. When Wuff realizes C-10 is not where he expects him to be, he calls—but C-10 has no radio. Wuff checks for smoke, fire, and scars on the ground in the target area then searches west toward the Laotian border. Not finding him, Wuff heads east toward their emergency rendezvous, an island just offshore.

C-10 manages to climb to five thousand feet, but the engine is banging away. He has to reduce power. C-10 uses the gravity-deployed slats on his wing to fly at the minimum efficient speed but gradually loses altitude. When he gets too low, he grits his teeth and adds power. The aircraft slowly climbs, but the engine protests with explosive bangs that shake the entire aircraft.

He flies over a good-sized city at about eight hundred feet, well inside the effective range of small arms, but he finally manages to cross the beach and head out over the gulf.

Making the water is a big deal. I take stock of what I do and do not have. That doesn't take long. I have an engine. I can add power and three things happen: I can climb a bit; the pointer on the EGT moves up toward the red line; and the engine explosions are louder and closer together. That is about all I can take, and I pull the power back. Three things happen: the plane descends; the EGT pointer backs out of the yellow arc; and the explosions subside a bit.

C-10 sees other aircraft flying toward the carriers above him and takes his heading from them. He takes off his helmet and tries to use his handheld survival radio, but the engine noise is too loud. He gives his position twice and puts the survival radio away. He flies most of the way with one hand on the secondary ejection seat handle between his legs so he can eject instantly if the engine fails or explodes. He nurses the bird back the eighty miles to Yankee Station. The first carrier he spots has the aircraft pulled back into the landing area ready for a launch. He chugs past and spots a carrier that is recovering aircraft. It's *Oriskany*.

As he approaches *Oriskany*, C-10 is down to a hundred and fifty feet, so he lines up behind the boat for a straight-in approach. Wuff arrives at the ship and spots C-10's aircraft. Wuff joins up on his wing.

After a quick inspection of C-10's aircraft, Wuff flies up on C-10's wing. When C-10 sees him, Wuff begins pointing back between their aircraft.

I shrug, indicating I don't know what he is saying. He points behind me again and I think, He can't possibly want me to fly back toward Vietnam. *I shake my head and point at the ship. He shakes his head and points behind me. I shake my head and point at the ship. He waves and flies off.*

Wuff is trying to tell C-10 that flames are shooting out of his tailpipe. He knows the carrier is not going to let a burning aircraft try to land, but C-10 doesn't know he is on fire. When C-10 intercepts the landing glide path, it's time to lower his landing gear. With the increased drag of the landing gear, he sinks below the glide slope. He adds power, then more power:

The explosions increase in intensity. I see the EGT pointer pegging in the red. There is an explosion. I let go of the stick and pull the ejection handle.

I remembered the ejection training saying that you should always try to beat the automatic separation from the seat and the automatic deployment of the parachute. I try and am late for both events. I look down and see the plane upside down in the water with some landing gear pointing upward.

I hit the water, go under, inflate my water wings, and come up to the surface. I have my helmet and mask on and am breathing [the emergency oxygen supply] through the mask just fine.

The one thing C-10 forgot to do was release his parachute as he hit the water. As a result, he surfaces in a tangle of shroud lines that still connect him to the chute.

I feel a presence above me and look up to see the Angel helo hovering quite low overhead. The pararescue swimmer is standing in the doorway looking down at me. I attempt to release my oxygen mask bayonet fitting to signal him that I am okay, but my gloves are slippery.

Just as C-10 gets his mask off, the swimmer jumps. The swimmer lands in the shroud lines and plunges under the surface, jerking C-10 under the water with him. C-10 thinks: *I made it this far and now I'm going to drown.* The swimmer grabs his collar.

> *[He] shoots me up out of the water. Shroud lines are everywhere. With one arm, the swimmer holds me about waist-high out of the water and with his other hand is slashing away at the lines with a knife. I pull my hands and arms in tight to my body in hopes I don't get knifed. He is very good at what he does, and it isn't long before he has me in the horse collar at (the end of the helo's hoisting cable).*
>
> *I am hoisted up into the helo and on my way to the* O Boat.

At the SDO desk, the talker reported a plane on fire in the landing pattern. I looked up at the closed-circuit TV in time to see an aircraft on approach pitch down. I see the ejection. A few minutes later, I hear the pilot is picked up. The word comes down—it is C-10.

When C-10 is aboard the helo, the air boss suspends the recovery of other aircraft long enough for the helo to drop him off on the flight deck. I get someone to cover my desk and head for the hatch pilots use to go to and from the flight deck. Having no official business on the flight deck, I stand just outside the hatch trying to look inconspicuous.

The helo lands. The CAG, Burt Shepherd, our squadron XO, the flight surgeons, and a couple of corpsmen scurry out in that instinctive half crouch everyone adopts when stepping under the arc of spinning helicopter rotors. Yellow Shirts (aircraft directors) sheep dog this gaggle of very important pedestrians to the helo.

C-10 climbs out of the helo still dripping. Multiple handshakes with everyone in a deep bow under the down blast from the rotor. They turn around and head back to the hatch, everyone still in their crouch. C-10 will be taken directly to sick bay for a checkup and some of the flight surgeons' medicinal brandy. As C-10 passes, he sees me. Over the roar of the helicopter taking off, he says, "It's going to be a long fucking war, Mule."

That evening, they tell C-10 he will be the squadron duty officer tomorrow to give him a day to recover from the ejection. After the movie in the ready room that night, the flight schedule is out. I look. Dick Perry and I will jump in with both feet. We are scheduled for the first and third launches. Both are to hit an assigned target and then conduct an armed recce.

I hit the rack. Time to sleep. Tomorrow is the day.

CHAPTER 10

DAY TWO

Author after a mission.

July 15

THE ALARM clock stuffed by my head in the mattress box kicks off day two at 0415. I fumble for it. Turn it off. Hit the deck. Shit, shower, shave. Clean underwear. Clean socks. Fresh flight fatigues. I head for the wardroom to get breakfast off the flight-line buffet. I like the smell of breakfast in the wardroom: a mélange of coffee, bacon, and toast. I grab a handful of bacon and run several slices of bread through the endless belt toaster, painting them from the bucket of melted butter, and burying them in the premixed cinnamon and sugar. No eggs. No grits. A mug of coffee and a large glass of orange juice.

0500

Off to air intelligence for the strike brief. We bow our heads and smell the two-page Ditto handout, some holding it up to their faces, sniffing the strike plan like fourth graders, while they tell us why someone who is not going with us thinks these targets are a good idea. Lots of talk about where to be and when, radio frequencies, code words, and a big map with too many flak sites to avoid or worry about. My flak avoidance plan for the day is to jink and pray. Next, a map with active SAM sites. Red, overlapping circles, each with a scale fifteen-mile radius. *Pay attention.* There are no active sites in our recce area, but there are some to the north and east, and one just south of our coast-in and egress route. I check the AI's chart against my SAM map. No changes.

0525

Back to the ready room. Check the flight schedule on the SDO's desk to find Dick and my aircraft numbers. Time for Dick's brief. Our target is a small bridge on a secondary road over a little river, about fifteen miles inland between Vinh and Thanh Hoa. Our aircraft are armed with six Mark 82 bombs for the mission, with our 20mm cannons in reserve. Dick's brief is matter-of-fact. Not much different than going out on the bomb range at Yuma. I know what to do. Done with that. Time for another smoke and piss. Stress is a diuretic.

Time to gear up. Into the flight locker compartment. Carry the gear to the ready room where there is room to put it on. G-suit first, zipping the waist on the right side, then the legs from ankles up the inside of the legs to the crotch. Then the Browning 9mm, a gift from my father for its thirteen-round clip, in a holster slung from a web belt, then the flotation gear, two small lumps slung under each armpit on a lightweight harness. Then, the survival vest hung from shoulder straps and a zipper up the front, with its numerous pockets, each custom fitted to its contents. Take out the survival radio, test it, put it back in the pocket on the front of my survival vest, next to the shroud cutter/switchblade knife, pencil flares and launcher. And the second pistol, a Smith & Wesson .38-caliber revolver with a two-inch barrel. It is my backup pistol now, but will become the Plan A pistol within a matter of weeks.

Last is the integrated aircraft and parachute harness. I fish the G-suit hose through the harness on the left and slip the Browning holster through on the right, then align the straps to fit around the other gear and make sure my junk is clear of the leg straps that will jamb upward when absorbing the full impact of my weight against the parachute's opening shock. I leave the chest latch undone for some momentary comfort. Check the reserve cigarettes and matches in the G-suit calf pouch (wrapped in a plastic bag, just in case I find myself in the one-man life raft stowed in the ejection seat-pan survival gear). Kneeboard in the helmet for now.

I fish one more cigarette from the open pack in the small pocket sewn onto my upper sleeve.

0550

A crackle of static from the squawk box: "Pilots, man your aircraft." Stand up, pull the sides of my harness together, exhaling to get the chest latch closed. The harness is fitted so tight that I walk with a hunch, like the old man I think I'd like to be someday. A deep breath against the harness just to prove I can. I grab the handles of the helmet bag and head out the back of the ready room, checking at the maintenance desk to find the deck spot of our aircraft.

In the passageway, we mix with the pilots from our sister A-4 squadron, VA-163, whose ready room is next door as we all line up to step onto the escalator. Installed just to transport pilots to and from the flight deck, it runs up during launches and down during recoveries. Go left, then down the short passageway at the top of the escalator, past the flight deck control shack, a small space with a back door leading directly to the flight deck so the deck crew can pop in like waiters checking in with the kitchen. The inhabitants move scale, plan-view silhouettes of aircraft about a scale diagram of the flight deck etched into a six-foot stainless-steel table. People hover over it sliding things about like a giant multiplayer Ouija board. The model flight deck fills the small space, leaving only enough room for the savants to crowd about it. The talkers are relaying orders to the flight deck directors, the lesser gods out in the wind, each dressed in the yellow jersey signifying their omnipotence within the boundaries of the flight deck.

I step out of the island onto the flight deck, scanning for movement and jet exhausts pointed at me, then grab a glance at the sky to double-check the meteorologists' predictions. Walking aft down the flight deck to man up, I feel a mixture of pride, confidence, and camaraderie, holding the apprehension at bay for a few more minutes—until it has just cause to demand my attention.

The boat has turned into the wind and is cranking on the knots. I lean back into the whipping wind as I walk aft and enjoy the fresh, salt air. Some days the air is smogged with the smell of stack gas because the boat is still running downwind to gain sea room within her operating box for the upwind run during the launch. After we are gone, she will run downwind again. When the next cycle launches, the deck crew will pull any aircraft left on deck forward, clearing the landing area for us to land when we come back. As soon as the last aircraft recovers, they pull everything left on the deck aft to clear the bow for the next launch.

We walk past the green-shirt squadron-maintenance guys, mostly standing about watching, a few scurrying to complete a repair at the last minute, and past the blue shirts, acolytes of the yellow shirt flight directors. Their hearing-protection Mickey Mouse ears stick out of holes in their cotton-helmet like caps. Everyone on the deck except the pilots are color-coded by job. We are camouflaged.

I spot my bird. Looking her over from a distance as I walk up, making sure I don't miss something obvious before I dive into the details of the preflight inspection. I greet the brown shirted plane captain. It is his bird that I am about to borrow for an hour and a half. I pass him my helmet bag, exchanging ritual pleasantries and assurances. I begin the walk-around inspection, nose gear, down the right side of the fuselage, around the wing and underneath again, then back to the tail, and up the other side ending at the ladder up to the left side of the cockpit, looking at everything, searching for leaks, hairline cracks, missing rivets, and unsecured hatches, caps, and connectors.

Done, I pause at the nose and write my takeoff weight on the nose-gear door with a grease pencil for the catapult crew. Then, I climb up the ladder to its little platform on top, next to the cockpit. Step out onto the left wing to check the doghouse doors on the top of the fuselage, check the settings on the bombing computer. We don't use the bombing computer because it depends on inputs from our radar altimeter. Rock Hodges, our squadron electronic warfare guru, tells us the radar altimeter uses the same C-band radar as the SAM missile. He says it can act like a flashlight, saying, "Here I am. Shoot *me*." Still, I check the settings and make sure the access hatches are all buttoned. Besides, I like the view.

All the birds are lined up on the deck edge, except the A-1s. They occupy middeck at the rear end of the flight deck, their wings folded like giant hands in prayer over their cockpits. The A-1s launch first because their flight-time endurance is longer than the F-8s and A-4s. Looking aft, I see the plane guard destroyer plodding alongside our wake like a tired dog on a long walk. On our masthead, a wind-tattered flag snaps hard in the wind, grimy from the stack gas.

Finished enjoying the view, I stretch to step back from the wing onto the ladder. Friends and family I have dragged out to look at an A-4 are always amazed at how small and cramped the cockpit is and how much stuff is crammed in it. Each bit of stuff is important because it controls or tells me something important. All of the aircraft's systems have to be managed. Each control must be in working order and set properly for engine start and reset for each segment of the flight. I must also monitor all the informational gauges from engine start until shutdown, regardless of the demands and stresses of everything going on outside the cockpit. Another reason the training command provided us with screamers. God bless them, everyone.

Before climbing in the cockpit, I squat and look down the port intake for any FOD (tools or other foreign objects that might damage the engine).

Then, I turn my attention to the cockpit. First, I check to make sure the ejection seat pins are out and the ejection seat safing lever is down. If the pins are left in, the seat will not fire when I need it. The safing lever is to make sure the ejection seat will *not* go off if I snag either of the firing handles while climbing in. Known as the "head knocker," it is deliberately designed to poke you in the head when sitting in the seat so you cannot help but notice it.

Satisfied that the seat is safe, I begin the contortions necessary to squeeze even my skinny frame, bulked out by the gear I wear, into the small cockpit. I raise my right leg over the canopy rail, twisting my hips to step onto the seat cushion like mounting a horse, pausing and leaning over to look back down the starboard intake for tools, etc. Then, facing forward, I hold onto the canopy frame and bring my left leg over the canopy rail, stepping down to stand one-legged to the left of the joystick on the tiny piece of deck between the seat and instrument panel. I lean left, maneuvering my right foot down from the seat, aiming it to stand on the right of the joystick so I can scrunch down onto the seat and stretch my legs out to the rudder pedals, scraping my knees under the instrument panel.

The ejection seat cushion is more than firm. It is hard. When the ejection seat fires, you want your butt to move with it and not let the seat get a head start and slam into your backside. The G-forces generated by the rocket that powers our Escapac ejection seat pushes our spines to the limit as it is.

I buckle the seat's hip straps into my harness fittings. The plane captain hands me the shoulder straps, so I can snap them onto my harness, then hands me my helmet. The helmet is a familiarity, imbued with my sweat, the foam pads shaped to my head by the Gs. I put it on, leaving the chin strap hanging loose for the time being.

The plane captain hands me my oxygen mask. I clip it to the fitting on the left side of my helmet and let it hang there while I plug in the radio lead. Then, the oxygen-supply hose goes into its fitting on the left console. I check the oxygen gauge to make sure the liquid oxygen tank is full and turn the oxygen on, holding the mask to my face to inhale the no-smell freshness of the oxygen as it pushes into my lungs under positive pressure. I let the mask hang, turn the oxygen off, and give the plane captain a thumbs-up.

I plug the G-suit hose into the left rear console. The plane captain hands me my gloves. I still wear the leather gloves; the new Nomex gloves are fireproof but stretch, sag, and itch. Then, he hands me my kneeboard stuffed with notes from the briefings and crib sheets for emergency procedures, radio frequencies, TACAN channels, code words, and bomb sight settings covering every weapon and type of delivery. I strap it on my right knee, a ritual signifying the watershed between getting ready and being ready. He hands me my empty helmet bag. I stuff it in the back corner of the right-side console, where it will not come adrift during the flight.

Waiting to start engines, looking aft down the angled deck.

The plane captain gives me the ritual "Good luck" and climbs down the ladder. If nothing else, he wants me to bring his plane back. He retreats down the ladder, unships it from the hole beneath the cockpit, and carries it off to stow someplace off the deck edge. The ladder will magically reappear on the bow when he meets me after landing. Strapped in with the plane captain clear of the cockpit, I put the head knocker up. The ejection seat is armed. In theory, if I eject while parked on the deck, I have a 50-50 chance of surviving.

I check the clips that hold the radar screen and other instruments in the panel. I heard from one of my squadronmates that, on a previous cruise, he had the radar screen's long-heavy housing come shooting back into him on the cat stroke. It slammed into his right forearm, rocking the stick hard left. He was quick enough to grab the stick with his left hand and right the aircraft. He managed to wrestle the radar screen back into its hole and finish the hop. The retaining clips that hold it in place had not been put back after the radar was serviced. Learn and live.

0605

I sit in the sleeping bird. Waiting again. Look left and right, up and down the line of A-4s parked six inches apart, wing tip to wing tip, along the port edge of the deck. The angled deck making it look like a long echelon formation. Each man alone in his cockpit, a known quantity. Each doing his private ritual, like a pitcher on the mound.

The 1MC crackles to life, the air boss' voice booms over the flight deck: "Standby to start engines. Secure all loose gear about the deck. Check fire bottles."

The yellow gear fires up, engines coughing and revving.

0607

The plane captain looks up. "Good luck, sir," just in case his first wish didn't take. The last audible words. More waiting for electricity and high-pressure air to start the engine—but no cigarette.

The moment of relative calm is broken: "Start engines. Check for FOD about the deck, Stand clear of propellers, intakes, and jet exhausts. Pilots, start your engines."

I tighten my helmet strap. Time to go to work. The A-1s start almost immediately. Electric motors whining to swing their huge four-bladed props, a plane captain standing by each with a fire extinguisher. The A-1s backfire and throw up clouds of smoke as their massive engines catch. They begin to trundle past in single file, spreading their long bomb and rocket-laden wings.

0616

"Launch aircraft." The first A-1 goes off. The launch has begun. I am still waiting while they start the A-4s to my right, those spotted furthest from the catapults. After the props go, the next off will be a KA-3 Whale, followed by the F-8s, who will top off their fuel from the Whale after they climb to altitude.

The A-4s launch last and are started last to save fuel. Minutes count. Even at idle, our fuel consumption is measured in hundreds of pounds per hour. First off among the A-4s will be the strike leader—not as a privilege of his position but because that way everyone in the group will have a little extra fuel to play with while trying to stay in formation. The same logic applies to every division and section leader. The wet-wing tanker goes off last.

The yellow gear works up the deck toward me. The smaller cart provides electric power to the aircraft when the engine is not running. To save weight and space, the A-4 has no battery. If the generator fails in flight, we have the ram air turbine (RAT), a little wind-driven generator that pops out and provides electricity for essential instruments and equipment. The second cart contains a small jet engine in its low-slung body to provide high-pressure air to spin our engine turbines up to starting rpm.

The two pieces of yellow gear race up to my aircraft. The plane captain signals, asking permission to plug me into the generator cart, then hustles up to do it. The bird wakes up, instruments coming alive as the cart driver revs up his engine to take the load. The gyro in the artificial horizon comes up to speed. I cage the gyro, forcing it to straight up and down and level, where it should stay throughout the flight, no matter how I twist, turn, plunge, climb, and roll the aircraft around it. A still point of reference in a universe of chaotic movement. Needles start coming off their stops on the other gauges, and the ALQ radar jammer lights up.

Time to test the ALQ. An inoperative ALQ is a down-gripe if not a death warrant. I push the button starting its self-test routine. Lights flash; the headset chirps: green light. Time to press the button that tests the "warbler," the electronic bird song that tells me my aircraft is in the guidance beam of a SAM. The warbler sings. I think: *This is not just for practice. This time it is for real.* My immediate reaction is, *NO! Damn it. Focus.* I herd the butterflies back into my anxiety closet.

The plane captain asks to hook me up to the ram-air cart. I give a thumbs up. Another signal from the plane captain, and the whine of the yellow gear rises as its little jet engine throttles up. I watch the rpm gauge climb to the start mark, then bring the throttle around the stop detent, rubbing it against the left side of the detent to make electrical contact with the engine igniters. I hear my engine catch and begin to wind up behind me. I move the throttle around the detent to idle, watch the rpm climb smoothly to idle. A thumbs up to say I have a start, and then scan the EGT (exhaust gas temperature), the EPR (exhaust/inlet pressure ratio), the oil pressure, hydraulic, electrical, fuel pumps, and the rest. *All good.*

I look up. The yellow gear is gone, starting the aircraft on my left. I go through the post-start ritual with the plane captain, responding to his hand signals by moving ailerons, rudder, elevators, speed-brakes, and flaps, ending by setting the flaps to the half-down position for takeoff. He ducks underneath the nose and wings to pull the safety pins from the three-landing gear. He reappears and holds the pins up where I can count them.

I pull the canopy down by the yellow nylon strap that secures it against a wind gust or, more likely, the exhaust blast from another jet. I close and lock the canopy. Time to turn on the air-conditioning, running it to max cooling trying to cut down on the sweat—not that temperature has much to do with it. I turn the oxygen back on and strap the mask to my face.

Sitting up straight, I lock the harness, jerking forward to make sure it is engaged, run the ejection seat up until my helmet bumps the canopy, then run it down a half inch. I want the maximum visibility while leaving room for me to sit up, back as straight as I can get it for the cat and, if it comes to it, an ejection. I check the radio mic by just tapping the transmit button and listening for the click in my earphones. A final thumbs-up to the plane captain. He and I exchange salutes. "Good to go." Waiting again.

Dick is in the bird on my right. The yellow shirt director takes him out and passes Dick to the next director up the deck and walks smartly forward until he is at my eleven o'clock. He stops, pointing both hands at me, *You belong to me.* My sole job at this point is to obey all his hand signals above his waist. Those below his waist are for the blue shirts. The yellow shirt crosses his fists above his head, *Brakes on and keep them on.* No parking brake. I lift both feet off the deck and put them on the rudder pedals, toes pressing forward and down, applying the brakes on both the left and right-main gear. He rolls one fist over the other below his waist, *Chains off,* to the blue shirt. Two minutes later, a blue shirt staggers out from underneath my aircraft draped in chains like the Ghost of Christmas Past. Both hands below the waist, fists with the thumbs out, moving them out to the side, telling a blue shirt to take the chocks out from both main landing gear.

The yellow shirt raises both hands up like a football referee signaling a touchdown, opening and closing his fists, off the *brakes,* then pulls me forward with both hands moving back and forward over his head, *Come ahead.* I push the power up smartly, get her rolling, and then back to idle, anticipating his right-hand down signal that will tell me *Left brake.* Braking on the left-main gear but not the right makes the aircraft curve left. I want the engine at idle as I turn, so I do not blow the deck crew on my right into something hard or overboard.

As I make the turn, I keep my eyes on the plane director, trusting him to keep me out of trouble. When my nose is pointing up the deck, he points with both arms to his right at shoulder level. I look in that direction and find another yellow shirt pointing at me with both hands and giving me the come ahead. He slows me and shunts me to the line for the starboard catapult then passes me to another yellow shirt. It's rush-hour traffic. We inch up one space every time someone is shot off ahead of us.

Finally, I am directly behind the jet blast deflector (JBD), a large steel plate that rises out of the deck behind the aircraft on the catapult to deflect its engine exhaust upward when the pilot runs up to full power for the cat shot.

Author waiting in line for the starboard catapult, eyes on the yellow shirt with hands on his hips. Note the raised jet blast deflector (JBD) for the port catapult on upper right.

A red shirt comes up, checking each fuze and arming wires one last time and pulling safety pins out of the ejector feet on the racks for each bomb, the centerline drop tank, and bomb racks themselves, in case we have to dump everything in an emergency. He comes out front and holds all nine pins up between his fingers on both hands. I count them and give a thumbs-up.

Our squadron checker, selected from the best of our plane captains, goes over my aircraft one last time to make sure everything is as it should be. He gives me a thumbs-up and then moves quickly to safety between the catapults.

0627

The pilot on the cat in front of me brings his engine to full power, my aircraft shudders in the blast that gets over the blast deflector to buffet my vertical stabilizer. The plane on the cat squats for half a heartbeat and is gone, his engine roar vanishing in a rapid Doppler shift. When he is halfway down the catapult track, the JBD drops flat. I see the wisps of steam leaking up from the cat track, whipping toward me in the wind. There is a yellow shirt standing next to the catapult track. He puts his finger to his nose: A blue shirt is putting a tiller-bar on my nose gear so he can turn the wheel on its caster swivel to make fine adjustments as I come on the catapult. Now, I must only use both brakes evenly. A hard brake application on one wheel can send the blue shirt flying or injure him where he stands. The cat shuttle comes sliding back down the track to the ready position. The yellow shirt gives me a come ahead.

God, this is fun. Adrenaline-fueled excitement is a wonderful thing.

The tiller-bar guy's job is to line me up on the catapult track. I just supply the power and brakes as ordered by the yellow shirt. My nose gear bumps up against the shuttle. The yellow shirt signals the come-ahead. More power, a quick hard burst, up and over the shuttle, off the power and on both brakes to stop and then ease ahead. A stop-and-hold signal. The yellow shirt signals—tiller-bar off.

Two of the cat crew scurry under the aircraft, each dragging one end of the heavy bridle made of steel cables that will tie my aircraft to the catapult. They disappear under my nose. Out of my sight, they drape the center span of the bridle over the shuttle, which has a curved lip on its front edge in the shape of a breaking wave, and then pull the two ends aft to hook the looped ends over the catapult hooks bolted to the frame inside both main-gear wheel wells.

Behind me, out of my sight, a member of the crew is connecting me to the hold-back cable, a thick wire rope that is fastened to the flight deck behind the catapult. There is a different cable for each type of aircraft. They are just long enough to reach the hold-back fitting underneath the rear fuselage. He carries a hold-back bolt, a small-steel bar with cylindrical heads on each end, like a dumbbell. One end of the dumbbell fits in the hold-back cable, the other in the hold-back fitting on the aircraft. The dumbbell is strong enough to hold my aircraft in place at full power. However, it is no match for the catapult. When the cat is fired, the dumbbell snaps in the middle, and I am gone.

The yellow shirt passes me to the catapult (cat) officer standing between the port and starboard catapults. He has just launched an aircraft from the port cat and is turning to do me the same favor. The cat officer holds both hands above his head, opening and closing his fists, *feet off the brakes*. Obsessively, I jerk forward, checking the harness lock, drop my heels to the deck, keeping the toes on the bottom of the pedals. Pushing the bottom of the pedals controls the rudder on the upright portion of the tail. He wipes an arm below the waist toward the bow, signaling the deck-edge cat crew to tension the cat by leaking a little high-pressure steam into the catapult. The shuttle slides forward, pulling the bridle taut, holding the aircraft in tension between the bridle in front and hold-back in the rear.

The cat officer twirls one hand above his head, *full power*. I push the throttle up, roll the friction lock tight, and pull the throttle holdfast down out of the left canopy rail. I hook my thumb and little finger behind the throttle's T handle and wrap my middle three fingers over the handle and around the holdfast bar, ensuring that my arm, hand, and the throttle will not slam to idle when the cat stroke hits. I will not move my left hand until I am off the bow. I check the gauges. She's turning and burning at full power and not complaining about it.

I wipe the joystick in a circle against all its stops, making sure it moves freely, watching the mirrors to make sure the control surfaces respond. Sounds silly. I just did this with the plane captain after we started the engine.

A day will soon come, when I finish this ritual by giving the stick a hard upward jerk before I salute the cat officer. I will start doing this because my friend Don Purdy will be on the cat when the stick came out of the floor after he saluted, signaling, he was ready to be launched. Don keyed his mic and, in a voice only an octave higher than normal, says:

"*Abort the starboard cat!*

"*Abort the starboard cat!*

"*Abort the starboard cat!*"

All will end well. The cat shot will be aborted. Don will be taken off the cat, turned around, and taxied aft weaving through the aircraft moving forward to launch, like a salmon going upstream. Don is one lucky man.

The author and Don Purdy.

But, for now, I just wipe the stick in a full circle one last time. I check the clips holding the radar scope again and throw my shoulders forward hard a couple of time to check my harness lock yet again— then I assume the correct posture for the catapult: lean back, spine straight, head against the head rest, heels on the deck, toes on the rudder pedals. This is also the correct posture for ejections. Convenient. All this is done in a few seconds.

I check the gauges once more, *All okay*. I salute the cat officer with my right hand, then place my right elbow in my stomach, open hand behind the stick to catch it on the cat stroke; otherwise, it will slam full back, pitching the nose too high and stall the aircraft. A stall off the cat means you eject or die—maybe both.

0628

I focus on the vertical speed indicator (VSI), which shows the rate of climb or descent. It is mounted on the lower left of the instrument panel. The cat officer is still signaling "full power," as he looks over his

151

shoulder to make sure his crew, who check the shuttle track after each launch, are clear. Turning back to me, he scans my aircraft one last time, turns again, and lunges toward the bow like a fencer, touching the deck with his outstretched hand, *Launch*. The "shooter" on the deck edge has been standing there with his hands up like it's a robbery. I take a deep breath and tense all my muscles.

Out of my sight the shooter lowers his arms, each hand reaching out to hit the two shoot buttons set far apart to avoid an accidental shot.

Wait for it.

Slam!–Pinned to the seat–gone!

Zero to 160 mph in 90 feet, 60 feet over the water—the first full-bore shot of adrenaline today. I love the cat.

As the nose gear reaches the bow, the catapult bridle falls free of the aircraft. As she lifts off, the nose wants to push up. I catch the stick in my waiting right hand and ease the stick forward to hold the nose at six degrees above the horizon. I am still focused on the VSI, waiting the agonizing half second or so for it to stop bouncing.

The needle points to the right. Below level means you are descending and—EJECT! Don't ask why—EJECT! The needle settles. It is above level; I am climbing. I snatch the gear up, check the airspeed and raise the flaps, then make a clearing turn to the right so the next guy will not launch into my wake of disturbed air.

Now, time to find Dick and join up on his wing.

0635

There he is. About half a mile ahead, just swinging right across my nose, climbing. I bank right to cut the corner. I love the rendezvous maneuver. Getting a pursuit curve. Holding him steady, a fixed spot on the canopy. He looks good, all loaded for bear. I glide in on invisible rails, slowly increasing my angle of bank, gradually matching my course to his. I come to a gentle stop just below him, tucked in on his left wing, my head level with and just behind his wing tip in the parade position. He sees me and nods. I push out into cruise formation.

0650

As we approach the coast, Dick checks us out with Red Crown, the guided missile cruiser that checks the friendlies in and out while keeping a close eye out for any MiG activity. "Red Crown, Magic Stone 411 is feet-dry with two." Then to me, "Robin, master-arm on." I double-click the mic button and reach around the stick to the bottom of the control panel to turn the master-arm switch on. Now, if I press the "pickle" button on the stick handle with my thumb, a bomb comes off. If I pull the trigger on the front of the stick with my forefinger, the two 20mm cannons will hammer away. I slide out to combat formation, begin jinking, and get my head on a swivel.

I watch the coast slide underneath us. The land is flat, more rural than I expected, and I don't see any rice paddies, something I did expect. There is a single paved road running north-south. It is their Highway 1 connecting Hanoi to Saigon, with a rough patch at the DMZ:

This is it. I am going to drop bombs on this place. I have known lots of bullies but never had an enemy. Now, everyone down there is my enemy and wishes me serious harm—stop it! Focus—do your job. Get your head back on a swivel.

I sweep the distant ground for the dust of a SAM launch, the close ground for muzzle flashes, the air around us for flak bursts and tracers, then run my focus out to infinity checking for MiGs—not that I have ever seen one except on recognition slides and flash cards.

Dick finds the bridge that is our assigned target. It is small. He rolls in. I stay on the perch to allow some separation and call any threats. A small flashing light catches my eye. It looks like a yellowish strobe light. The penny drops:

Someone is shooting at Dick.

"Batman, you have flak, a hundred meters at one o'clock from the target."

The response is a double click of his mic. The gunner misses Dick. Dick misses the bridge by about fifty feet at seven o'clock (short and a little left), close enough to get an "E" (excellent) on a bombing range but not close enough to bother this little bridge.

My turn. I figure out the gunner has a 12.7mm heavy machine gun, the equivalent of our .50-caliber. Not exactly flak, but it can kill me and my bird. He can't reach us at our roll-in altitude of ten-thousand feet, but we dive into his effective range on the bomb run.

I'm in. As I pass through six-thousand-feet on the way to the release point at five-thousand-feet, he starts shooting at me. The tracers float up slowly, appearing to curve in as they get closer and then whip past. Close enough to give a sense of speed and excitement—not close enough to threaten.

Focus. Ignore him. Make a good run.

I manage to ignore the tracers. My two bombs miss left.

Up and off. Breaking away from the gun on the ground. Dick is climbing for a second run. Ordinarily he would put the gun at his three or nine o'clock, maximizing the gunner's lead problems, but our best chance of a hit is to run in at a slight angle to the bridge's long axis. We are more accurate left and right than short or long (except for me), so he keeps the same run-in line, leaving the gunner at one o'clock with a smaller-angle-off and easier shot. I follow him up toward the perch. Dick's second pair of bombs do the job. We are off to find something else, leaving the gunner to figure out why he missed. He will do better next time. There will be a next time. They will repair his little bridge and, eventually, we will be back to drop it again.

As we go off to find other targets, I think:

I did it. I've been shot at and did my job. I can ignore the tracers and deliver my bombs.

I am mildly surprised at how easy it was—and immensely relieved.

I passed the test.

Ha! I have no idea what the test is. They are just passing out the number two pencils.

We complete our recce and find no significant targets. We drop our bombs on another tiny bridge.

0712

We go feet-dry. Dick checks us back in with Red Crown, and we head for the ship. We check each other for damage. No holes. *Oriskany* is just starting to launch the next cycle, so our signal is "Delta" (hold at max conserve). Ten minutes later, the launch is complete. Looking down I can see them pulling the aircraft still on deck forward, clearing the landing area. Minutes later our signal is Charlie (land).

Dick lowers his tailhook, a signal for me to do the same and to close up into parade position on his starboard wing. Dick starts a steep descent to a point about a mile aft of the carrier, making wide turns to check for aircraft under us. He leads me up the starboard side of the ship at five-hundred feet and three-hundred knots. I am tucked in tight. I see the ship flash into view under Dick's plane.

As he passes the bow, Dick looks at me and tells me he is leaving the formation by blowing me a kiss. He snaps left into a sixty-degree bank and pulls hard away from me. I make a quick check for other aircraft as I count, *One potato. Two potato. Three potato* and break left. Chop the power, speed-brakes out, slowing and descending. At ninety degrees of turn, I put down full flaps then lower the landing gear, pushing up the power to slow my descent and catch my speed at 140 knots. I check my distance from the ship as I fly by on the opposite course. As I pull abeam of the stern of the ship, I check Dick's position ahead of me. He hasn't completed the first ninety degrees of his approach turn, so I hold my turn to make sure he will have enough time to clear the landing gear before I arrive at the ramp.

Into the turn, I cross the wake and rollout with my nose pointing at the crotch of the angle deck. "Magic 409. Ball, 1.9." The LSO comes back, "Roger Ball."

A few seconds later and, thump, I am on the deck. Speed-brakes in and full power. The hook catches and I am slammed to a stop. Power to idle, hook up, flaps up, find the yellow shirt, right brake, power up to get clear of the landing area, hurrying across the foul-deck line.

I did it. I am a combat pilot.

I can't remember where we went or what we did on the second mission that day. I remember seeing my first flak bursts, thinking, *They are pretty much just like all the World War II films I have seen.* On this day, none were close enough to worry me.

AH 406 with an AGM 45 Bullpup on its wing.

WHILE DICK and I are flying our first two hops, Wuff is leading C-10 back to Happy Valley. Wuff had managed to persuade someone to give him an AGM 12 Bullpup B. Wuff is going to teach the flak site that shot down his wingman not to shoot at airplanes with orange boomerangs on their tails.

Wuff keeps a list of flak sites that are too successful or too good. He usually saves a bomb on each mission. When he has hit the assigned target, he flies that bomb over to the nearest flak site on his list. The flak site only gets off the list when, for one reason or another, they stop shooting at him. He tells C-10 he could save a bomb or not as he wishes. C-10 opts in.

Later that day, we lose Lt.j.g. Robin Cassell from VA-152. He was leading a section of two A-1s. While attacking some small boats, he radioed he had been hit by small arms fire. Within moments, his A-1 hit the water and exploded. He was still in the cockpit at impact. I don't know Rob but feel a "'there but for the grace of God" twinge. If they hadn't closed the Spad pipeline, I would be doing what he did.

CHAPTER 11

DAY THREE

Parade Position.
The patches on 404 are temporary corrosion control
awaiting the break between line periods to repaint the aircraft.

July 16

ON DAY THREE, Dick and I fly another armed recce, this time into Happy Valley up against the Laotian border, where C-10 took the hit on Day One. It is too soon to call the mission routine, but the flak is light. My bombing is still erratic.

While we are hunting across the panhandle, others are in the northeast. Lt.Cmdr. Butch Verich is flying a flak-suppression mission in his F-8, providing cover for A-4s attacking a railway yard thirty miles south of Hanoi. He is targeted by a SAM site. Butch evades the first two missiles but is hit by the third. The F-8 is done for.

Butch has a good ejection and lands on a karst (limestone) ridge without serious injury. He is in a remote area, but this is a wholly different problem than when C-10 made it feet-wet and ejected behind the carrier two days ago. Butch is within the Hanoi defense area and is eighty miles from the Tonkin Gulf. It is too late in the day to get a helo to Butch before dark. They tell him to hang in there and "we'll be back." Butch finds a cave to spend the night.

That evening, the admiral is reluctant to order a rescue attempt that deep into North Vietnam. Lt.Cmdr. "Marvelous" Marv Reynolds of the VA-163 Saints convinces his skipper, Cmdr. Bryan "Magnolia" Compton we must at least make the attempt. The two of them go to the CAG and make the case. The CAG agrees and goes to the admiral. The admiral is convinced. They start planning the SAR for first light.

I am told we have a foreign movie tonight. French.

WHEN THE Vietnam War began, the navy had no helicopter squadron dedicated to search and rescue from combat zones. It soon became clear that this omission must be remedied. The navy ordered some Sea Kings modified with armor and armament and began to train up a new helicopter squadron dedicated to the task.

In the interim, the navy detailed a detachment of Sea Kings from HS-2, an antisubmarine squadron (ASW) flying the HS-3A Sea Kings from USS *Hornet* (CVS 12). The *Hornet* is an anti-submarine carrier that has been stationed at the entrance to the Tonkin Gulf to provide ASW protection for the three attack carriers on Yankee Station. The SAR

HS-3A helos were assigned the call sign "Big Mother." Each Big Mother had its expensive and secret ASW gear removed and door-mounted M-60 machine guns installed.

The Navy also modifies some of the smaller UH-24 Seasprites that usually operate in an anti-submarine role from the tiny decks on the stern of destroyers. Call sign Clementine, they operated from the northern and southern SAR destroyers close offshore.

In July 1967, the Big Mother detachment operates from the big deck of USS *Constellation* on Yankee Station to reduce their reaction time in case of need. On the night of July 16, Lt. Neil Sparks and his crew from the HS-2's det aboard *Constellation* are tapped to attempt Butch's rescue. Sparks decides to go feet-dry well south of the direct route to Butch's location at a place where the coastal defense belt is the thinnest. He will fly west into the sparsely populated and defended hill country before heading north.

2100

MEANWHILE, I SIT in our ready room watching *A Man and a Woman*, nice woman, nice car, nice music. When the movie ends, the flight schedule is out and sitting on the squadron duty officer's desk. Guys wander by, glancing down as they leave.

Quit stalling. Go look at it.

There's an extra launch. Early. Butch's SAR before sunup, followed by only three more launches on the page. That means Alfa Strikes.

An Alfa Strike is a mission against a single high-priority target. High-priority for us means heavily defended by them. I scan down the page for my name. The first Alfa Strike launch is 0800 hours. Dick is leading a division of four strike bombers. I will fly his wing in the number two position. The target is a railway bridge southwest of Hanoi, out on the edge of the thickest defenses. At 1200 hours, I am scheduled to fly the wet-wing tanker backing up a strike against an army barracks south of Hanoi. 1600 hours, last strike of the day, I will man the spare aircraft for a strike on a highway bridge south of Haiphong. As the spare, I will fill in if a strike or flak-suppressor aircraft goes down for a maintenance gripe after "start engines"

Well, now I know—and now it's time to sleep. Good luck with that.

2120

In the rack. Start the sleep ritual: read the book, nod off, turn the light off, think of the time in Yosemite, sitting on a rock in the leaf-dappled shade, looking up at water tumbling off the cliff hundreds of feet above. Quiet except for the falling water and a mountain jay in the tree above. Nothing to do. Just sit there and let the world drift away.

2157

Sleep—at last.

0221

"Bong! Bong! Bong!"
Vault out of the bunk
"Fire! Fire! Fire!"
flight suit and boots
"Class bravo fire on the hangar deck.
Port side, forward. Frame 21"
That's us. Get clear
"Away the duty fire and rescue party"
All four of us are out
pounding up the ladder
heading forward along the passageway
towards a chain of ladders up to the flight deck.

0236

Standing on the flight deck in the dark. A thousand and more of us, rousted from sleep, talking in low murmurs carried on the breeze.

The 1MC gives the all clear: "Secure the fire and rescue party. Set condition Yoke throughout the ship."

Back down to our hole. Back in the rack. Back to sleep, if I can. If two hours are enough to forget tomorrow—again.

CHAPTER 12

DAY FOUR

Strike group headed feet-dry.
F-8 fighter escorts climbing through in lower-left corner.

July 17

DAWN FINDS "Marvelous" Marv over Butch Verich's cave. They establish radio contact. Marv tells him he'll be back in half an hour. Lt. Sparks and his crew get the green light.

My alarm goes off at 0415. I am groggy but awake. Then I remember. *Alfa Strike today.* I rub my nose with the sides of both thumbs.

0500

Off to AI for the brief. The brief is longer and full of details. We use a different system of call signs on Alfa Strikes. Instead of everyone using their sections leader's personal call sign, we use our squadron call sign and a number based on our position in the strike group. Dick is Magic Stone One; I am Magic Stone Two. John Davis and George "S-10" Schindelar, the fourth man in my stateroom, are Magic Three and Four. I need to remember the call signs of all the aircraft and their places in the formation so that if I hear "Old Salt Five, warbler," I will know where and how far away he is from us.

This target is right on the edges of several red circles. *Hmmmm.* I stare at the AI's chart, memorizing it. I have flown only four combat missions but have figured out that, once I cross the beach, there is no time to fish out my missile site map. Against all expectations, all those last-minute cramming sessions in college come in handy.

WHILE I am briefing, Sparks and his crew, escorted by Spads from VA-152, fly to Butch Verich's location with a minimum of opposition. As the helicopter slows to hover over Butch's position, they receive heavy small arms fire from local militia troops who have flooded the area. Aviation Antisubmarine Technician, Third Class (AX3) Teddy Ray and Aviation Machinists' Mate, First Class (AD) Al Massengale in the helo's cabin return fire with their M-60s.

Big Mother begins to take hits. One of the two generators is destroyed, causing them to lose some avionics. They can continue the mission without them, but, if they lose the second generator, they will have only about 15 minutes of flight time on their battery—not nearly enough time to get feet-wet. A bullet enters the cockpit and shatters an airspeed indicator on the instrument panel. Another round goes into the hydraulic equipment cache immediately behind the pilot's seat. It destroys the automatic stabilization gear (ASE). Without the ASE, the helo is hard to control in flight, even harder to hold in a hover. Worse, the damage to the hydraulics makes the flight controls sluggish, compounding the pilot's problems of flying the unstable helo without the ASE.

As co-pilot, Lt.j.g. Robin Springer is responsible for communications with the support aircraft and Butch Verich. A bullet takes out their UHF radio. Robin is unable to contact anyone outside the helo. He jerks the handheld survival radio out of his survival vest, takes off his helmet, and establishes contact by shouting over the noise of the rotor, engine, and gunfire.

When a SAR helo arrives on scene, its crew must pinpoint the pilot's location, come to a dead stop, and then hover a few feet above the ground while they lower the hoisting cable and wait while the pilot opens and climbs onto the jungle penetrator (a collapsible seat). They must continue to hold their hover until the pilot is winched up clear of the trees, before they can get out of Dodge.

But Neil Sparks has an almost unflyable helicopter. He does not sheer off, abandon the rescue attempt, and head for the water. He stays and wrestles it into a hover. It takes an interminable twenty minutes to get Butch safely on the cable and hoist him aboard. Once the pickup is made, they leave the immediate area.

Because of the damage, retracing their flak-free but roundabout ingress route is not an option. Sparks heads straight for the Tonkin Gulf. En route, he is blocked by an active flak site. Marv Reynolds smothers the site with ordnance. The flak site goes quiet as Big Mother lumbers past.

Big Mother 67 and her crew get feet-wet almost two and half hours after they went feet-dry. They drop Butch off on *Oriskany* and then head directly home to the *Hornet* where HS-2's maintenance department can begin repairing the damage.

Neil Sparks and Marv Reynolds will both be awarded the Navy Cross for their parts in the rescue.

THE WORD comes down while we are waiting to man aircraft: They got Butch Verich out! We are ecstatic and think all those practices in Nevada paid off. I decide:

We are really good at this stuff. So far, we lose four aircraft, but we get three pilots back. We would have got Cassell if he had an ejection seat.

Okay. You go down, they come get you. The flight surgeon checks you out and gives you a couple of little bottles of "medicinal" brandy, and you are good to go. Scary, but I can deal with it.

0525

Back in the ready room, I check the flight schedule on the SDO's desk for our aircraft numbers. Then, the division brief with Dick, time for another smoke and trip to the head. Check the clock. Time to gear up, smoking another cigarette while I do.

0550

"Pilots, man your aircraft." Time to shuffle off to Buffalo. Up the escalator. Across the flight deck. Preflight the bird. There are a lot more pilots up here today. I climb up and strap in. Then sit and wait.

I could use a cigarette about now.

0605

"Standby to start engines. Secure all loose gear about the deck. Check fire bottles."

The noise level jumps up. The yellow gear fire up and start scurrying about. The plane captain looks up. "Good luck, sir," his voice carried off by the wind.

0607

"Check for FOD about the deck—Stand clear of propellers, intakes, and jet exhausts—Pilots, Start Your Engines."

The A-1s roar to life. The first jet engines whine to a growl. Helmet on. I get started. Close the canopy. Everything checks out. Wait to taxi.

0614

"Launch aircraft."

The first Spad roars off the cat. Rush hour starts. Eventually, I taxi forward and am put in line for the port catapult.

0621

I am sitting behind the JBD, next in line for the catapult. I realize:

I am the tip of the spear—the thirty-five-hundred men on this ship, the thousands in the RAG and training command, all the Navy training squadrons and schools do what they do just to put me in this cockpit and launch me against the target.

I get goose bumps. Pride and excitement have routed fear and anxiety.

I am ready.

The JBD drops, and I am hurried forward, then push the nose gear over the catapult shuttle. Hold-back in. cat tensioned. Full power. Left-handed death grip on the throttle. Check the gauges, wipe the cockpit. Head back, salute the cat officer, right elbow in my gut behind the stick. And—*off we goooooooooo!*

I lock onto Dick, gliding in on him, stopping with a little dip of the wings to match my curve to his. Pause and then slide back and under him, taking up a parade position on his right, leaving room for John Davis. I settle in. Glancing under Dick's aircraft, I see John gliding up, with S-10 following. A wordless ballet.

As S-10 slides into place, Dick eases out of the rendezvous turn and brings us up toward the strike group. He slides all four of us into place.

Our TARCAP (target combat air patrol) fighters overtake us from behind. Two sections of two, climbing above us. Long sleek bodies, reminding me of sharks, moving effortlessly in opposing scissor sweeps to keep their speed up without overrunning the slower strike group.

Commander Burt Shepherd, our CAG, is the strike leader. He briefed a left roll-in, so the flak-suppressor section is out on the left end of the line, where it can get in first and, hopefully, make some gunners duck. The two lonely A-4 Iron Hands, with their Shrike anti-radar missiles, are above us, outboard of everyone, one on each end of the line, waiting for their F-8 fighter escorts to join up after topping off from the Whale. Strike lead starts a slow climb, his power at ninety-five percent, leaving us five-percent to play with while staying in formation. The fighter escorts for the Iron Hand sections slide into place. We are complete. Without a word spoken.

This is so damn exciting I can hardly stand it. The strike group coming together, four strike divisions spread across almost a mile of sky.

0655

The coast drifts toward us. About five miles short, CAG calls for master-arm switches hot. He checks us out:

"Red Crown, this is Old Salt 302, feet-dry with twenty-eight."

"Roger, Old Salt 302."

We shake out and begin to jink. I get my lookout scan going. I hear crickets in my headset: the air defense search radars. They know we are coming. I can imagine the phone ringing at the flak sites ahead of us, the crews putting away their breakfasts and letters from home, gunners climbing up onto their seats, loaders readying the stacks of reloads.

Dead on time, we cross the beach, going feet-dry climbing eleven-thousand feet above the ground. Strike lead continues the slow climb until we turn north toward the target. We are hoping for fourteen-thousand feet or better so we can trade the extra altitude for speed on the final run in to the target.

The jinking is constant. Each division, each section, each aircraft constantly moving at random. Each in their own box of airspace, trying to prove the AAA computers' predictions and the gunners' guesses wrong.

Another wave of adrenaline surges through me.

My heart rate spikes
My senses expand, absorbing everything
Concentrate
Slow breathes
The world slows down
my body and aircraft vanish
my focus stretches out

encompassing the limits
of my perceptions
head on a swivel
Jink and think
paring avoidable risks
to the minimum

We go west, passing below Big D Island in the Red River, south and a little east of Hanoi.

0713

Turning north now. Strike lead begins the long slow descent to the roll-in point, building our speed. The Iron Hands and their escorts move ahead, waiting for the missile sites to paint us. They will each suppress one site for a few seconds while we close on the target, and maybe a second site while we roll in, hoping to shred their radar antenna, or better, they'll follow the Shrike's smoke and put bombs on the missile site. I piece out roughly where the target is by the shape of the river and the karst ridges running to the northeast, picking more precise landmarks as we close on the target.

My ECM gear gets noisier, a plague of hoarse crickets in my ears.

"Missile launch Eleven o'clock, ten miles!"
I look
See nothing
"Magic Three, warbler"
that's Davis
"Old Salt One, warbler"
"MISSILE LAUNCH ELEVEN O'CLOCK, NINE MILES."
A second missile?
I can't find it
My ECM gear begins a slow warble.
Shit
I key the mic: "Magic Two, warbler"
Where the fuck are they?
"Magic Ten, shotgun"—a shrike launch

I squirm and twist against the harness to see
around the one-half-by-three-inch angle of attack indicator,
the canopy frame,
the gunsight mount.
It's out there
but where?
I keep Dick in my peripheral vision,
expecting him to break into a missile evasion maneuver.
A voice, "Old Salt Five, break left, NOW!"
Old Salts. I look left.
There!
The SAM overshoots the Saints
It explodes
A miss
There—the second missile!
Trying to follow the Old Salts down
it bursts over and behind them

Nothing but two ugly orange smears in the sky behind us. All in
about sixteen seconds from launch to detonation. Old Salt Five's
division has recovered from its evasion and is climbing back to rejoin
the strike group. I can't believe I'm doing this.

"Old Salt One is in"
"Magic Nine, shotgun"
The other Iron Hand is taking a shot
My eyes follow the shrike smoke trail
Focus—god damn it—focus
I snap my head back to ten o'clock level
CAG has started down the pipe
flak blossoming around him
his division follows, plunging one after another
I scan the sky behind for MiGs
and out front for a third missile
Dick is climbing
sliding left to get on the roll-in cone earlier

I slide to his right
the Old Salt division still climbing back
Sliding behind us
A glance at the target
Stale flak bursts hang in the air
New flak crumping into life around the roll-in point
Find the target
A glance down
Erupting brown clouds obscure the target
shockwaves of bursting bombs flash out through the dust cloud
It should be—about—there
Dick is in
Here we go
Eyes sweeping the sky for other A-4s
No one above whose bombs will fall on me.
No one below that my bombs might fall on.
No one left or right
who will pull out at the same moment as I
rolling 135 degrees, pulling into the dive
pulling the nose down below the target
Rolling out in a 45-degree dive
putting the gunsight plumb line—*There*
start tracking the pipper toward—*There*
Airspeed—450
dive brakes out, power back to 85%
Check airspeed–dive angle–altitude–wings level
matching the altimeter against the pipper's crawl up to the target
Too slow
I'll be at release altitude before the pipper gets to the target
Tracers almost head on—forget them
Airspeed at 450
Okay
Dive angle about 50 degrees
too steep
I'm still going to be at release altitude too soon
just a tad back on the stick

flattening the dive, a little
to hurry the pipper crawl
Tracers in the peripheral vison
Ignore them. Focus
Tracking, tracking, tracking
Pipper sweeps toward the target—*Wait—now*
Thumb on the pickle button
push once
the bombs ripple off in three pairs.
Three thumps, felt not heard
Pull—hard—speed-brakes in—slamming the throttle up
Strain and grunt
six and half Gs
nose coming above the horizon.
Ease to three "Gs"
roll left to 60 degrees angle of bank
put the Gs back on
Look back over my shoulder
I see what I think are Dick's bombs going off
on target
then mine
about seventy yards wide right.
Shit.
Maybe someone else's bombs.
Nose above the horizon
There are A-4s everywhere
Slack off the Gs
clear the space and
quick roll left and pull
look right—off the Gs—roll 120 degrees—Gs back on
level out at 6,000 feet
reverse again
Find Dick
There
Right where I expect him to be
Follow him out

scissoring behind him
Punching out chaff like I own stock
to confuse the radars
Twisting to see what's behind us
More A-4s coming out
We are out of the dense flak now.
F-8s above us
high cover

Dick leads us to feet-wet. Back out over the gulf—surfing the adrenaline, euphoric. Dick checks us inbound: "Red Crown, Magic Stone 404, feet-wet with two."

A few seconds later I hear John Davis, "Red Crown, Magic Stone 408, feet-wet with two."

John and S-10 are out.

Dick stops jinking. I move into cruise formation. A hand signal tells me to check him for battle damage. I close into parade position on his left wing and let my aircraft float to a stepped-up position so I can see the top of his port wing and fuselage, then sink to check the underside of his wing and fuselage, drop aft to check the tail, and slide under to his right side, repeating the process in reverse. I settle into parade position on his right. No holes, nothing leaking or fluttering—I give him a thumbs-up. He passes me the lead and checks me out.

He gives me a thumbs-up. I pass the lead back to him. He asks my fuel state by raising a fist to his oxygen mask, thumb out, and mimics drinking. I give him the pounds of fuel I have left on board with the fingers of my left hand. Vertical for "one" through "five," horizontal for "six" through nine," a fist for "zero." I have 2,100 pounds of fuel. Enough.

On the way back my euphoria is overtaken by anger. I am furious with myself. I did not see the incoming missiles. Worse, I was gawking at the first missile while the second was inbound. I forgot all about the second missile until it flew into my vision while I was watching the Old Salts. If I can't see and track the SAMs, I am going to get us both killed.

A-4 at touch down.
Note the one wire behind the aircraft,
and the hung 500# MK 82 bomb on the starboard wing.

After we debrief with the air intelligence guys, Dick and I go back to the ready room to talk about the flight.

I tell him, "I didn't see the missile until it was on the Salts."

He tells me, "Look quick when you hear a launch call. Don't try to focus on a spot, just scan for a dust cloud and the booster's hundred-foot tail of fire. Given the lag between someone spotting the launch, making the call, and your reaction, you only have a second or so to see the booster's tail. If you see it, focus on it. When it goes out, keep your eyes moving along its apparent path looking for a pale glow, pink maybe; that's the main motor hiding behind the body of the missile. If you can't see it, loosen your focus and keep tracking where you expect it should be by then. Keep running up and down the line of flight moving closer until you spot it."

He looks at me. I must not be radiating confidence.

He laughs and says, "Once you see one, it gets easier. You'll know what to look for. It gets almost automatic—you look, your eye snags on it, you see it."

Dick is right about that. Fifty years later, I will still see them in my dreams, and awake when little flashes and small, quick movements snag in my peripheral vision.

172

I tell him I forgot about the second missile when I finally saw the first.

"Don't do that."

"Okay."

"Look, if a missile is pointed at us, don't take your eyes off of it. It is the immediate threat. If it is going after someone else, forget it. If there are two missiles launched seconds apart from the same site, they are going to the same target. The second will follow the first. Keep your eyes on the first; when it's past, look for the second. If the first missile isn't tracking us, neither is the second. You can forget it too. Worry about another missile from a second site."

Learn and live.

I nod, but I must look doubtful or worried (I certainly feel both) because he says, "No one sees them at first. They say if your first missile is shot at you it will kill you. It wasn't. You weren't. Next time you will do better."

I try to look more confident and nod.

CHAPTER 13

DAY FIVE

UH-2 Seasprite "Clementine" launching from deck of a destroyer.

July 18

DICK HARTMAN grew up in Brunswick, New Jersey. In 1957 he graduated from the Naval Academy. Over the next decade, he earned his wings and did a Mediterranean cruise aboard USS *Independence*. Rotating to shore duty, he earned a master's degree in aeronautical engineering at the Naval Postgraduate School in Monterey, went to the A-4 RAG at NAS Lemoore, and received orders to the Ghost Riders.

He survived the '66 cruise and fire, emerging as one of the combat veterans who are the heart of our squadron. Duthie is his wingman and thinks the world of him.

Richard Danner Hartman.

ON JULY 18, Dick Hartman and Larry Duthie, are scheduled on an Alfa strike against a bridge over the Red River near Hanoi at a place called Co Trai. I am not on the mission but hear about it as the day unfolds. As they approach the target, Hartman and Duthie are forced into steep-diving turns to evade first one, and then a second SAM. The SAMs follow them down, impacting a karst ridge behind Duthie. They are at low altitude close to the target.

Hartman knows they won't be able to climb back to the roll-in altitude of ten thousand feet before they reach the target. Rather than flying to the target and having to orbit in the flak as they complete their climb, he makes a climbing turn away from the target. His new heading will carry him across a karst ridge and over a small valley. Hartman knows the valley from the '66 cruise, when he flew over it several times and never drew anti-aircraft fire. True to form there is no flak from the valley as they climb. When they are about halfway to the roll-in altitude, Hartman makes another climbing turn back towards the target.

Larry Duthie

Approaching the target, they pass A-4s from the strike group that have dropped their bombs and are headed back to feet-wet. Hartman's and Duthie's warblers begin to sing again. Two more SAMs track them. Hartman leads Duthie into another missile evasion maneuver.

This time the missiles drive them down to 800 feet. Hartman, heads back to the valley to climb back for a third try at getting to the target.

As he skims over the top of the ridge, into the little valley, Hartman's aircraft is enveloped in a maelstrom of anti-aircraft fire. His aircraft is hit. It is unflyable. He ejects almost immediately, landing unhurt on top of a karst ridge.

There are no good places for an American pilot to land in North Vietnam, but on top of a karst ridge is better than most. With nearly vertical limestone sides and few routes up to their tops from the surrounding flat land, they are usually uninhabited. Most also have vegetation and caves on the top. Good places to hide.

Duthie cranks his plane around, turning hard to circle back and begin the SAR effort for Dick Hartman. Within minutes—*BAM!* Duthie's aircraft is hit.

His aircraft is badly damaged and on fire. Duthie heads for the gulf. He only makes it about ten miles before he loses all his flight controls. Both hydraulic systems and the backup manual system are gone. His aircraft rolls into an inverted dive and heads for the ground at five-hundred knots or better—too fast for comfort on an ejection, but Duthie has no choice. He pulls the handle and is rocketed into the five-hundred-knot slipstream.

At that speed, the opening shock of the parachute is brutal, but Duthie and his parachute both survive impact. He comes down on the side of a karst hill. He plunges into a tree top and manages to avoid straddling any branches as he falls through the tree. He stops with a jerk as the chute canopy snags on the treetops. His body is flooded with adrenaline.

Duthie looks down. His feet are about six inches above the ground. He releases his harness and drops to the ground still on his feet. The ejection seat-pack that comes out with the pilot is hanging from the shroud lines next to him. The seat-pack is full of survival gear for all types of situations. Duthie wants the relevant gear, but it is behind a fabric cover that is neatly stitched to the pan. He reaches for his brand-new Buck Knife. He finds the paracord he used to tie the knife to him so he wouldn't lose it. The paracord is short with a frayed end. Paracord has a 250-pound-breaking strength but was snapped in two by the opening shock. He reaches for the shroud cutter Velcro'd into a pocket on the front of his survival vest. He finds only the bitter end of its paracord leash. Duthie sets about picking the stiches on the seat-pack fabric with his fingernails. He gets it open rifles through the contents, tossing the shark repellant, life raft, ocean-dye markers, and other water survival gear.

Duthie finds a can of emergency water. He is thirsty, but the little key that opens the can is gone. Duthie considers shooting hole in the can with his pistol. He thinks better of it.

DONE WITH the seat pan, Duthie realizes the big white parachute is likely to draw unwanted company. Putting some distance between himself and the parachute seems like a good idea. He turns and heads up the hill.

After only a couple of steps, he falls down.

Duthie stands up. He falls. Tries again. Falls again. "Damn leg isn't working." He manages to get vertical using his good leg and hobbles up the slope away from the parachute.

He doesn't get far before he hears voices behind him. Several members of the North Vietnamese militia have discovered his parachute. He knows they are likely to be armed with AK-47 assault rifles.

Duthie realizes that at least one of them is heading up the hill in his direction. He flops down out of sight behind a log. He is armed with a snub-nosed .38-caliber revolver—a gun with which he had been unable to score a single hit on the combat pistol range, including a point-blank shot at a life-size target. Nevertheless, Duthie thinks, "If the man coming up the hill gets too close, I will sit up and try to shoot him." Luckily for everyone involved, the man walks past Duthie's log and continues up the hill.

WITH TWO pilots down, the navy SAR helos head for the scene to pick up fallen strangers. The closest is a Clementine on the Northern SAR destroyer stationed just off the shore.

Meanwhile, Big Mother 67 is launched from the SH-3A detachment aboard USS *Constellation*. Both helos pick up A-1 escorts on their way to the beach.

THE AIR FORCE was ahead of the curve and already had squadrons specifically dedicated to performing combat rescues. Their motto is "These Things We Do, That Others May Live." They fly the Jolly Greens, an Air Force version of our Big Mothers. Their HH-3Es are specially equipped with self-sealing fuel tanks, drop tanks, an in-flight refueling probe, some armor, and M-60 machineguns mounted in the cabin doors.

Based in Thailand, the Jolly Greens stage through clandestine CIA bases in northeastern Laos along the border with North Vietnam. They operate in pairs. One goes in low to make the rescue. The other flies high cover, so if the first is shot down trying to make a pick up, the cover Jolly can try to rescue its crew. The Jollies are escorted by the Sandies. They use the A-1E, a three-place Air Force version of the A-1 pressed into service as a single place attack aircraft.

STARTING CLOSEST to the beach, the Clementine will arrive first. At this point, they know Dick Hartman's location as reported by Duthie, but no one has located Duthie. The Clementine is sent for Hartman.

Big Mother 67's crew is led by Lt. John Bender. He and his copilot, Lt. John Schloz, swap seats every other mission so both will log command pilot time. In the back, they have AX2 David Chatterton and AX3 Wayne Noah, manning the machine guns and hoist.

Unlike fixed-wing aircraft, in helicopters the pilot sits on the right side, the copilot on the left. On July 18, it is John Scholz's turn in the right seat. John Bender sits in the left seat and serves as copilot.

An F-8 pilot is able to pinpoint Duthie's position. Big Mother's route to Hartman just happens to take it directly over Duthie. With the Clementine ahead of them and already committed to picking up Hartman, they decide to go for Duthie.

The helos are incredibly vulnerable. They are low and slow coming and going and therefore much easier to hit than even the A-1s. Much of the time, they fly within the effective range of small arms. Hel[...] have little or no armor. Their aluminum skin is so thin that even smal[...] arms rounds go right through it seeking out flesh, or engine, or fuel, or hydraulics, or any of the other vital equipment crammed into it. Tough duty, but what happens between getting in and back out is even more dangerous. When a pilot goes down, the North Vietnamese flood the area with troops and militia and wait for the helicopter.

Jolly Green and Sandy Air Force SAR team.
The Sandy, three-place A-1E Skyraider is in the foreground armed with
rockets on its multiple wing-stations, flying alongside a HH-3E Jolly Green.
Both are equipped with drop tanks to extend their range and loiter time on
missions.

When the radio calls generated by Hartman's and Duthie's ejections go out on the guard channel, two Jolly Greens launch and head east from Laos. The Jollies are accompanied by two sections of Sandies.

Sandy One is flown by Maj. Theodore Broncyzk with Capt. Bill Carr on his wing. The second section is flown by Capt. Paul Sikorsky and Capt. Jimmy Kilbourne. The Jollies are held near the North Vietnam boarder with Laos. They are told to orbit, save fuel, and await developments. The low Jolly Green does just that. The high cover/backup Jolly is flown by Major Glen York, with First Lieutenant

e as his copilot. Glen York's idea of a holding orbit is a
 leg toward the SAR scene, a 360 degrees pirouette, followed
ner thirty-mile leg.

hen a flight of F-4 Phantoms arrives to fly high cover for the
ies, the Sandies are released to fly close air support for the Navy's
attempt to pick-up Hartman and Duthie. North Vietnam is shaped like
a porkchop. To reach Hartman and Duthie, they must fly across the fat
part of the porkchop.

The Clementine finds Hartman and goes into a hover. While
lowering its jungle penetrator, Clementine is hit by small arms fire. The
helo begins to shudder violently. The vibration is so severe, it shakes
the instrument panel off its mounts. The panel will eventually fall on
the pilot's legs while he struggles to control the crippled bird. Unable
to hold the hover, the pilot aborts the rescue and heads for salt water,
leaving Dick Hartman still on the ground.

Meanwhile, the Sandies flown by Major Broncyzk and his wingman
arrive over Duthie's position. They are soon joined by the second pair
of Sandies, followed minutes later by three Locket A-1s from VA-152.
Major Broncyzk takes command of the SAR effort. The A-1s suppress
flak sites and attack the militiamen climbing the hill towards Duthie.

Big Mother 67 gets eyes on Duthie and comes into a hover over a
nearby clearing. It, too, takes heavy fire. Notwithstanding the best
efforts of the A-1s, Big Mother 67 is shot-up. The door gunner, AX3
David Chatterton, is hit in the chest. Lt. Bender has to abandon the
rescue and fly his damaged helo back out to sea to find a deck with a
doctor aboard.

The Northern SAR destroyer leaves station and heads toward the
beach at flank speed to shorten the distance for the damaged helos.

As Big Mother heads for feet-wet, Major Broncyzk sends a Locket
to escort it out. He and the other A-1s continue to attack the flak and
militia around Duthie's position.

Inside Big Mother 67, David Chatterton is laid on the cabin deck.
He is conscious and tells his crewmates:

"I don't want to die."

Within minutes, he bleeds out and is gone. Dave Chatterton gives his life to save someone he never met, and who would never get to know him, someone who has never forgotten him.

Clementine and Big Mother are nursed back to a friendly deck. Dick Hartman and Larry Duthie are both left where they are. But the day is not over.

WITH BOTH Navy attempts abandoned, the Jolly Greens are cleared in. The low Jolly is still orbiting far off to the east and does not have enough fuel to reach the SAR site, make a pickup, and go back to base. It has to go back to Laos to refuel.

Jolly 37 flown by Glen York, however, has "drifted" much closer to the downed pilots. He has just enough fuel in hand to fly the rest of the way in and attempt a rescue. Notwithstanding the lack of a covering Jolly and in the face of what just happened to Big Mother 67, Glen York decides to try to rescue Duthie. He drops down and heads in skimming over the tree tops, escorted by the flight of Air Force F-4 Phantoms.

Jolly 37 has barely started, when Sandies One and Two are jumped by two MiG 15s. The Sandies immediately clean their wings of drop tanks and their remaining rockets to reduce drag and maximize their maneuverability against the MiGs.

The F-4 Phantoms escorting Jolly 37 race ahead to engage the MiGs. When the Phantoms intervene, the MiGs disengage and head for home, but both the Sandies have been damaged by cannon fire from the MiGs. One of the Sandies is on fire. The A-1 is a tough bird, but it is time for Sandy One and Two to head for home. The Phantoms are also low on fuel and head west towards Thailand.

Glen York and Jolly 37 keep coming.

In the back of Jolly Green 37, Staff Sgt. Ted Zerbe and Airman 2nd Class Randy McComb are manning the machine guns, ready to hoist Duthie off the karst—if they can find him.

A-4s from the Ghost Riders and Saints who still have ordinance stream in and join in the suppression effort. F-8s from the O Boat also arrive to provide fighter cover.

Jolly 37 manages to survive the flak and find Duthie in the thick vegetation. They go into a hover over a nearby clearing in the trees and wait while Duthie makes his best speed to reach the spot. They snatch Duthie from the hill under fire.

With Duthie aboard, Glen York veers off, dropping below the far side of Duthie's hill. Out of immediate danger, they ask Duthie where Hartman is. Duthie shows them on a map. Glen York asks his co-pilot, Billy Privette if they have enough fuel to rescue Hartman. Billy says, "Barely—maybe just enough."

Glen York makes the decision to try.

They hand Duthie an automatic rifle, point to an open hatch, and tell him to shoot back when shot at. They make one pass down the karst but don't spot Hartman, and can't raise him on his survival radio. Billy Privette says they are past bingo. Past time to leave.

They head for a CIA airstrip in Laos flying under overcast skies. Helos prefer to hide in the weeds. They are especially visible and vulnerable at altitude, but Glen York has no choice. At higher altitudes the Jolly Green gets more miles per pound of fuel. If they are going to make it back to base, they must climb through the overcast to above ten-thousand feet. As Jolly 37 and its Sandy escorts head west, more MiGs are sent out to intercept them. The MiGs, however, are looking down below the cloud deck at treetop level. The radar track shows them flying by underneath Jolly 37.

By the time Jolly 37 reaches the airstrip, they are flying on fumes. When they land, they immediately start refueling by hand. Fueled up, they are going back for Hartman.

They tell Duthie, "Stay here. Someone will come get you."

Duthie begs to go.

"Nope. We got you out. We aren't taking you back."

Duthie is left in a shack at the end of the runway.

When Glen York and his crew get back to Hartman's area, they ask the admiral in command of Yankee Station, call sign "Jehovah" for clearance into the Hartman's location. Jehovah says:

"Negative. Negative. The Navy takes care of its own."

He will not permit them to proceed. Glen York and Jolly 37 crew head back to Laos.

That afternoon, another Clementine is launched from the southern SAR destroyer to rescue Dick Hartman. Escorted by two A-1s from VA-215, it too is shot up and has to abandon its attempt to rescue Dick Hartman. The second Clementine makes it back safely.

Bud Edney

IT IS NOW late in the day, and this Jehovah cannot stop the sun from setting. It is too late for the Navy to mount yet another effort to rescue Hartman. He will have to spend the night on the karst.

An Air Force helo picks up Duthie in Laos and takes him to Thailand. We will try another "Butch Verich" rescue at first light.

The Ghost Riders will lead the air support effort. Planning and leading the mission falls to Lt.Cmdr. Bud Edney. "Budney" is a skilled tactician and combat pilot. He is also Hartman's friend. They knew each other at the Naval Academy, and share a stateroom on *Oriskany*. The planning runs late into the night.

The North Vietnamese are also busy during the night of July 18–19. They move more antiaircraft weapons up to the foot of Dick Hartman's ridge.

Hartman spends the night moving down the karst ridge to put as much distance as he can between him and the hornets' nest of flak on the valley floor.

On *Constellation*, Lt. Dennis Peterson and his crew are selected to make the dawn attempt to rescue Hartman. Peterson sets about planning a circuitous route to Hartman's ridge that will avoid known flak sites. Meanwhile, maintenance crews work through the night to patch and repair the twenty-seven bullet holes in Big Mother 67 and clean up the blood in the cabin.

Day five is over. Only sixteen more to go on our first line period.

CHAPTER 14

DAY SIX

A Big Mother of HS-2.
Stripped of ASW gear and painted in camouflage
for combat SAR operations, it waits for a call on the deck of a destroyer.

Greater love hath no man than this,
that a man lay down his life for his friends.
—John 15:13

July 19

BIG MOTHER 67 is patched up and ready to go before dawn. Dennis Peterson and his crew launch in the predawn gloom. They will try to make good on Jehovah's boast.

Big Mother 67 is escorted by Locket A-1s from VA-152 off the *Oriskany*. Peterson goes feet-dry at low altitude well south of Hartman's location. He will skim along the tree tops from one karst ridge to the next like a squirrel jumping from tree branch to tree branch while flying a wide arc to approach Hartman's ridge from the south. Peterson hopes to remain undetected until the last few minutes when he has to cross a valley to reach Hartman's ridge.

As Big Mother 67 approaches, A-4s from the Ghost Riders and the Saints, and A-1s from *Oriskany* and *Constellation* are already on scene. The *O Boat's* F-8 squadrons provide a covering combat air patrol in case the MiGs try to intervene. The A-4s chum up the flak on the valley floor, attacking anything that shoots.

Bud Edney is the on-scene commander. He makes contact with Hartman and pinpoints his new position on the ground. Bud passes the word to Big Mother. The A-4s begin to pound the flak sites on the valley floor.

BIG MOTHER'S hoisting gear and machinegun are mounted at the main hatch on the right side of the helo. Therefore, once the downed pilot is located, the norm is to keep him inside a righthand orbit, where the pilot and hoist operator can both see him and the jungle penetrator, as they maneuver for the pickup.

The Big Mother flies along Hartman's ridge from the southwest to northeast. Bud Edney and the other support aircraft are taking fire from the valley to the southeast of the ridge. The helicopter overflies Hartman but does not spot him. Bud Edney tells them to circle back to the left, but, in the moment, Dennis Peterson swings the helo around to the right.

The turn carries the helo off the top of the karst ridge and over the little valley crammed with flak. Big Mother is hit, explodes, and drops onto the valley floor in a ball of fire.

Big Mother has a crew of four. Men we never knew who have come to save one of us from a place where one of their own has already died. They are:

Lt. Dennis Peterson,

Ens. Donald Frye,

AX2 Don McGrane, and

AX2 Bill Jackson.

All four perish.

At this point, all the aircraft on scene are low on fuel and must head feet-wet. John Davis barely makes it to a tanker. Barry Wood, once "The World's Most Powerful Ensign" is flying on our Ops Officer, Bob Arnold's wing. Barry makes it to the water but not to a tanker. He ejects near the southern SAR and is rescued.

Bud Edney is low on fuel and must also leave. Dick Hartman makes a last radio call to his friend:

"Guys, please don't leave me here."

LATER THAT AFTERNOON, yet another Big Mother launches off *Constellation* escorted by Spads to make another try. In Thailand the Jolly Green command decides it will also launch another attempt to rescue Dick Harman. Glen York and Billy Privette volunteer to fly the mission. Where does anyone find men such as these?[11]

Jehovah is all powerful on Yankee Station, but there is an admiral more than four hundred miles away in Saigon who is his boss. The Saigon admiral has had enough. There will be no more attempts to rescue Dick Hartman. The Big Mother and Jolly Green are recalled. The Saigon admiral orders everyone to abandon the rescue attempt.

Back on the ship, we stuff a blivet (a drop tank converted to carry cargo) with water, food, radios, and batteries, and whatever else we think might help him evade capture. No one believes that will happen, but we have to do something. The blivet is dropped near Hartman's position. We all think abandoning Dick Hartman to be captured is unconscionable, even if it is the right decision.

Duthie is flown back to us on the *O Boat*. He tells us that when he ejected at more than five-hundred knots, his lower leg got caught in the slipstream and spun around his knee like a windmill. The ejection

189

and/or the opening shock also "tweaked" his back. It is going to take more than the flight surgeon's brandy to fix his knee and back. We are glad to see him, but, after two days or so, he is off again, this time to the naval hospital at Cubi Point in the Philippines.

MORE THAN forty years later, partial remains of all four men in Big Mother 67's crew will be repatriated. Their families will decide that because they flew together and died together, they should be buried together. Their remains will be placed in a single coffin and buried in Arlington National Cemetery with full military honors. Paul Engel, Bud Edney, and the surviving JOs will attend to remember their courage and sacrifice.

Just typing their story makes me weep.

SOMETHING ELSE happens on July 19. Another man is killed. A man I don't know well, but I know him. He is one of the original seventy-two A-4 and F-8 pilots in our air wing who fly the strike missions. I work with him. He is one of us. Like Dick Hartman, Larry Duthie, and Barry Wood, he is a man—not a statistic or cartoon character. He has a family, friends, plans, and hopes. His death will cause grief, leaving a massive hole in the lives of those who know and love him. Like every one of the fifty-eight-thousand names on the polished granite wall, he was a human being. This is how he died:

On the afternoon of July 19, I am flying a wet-wing tanker to provide extra fuel to battle-damaged aircraft if needed. I monitor both the last gasp of the Hartman SAR effort and a strike in progress. Cmdr. Herb Hunter, skipper of VF-162, is leading the TARCAP fighter escort. He is a former Blue Angel, the Navy's flight demonstration team. By definition, Herb is one of the best of the best. His F-8 Crusader is hit by AAA. He is still flying with no fuel leaks. He doesn't need my services, but I continue to track him on the radio—just in case. He nurses the crippled bird to feet-wet, but he needs to put her down sooner rather than later.

Because of the damage, any landing will be at a higher-than-normal speed. Although risky, a carrier landing is theoretically possible at his new minimum flying speed. He has two options, a controlled ejection near a helo or try to get it aboard. Cmdr. Hunter will land it. *Oriskany* does not have a ready deck, but another carrier is landing aircraft. It will take Herb after all its aircraft have landed.

Herb's damaged engine holds together until he gets signal Charlie. He begins his approach. As he gets in close, his speed carries him high. He makes a late correction and is coming down fast at the ramp. He hits the deck hard—so hard the landing gear collapses. His aircraft bounces into the air and over the arresting gear, careening off the port side of the flight deck heading into the water.

We are all trained to eject if we head over the side without flying speed, wire or no wire. Herb ejects. His body is found floating with a partially deployed parachute.

I listen to this as it happens. *Why the fuck didn't he eject instead of trying to land?* It is all second-guessing, but I think, *Ejection seats mostly work. A carrier landing is hard enough, dangerous enough at a normal approach speed in an undamaged aircraft. Why risk it? Why not make a controlled ejection, wings level, slow speed, at an altitude that gives some margin of error?*

I think of C-10 who was determined to attempt a landing in his barely flying aircraft on day one. I decide pilots are reluctant to eject because it means giving up our ability to control the situation. We are pilots, not paratroopers.

I won't make that mistake.

It won't take long before I break that promise to myself and rethink my internal criticism of this valiant leader, but that is what I thought on July 19, 1967.

CHAPTER 15

DAY SEVEN

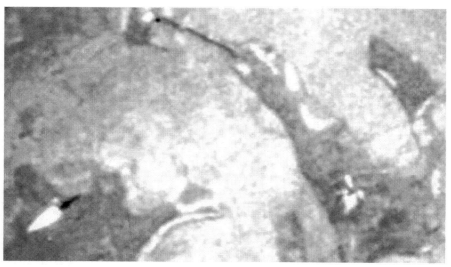

SA-2 SAM in the lower left corner
The missile's booster has fallen away. Seen in profile, the missile is tracking
someone else. The still picture cannot convey the missile's speed. It would cross
the frame of this picture faster than a blink of your eye.

July 20

ON DAY SEVEN, the air wing is tasked with three more Alfa Strikes. Dick Perry and I launch on a mission against Haiphong, deep in the heart of their air defenses. Aircraft are in short supply. The Ghost Riders cannot muster eight strike aircraft, so Dick and I will fly as an independent section. Dick will be Magic Four, and I Magic Five.

The AI briefings are quickly becoming familiar if not routine. There is always a sermon, a few weary words to stir our souls. It is a tough sell. When we are sent against three targets every day because someone up the chain of command thinks they are worth our lives, no target is more or less important—any more than any one of our lives is more or less important. It is just what we are going to do next.

Briefing done, we hang out in the ready room: smoking, taking a last trip to the head, and gearing up, waiting for the call to man aircraft. Then, it's the slow escalator ride to the roof and the banter as we walk down the flight deck, just to show we are Zen with it all.

The preflight rituals and engine start. The slow crawl up to the catapult and the E ticket adrenaline jolt as I am shot off the bow. I rendezvous with Dick, we join up with the strike group, climb to feet-dry, and from there the long aerial cavalry charge to the target.

0734

We are about twelve miles out. Both Iron Hands have engaged missile sites. My system is flooded with adrenaline—everything in slow motion. A voice I don't recognize:

"Missile launch! Two o'clock, eleven miles"
I see it
The booster flame
just for a second
The missile!
maybe fifteen or twenty degrees off to our right
the hundred-foot exhaust flame winks out
as the booster falls off
my warbler begins to sing

two others make the call

I scan the distant ground, with only glances up–down–and behind. My heart rate screams up over two-hundred beats a minute. Time flowing like taffy.

There!
Maybe a thirty-foot tail
the missile curves
turning toward
me
the exhaust flame goes into eclipse
The glow!
the corona of the tail
bulging out behind
the oncoming missile
I glance away
scanning out left and behind
I look back
Nothing
Where is it?
Can't find it
Look at the same spot on the canopy
It's on an intercept course.
It has to be there—
Got it
closing fast
drifting right
away from us
"Magic One, break left now!"
our first division breaks down under us
Dick slides left and up
I move to his left wing
the missile tries to follow Magic One down
it's on us in a flash

195

passing five-hundred feet below to my right
BOOM!
I wince—hear it—feel it
Jesus, that's close
quick check
no flashing lights
all the needles where they should be
controls work
no holes I can see in wings or nose
no one in Magic One's division falls out
no "I'm hit!"
Dick edges up and right
next to the trailing Old Salt division
leading us into the slot Magic One's division held
knowing they will lose speed
climbing back up to the strike group
"Old Salt One is in, off left"
flak blooms silently ahead
around the Old Salts
They are targeting the roll-in
gray and brown smoke
57 and 37mm
Crump! Crump! Crump!
another salvo—closer
Roll in, Dick, roll in!
CRUMP! CRUMP! CRUMP! CRUMP!
a salvo erupts just below us
a quick check
I'm okay
No smoke from Dick's airplane
Scan our division
all okay
We'll never make it to the roll-in
Dick is in
CRUMP! CRUMP! CRUMP! CRUMP! CRUMP!
These fuckers can shoot

I'm in
Warbler!!!
I hurry it
I want to get down in the grass
where the SAM can't see me
It is a fucked-up run
I salvage it as best I can
I have no idea where my bombs go
I am off a second behind Dick
pulling hard
chaff–chaff
rolling
chaff–chaff—chaff–chaff
reversing—chaff–chaff—chaff–chaff
The damn warbler won't shut up
chaff–chaff—chaff–chaff—chaff–chaff
twisting in my seat on each jink
looking over my shoulder
as I roll reversing each turn
scared stiff a SAM
is tracking from behind
where I can't see it
I glance ahead at Dick
He's going out at three-thousand feet
I am dancing behind him
like a frenetic squirrel
still pushing the chaff button
still looking over my shoulder
on every jink

0736
We are out of the flak
Time to get the hell feet-wet
Don't let down!
Head on a swivel
Jink and look

197

They haven't
given up
trying to
kill us

0741
Check the instruments
engine sweet
fuel state?
Twenty-eight-hundred pounds
enough

Here comes the beach.

Feet-wet

a mile off the beach
Dick stops jinking
"Thank god."
master-arming switch off
slide into a loose cruise position
flight suit drenched
in sweat
shivering—cold
in the air-conditioning blast
Run the temp up
I am wired
Legs vibrating up and down
both feet off the rudders
plant them on the
cockpit deck
Control the breathing
calm down
Hold left hand out
No shakes

I float on the rising euphoria as the adrenaline subsides. Dick checks us in with Red Crown and starts an easy climb. He waggles his wings: time to check him for damage. I slide in close, scanning for any holes, bloody streaks from leaking hydraulics, wisps of smoke or vaporizing fuel, I sink a few feet, I drift under him, crossing to the other side, then rising to his wing tip. No damage.

I give him a thumbs-up. He passes the lead to me. And sinks out of sight as he checks me over. Up on my other wing—thumbs-up and asks for my fuel state. I flash the numbers. Dick signals a switch to *Oriskany*'s approach control radio channel, and pushes me out to cruise formation. He levels off at eight-thousand feet and throttles back to max conserve as we head for the carrier.

0756

It is a beautiful day. Unlimited visibility. The crystalline sky dotted with fair weather clouds. My eye snags on a creaming streak of white on the blue water ahead. At this distance, she is a small gray smudge at the narrow end of her wake—home. She is still running downwind, with the destroyer flying wing, drawing its pencil-thin wake on the blue tabletop.

"This is Child Play. Signal Delta." The air boss wants us to wait and conserve fuel. Dick puts us into a wide orbit around her.

Time for a smoke. I undo one side of my oxygen mask, letting it dangle on my chest. Oxygen off. Band-Aid can ashtray out. I fish out a cigarette and a match book from my pocket sleeve. Flying with the stick between my knees, I light up and take a long, slow drag.

Still alive—again.

Beyond that, I just enjoy the bright blue sky with Dick's bird balanced on my horizon, looking about as the others gather, enjoying the nicotine seeping back into my system.

0810

The *O Boat* is turning. As she straightens with her nose to the wind we hear, "This is Child Play. Signal Charlie."

Dick puts his hook down. I do the same. Time to land. I put out the second cigarette, Band-Aid can back in the G-suit pocket, oxygen on, mask on. No more floating on the tide of endorphins. Time to do. Time to get her aboard again. I lock my shoulder harness and throw my weight against it to make sure it engaged. I scribble the high positive and negative Gs I demanded of the aircraft on my kneeboard before the arresting gear pegs it in both directions. We both dump excess fuel to get down to our maximum landing weight.

0817

"Signal Charlie"
Oriskany *is visible between the aircraft.*

Dick gives me the speed-brake warning signal; a pause and he nods his head—we both thumb the speed-brake switches on our throttles—decelerating in tandem. He tosses his head back and pulls the throttle back to almost idle, taking us down to five-hundred feet in a long graceful curve to a point about a mile behind the carrier. We slow to 250 knots, speed-brakes in and throttle up, as he takes us alongside the wake, working hard to look good as we roar past the ship's starboard side.

We pass the bow. Dick's head swivels left checking for aircraft in the pattern, looks back at me, kisses off, and breaks left. I scan the pattern while counting: *One potato, two potato, three potato, and* . . . snap

200

into a sixty-degree bank. Right hand pulling the stick, bending it into the turn. Left hand pulling the throttle to idle. Speed-brakes out. At 180 knots–flaps down; jockeying the turn to maintain separation from Dick. At 150 knots–gear down. Power on to hold the speed and altitude. One hundred eighty degrees of turn and I rollout, wings level, running downwind on a course opposite that of the ship.

0819

I hit the 180 abeam the LSO platform on the aft end of the flight deck, on speed and on altitude. Check the gear and flap indicators. Throw my shoulders forward to make sure the harness is locked for the trap—again. If I am obsessive about the harness lock, it is because I know someone who forgot and ended up with his head jammed under the instrument panel. Took two sailors to pull him out ass first to the laughter and cheers of everyone on the flight deck. An embarrassment I do not wish to experience. I check for spacing from Dick. He's at the ninety, halfway through his approach turn.

Wait a moment
give him some more room
Okay
Here we go again
Adrenaline again
Approach turn—on speed—descending
passing through 450 feet at the ninety

0821
Crossing the wake
Passing through two-hundred feet
Slowing to 138 knots
catch it at the optimum angle of attack
Rollout in the groove
Gunsight pipper in the crotch of angle deck
Start her down
the ball showing me low—*little power*

thumb the radio: "Magic 314, Ball, 1.9."
LSO comes back: "Roger ball. Power, you're low"
little more power
Center ball
Take half the power correction out
Meatball–angle of attack–line up–meatball–angle of attack–line up
checking all three
meatball–angle of attack–line up
every second-and-a-half
meatball (high or low–power)
angle of attack (fast or slow–attitude)
line up (left or right–bank)
anticipating each correction
before I need it
meatball–angle of attack–lineup
a little power for the burble
meatball–angle of attack–lineup
out of the burble, take some power off
meatball–angle of attack–lineup
in close
ball sinking–power
at the ramp
meatball
lineup
meatball ball rising
pull a tad of power
committed now
wheels thump
full power
speed-brakes in
No stop
LSO: "Bolter, Bolter, Bolter!"
Shit
off the angled deck
holding the angle of attack
a climbing left turn

into the bolter pattern
to do it again

0827
wheels thump,
full power, speed-brakes in,
WHAM—into the shoulder straps,
Trap!—dead stop
Elation
a big smile hidden behind my mask
Check the brakes, look right, hook up
Yellow shirt signaling, Off the brakes
arresting gear pulls me back
putting slack in the cable
A blue shirt with a pry bar sprints toward my tail
to knock the cable off the hook
Yellow shirt wants brakes
to stop the backward roll.
Now he wants right brake and come ahead
power up
pivot right
off the right brake
fast taxi
charging across the foul-deck line
to get out of the way
left hand finds the flaps lever without a look
pull it up retracting the flaps
Across the foul-deck line
I'm clear
Power to idle
brakes
deck clear for the man behind
slow it down
Passed to another yellow shirt up the deck
He slows me and passes me to another
Park it up on the bow—six inches wing tip to wing tip

The tired blue shirt shambles over
still draped in Marley's chains
He ties the bird down
Chocks in
Throttle around the detent
Shutting it down
Noting the engine
rundown time
It's over.

0829

I check the eight-day clock, an hour and forty-two minutes deck-to-deck. I note it on the kneeboard: 1.7 hours flight time. Plane captain appears carrying the ladder. I pop the canopy with one hand and catch it with the other to prevent it slamming open in the wind. Get the gust strap from its little bag on the canopy rail and hook it to the canopy, letting the strap feed through my fingers.

Chief Mac walks up. He is the leading chief in our maintenance department. Short, wiry, and pushing past fifty. He has been in the navy since he was eighteen. He is the heart and soul of the squadron. He is why we will maintain such a high availability rate even when our aircraft grow old before their time, why our ejection seats work and parachutes deploy when we need them, why we will have an ordnance success rate nearing one-hundred percent (everything shoots, falls off, and goes boom when it should). He wants to know if there is a problem with my aircraft. I give a thumbs-up. (*A good bird. Bomb it, gas it, and turn it for the next go.*) Head knocker down, oxygen off, mask off, unhook the oxygen hose, radio leads, and G-suit; zero out the G-meter, which is pegged from the trap. Unstrap lap and shoulder harness, and unstrap the kneeboard. I grab the helmet bag, stand up, stand on the seat, step onto the ladder and climb down. I say "Thanks," to the Plane Captain, "good bird."

Cacophony, everything in motion
head back on a swivel
aircraft hurrying to cross the foul-deck line

taxiing aircraft
with props to chop me
intakes to swallow me
jet exhausts sweeping the deck
to blow me away
Duck into the island.
Safe.

0831

Helmet off. Down the passageway to the escalator. Down another passageway to the ready room. Stop in the head. Then through the ready-room backdoor across the passageway. Stop at the maintenance desk, light a cigarette, and fill out the yellow gripe-sheet, noting the flight time, maximum Gs, and any problems with the aircraft. Walk in and strip off my gear under the air-conditioning vent, enjoying a cold air shower. Cigarette out, stow the gear, and back to the ready room for a fast smoke before I go off to the AI spaces to debrief.

0849

Back to the ready room. The euphoria melts away, leaving me drifting on a pool of lassitude. C-10 appears at my elbow.

"*Ja' jeat 'jet?*"
"*No, j'ou?*"
"*Squ'o.*"

The wardroom is still serving breakfast. *Good.* I love breakfast.

0910

I'm the aircraft division officer and have an hour. I should check the aircraft division shops to see if I can help. It is the same in every shop; they need me only to get out of their way while they hustle to get the birds up for the next go. I listen and watch, hoping to learn something.

0950

I'm on the next launch. I wander back to the ready room in time for a smoke before we head to the AI spaces for the pre-launch briefing. I'm pleased with myself. This is only my sixth day of flying combat missions, and I saw the missile launch (if only after someone else called it). I kept it in sight after the booster separated, found it again after looking away—while there was still time to do something about it. I stayed with Dick as we danced through thick, accurate flak. I am over the top. "Excited" doesn't say it. For the moment, I skip over the fact that I ended up flinging the bombs more or less randomly at Mother Earth. I look around the ready room at my squadronmates.

I am one of them. I have a lot to learn, but I can do this. I belong here.

DAY SEVEN is not just a big day for me. Jim Nunn, a JO in VF-162, gets a "cold cat." His F-8's ejection seat is not as capable as the A-4's at low speed and low altitude, so he stays with the bird. He hits the water just in front of the ship. His F-8 sinks like the metal pipe it is.

On the *O Boat's* bridge, they immediately throw the wheel hard over, count a set number of seconds and then throw it hard in the opposite direction. This has the effect of kicking the stern and the ship's massive screws clear of the aircraft wreckage—and the pilot.

Jim will later tell Duthie that when he hit the water: "I thought I was dead. I wasn't. So, I ejected."

The cannon shell under his Martin Baker seat fires him through the canopy, but the sudden stop when he hits the water fractures vertebrae in his neck. He manages to get out of his parachute harness and inflate his flotation gear. Jim pops to the surface in the ship's wake and is rescued by the helo on angel duty.

Lt. Russ Kuhl's day also goes sideways. Russ is a pilot in our sister squadron, VA-163. He was hit by flak northeast of Haiphong. His wounded bird carried him back to feet-wet before it died.

His ejection did not go as advertised. When he, his parachute , and seat pan separated from the seat, he looked down at his feet and was surprised to see nothing but blue sky above(?) them. He was falling upside down with his streaming parachute above him. When the parachute canopy opened, it "cracked me like a bullwhip." The hand-held survival radio shot out of his survival vest and walloped him on the chin. The radio is smaller but heavier than a common brick. It hit Russ hard enough to break his neck. Broken neck or no, Russ got clear of his chute in the water and was rescued.

Russ Kuhl's ejection requires I do something. I am responsible for the parachute riggers who supply and maintain all of our safety and survival gear, including the survival radios and survival vests. I head down to the riggers' shop off the hangar deck. They have talked to the Saints' riggers and are already on it. More Velcro. The riggers point out that we take the radios out to make sure they are working every time we gear up. We need to make sure the flap is pulled tight and the Velcro is pressed down *firmly* with no wrinkles when we put the radios back in our vest. I pass the word in an APM (all pilots meeting) that night before the movie.

Jim and Russ are flown off to join Duthie in the Lucky Few Club at the Cubi Point naval hospital.

AS SOON as Russ Kuhl and Jim Nunn are out of traction, they find Duthie. They check themselves out of the hospital, and move into the BOQ. When *Oriskany* comes off the line, the flight surgeons are dismayed to discover that all three of their patients have disappeared from the hospital. They track all three down, readmit them to the hospital. Russ and Duthie will be sent to Oak Knoll Naval Hospital in Oakland, California, for treatment and rehabilitation. I am glad Duthie is back and safe, but will miss him.

That night, as I am trying to sleep, I start thinking about Jim and Russ. It occurs to me, *The pace of losses seems to be picking up.* I grab hold of myself.

Stop it! Didn't happen to you. I have learned what I can from it. There's no going back. No looking back. I'm in my bunk, safe as houses. Now, go to sleep.

CHAPTER 16

DAY EIGHT

A-4 buddy tankers topping off F-8 Crusaders after launch.

"They're trying to kill me," Yossarian told him calmly.

"No one's trying to kill you," Clevinger cried.

"Then why are they shooting at me?" Yossarian asked.

"They're shooting at everyone," Clevinger answered. "They're trying to kill everyone."

"And what difference does that make?"

—Joseph Heller

July 21

BETWEEN being shot down and surviving the fire during the '66 cruise and going for a swim in the Tonkin Gulf on day six of the '67 cruise, Barry Wood is done with airplanes. He has waited two days but now goes to the skipper and turns in his wings. In my memory, they had him off the ship in nothing flat. He was gone before I had a chance to say good-bye to him. This is wrong. When Jim Waldron reads an early draft of the book, he tells me, "They made Barry the permanent squadron duty officer for a week before they got him off the ship." That makes sense. Our skipper, Doug Mow, would have given Barry a few days to change his mind. I am sure Jim is right, but I don't remember Barry sitting at that desk for a week or sleeping in the bunk below me. He was invisible to me or at least to my memory. The only truth in what I originally wrote was "I never said good-bye to him," even though he slept in the bunk below me.

That was not out of animus toward Barry for turning in his wings. The reality is I probably was embarrassed for him. I may also have had an irrational fear that turning in your wings might be contagious, so I just avoided him. If these were sub-conscious motives, I also consciously worked to walk past him without a thought. Hartman, Duthie, and Barry were the first losses in our squadron and a turning point for me. I learned that to be a warrior I must go forward, regardless of the losses.

I work at putting our losses behind me every day. John Donne be damned: I set about busy digging an emotional mote, making myself an island. Dead, captured, wounded, or turning in your wings are all the same. Gone is gone.

I can't imagine how Bob Arnold must feel. All three of the pilots in his division that he trained and led into combat a week ago are gone.

Closer to home for me is the awareness that we have lost Duthie and Barry, our only two combat-experienced JOs. Glad I don't believe in omens.

Barry is done with flying but not with the war. He asks to go to Swift Boats in the Riverine Force, guys in little plastic boats fighting the VC and regular North Vietnamese army in the Mekong Delta. His request is granted. Years later, I will be told Barry earned a Silver Star fighting in the delta. In my experience, most Silver Stars went to the senior officers for leading strikes. Of the few JOs who were awarded a Silver Star, most wore them in their coffin—assuming we got his body back.

After Vietnam, Barry will ask for and gets his wings back. He will fly photo reconnaissance in RA-5C Vigilantes. He will die still a young man whose life was filled with ghosts and demons.

Don Purdy moves from the JO bunkroom into Barry's empty bunk. Sometimes I beat Don out the door on a fire alarm.

DAY EIGHT is Also the day I fly the buddy tanker on a mission during which nothing happens but which inalterably changes me.

It is the day I total up our losses and figure out how many of us will be gone by the end of the cruise. The numbers are not good. Barry's departure makes it four Ghost Riders shot down and three gone. Only nineteen of us left. That's one-seventh of us in just the first of the fifteen weeks we will be on the line during this cruise.

Wayne said, "always double-check your numbers." Sitting in the cockpit, I do the arithmetic for the third time. The numbers don't change. As near as I can tell, the overall loss rate for our Air wing is no better. At this rate, all of the A-4 and F-8 pilots will be gone long before the cruise is over.

I am not going to survive this cruise—never mind the next.

I sit in the cockpit, flying the tanker in its go-nowhere loop— staring my death in the face.

Aw shit!

Being here is the last thing I will ever know or do.

I'll never make love to my wife again.

I'll never see my child.

I'll never see my parents again or my sisters and brother.

Hell, I'll never drive a car again.

Well, what now?

I can do what Barry did; I can turn in my wings. If I do, I am out of here. I'll have to serve out my enlistment, but it won't be flying against Hanoi and Haiphong. I'll survive.

It doesn't take long to decide. Five, maybe ten seconds.

I can't quit. I cannot leave these guys to die without me. I am where I want to be, doing the most important thing I will ever do. This is where I belong.

I realize, if I leave, they will replace me.

If I quit, someone will die in my place. I cannot live with that. I am staying.

I feel good about the decision to stay, I am not afraid of dying—but I feel hollowed out. I think of my childhood. It was filled with the small magics of everyday life. Ants talking to each other as they come and go from their anthills. The magic of a cocoon spun by a caterpillar on a bush in our backyard, its twig carefully picked and placed in a jar with holes ice-picked into the metal lid and, in the spring, coming home from school for lunch to find the jar on the kitchen table with a butterfly struggling to emerge. Knowing that Raggedy Andy really does come alive in the night and plays with my toys, because when I asked my mother if it was true, she asked me, "Do you believe that he does?" And when I said, "Yes." She smiled and said, "Then he does." I never wanted for anything I truly needed, especially love and attention.

I have no complaints. I've had a good life.

I will miss home, being with my wife, raising our daughter, more kids, Mom, deep-sea fishing with Wayne—Stop it! I won't let my squadron brothers down. No one will die in my place. I will not quit.

I take a deep breath. I'm done thinking.

If I die this afternoon, I can't say I've been cheated. It's okay.

Sitting in that cockpit, I am at peace. I have no fear, no regrets. Death is just another experience. I didn't know what was happening when I was born, but I will experience death head-on—awake— alive—leaning in. I wonder what it's like?

Death will be—interesting.

I wonder if I will remember it?

Those few minutes boring holes in the sky are the pivot point—the fulcrum of my life. There are a lot of things I am afraid of, but death is no longer one of them. Dying is just another experience, another part of life.

I WILL NEVER second-guess the decision to stay. Nor will I ever regret it, not even in my darkest moments. I admit that, sometimes, I will regret I did not die there—then—regret that I outlived my moment. But staying *was* the best thing I ever did, and my death there and then would not have changed that. Nor will the decades of living with the aftermath of combat.

SITTING IN the cockpit, I realize that, if I am to do this, I cannot allow myself to predict or project beyond the moment. I must live in the soap bubble of now and never worry about the moment my bubble will burst. Making up my mind to live in the moment is the easy part. In the beginning, I am tested every time the bell tolls. But I press on and do what I must do.

Just because I accept my death does not mean I want to die. Brother Death will have to work to take me. I will fly my life into the ground until it comes to a dead stop. Nor will I let Death cast a shadow across my life. When Death has retreated beyond arm's length for the moment, I will not worry. I will not think about what almost happened or might happen next.

I begin shrinking my world down to now. I abandon my past, discard my future.

My world becomes the Ghost Riders, the cockpit, the thirty-mile horizon, and infinite dome of sky where I carve curves in the air, conforming to my leader, improvising on his theme, not mimicking, head and eyes moving constantly, registering each threat, ascending to the perch, plunging on the target in razor-straight dives. More alive than I have ever been or ever will be again. Adrenaline highs, post-adrenaline euphoria, losses ignored, and grief ruthlessly suppressed. During the interludes between debriefing and briefing, I drift in a languid sea of mindless chatter, laughter, reading, eating, watching a movie—never counting the seconds until it is time to strap an aircraft on my back and have at them again.

THROUGH THE YEARS that follow, I will never tell Mom about the moment I chose to stay and die, much less why. But, decades later, I will witness her accepting death while holding on to life until she was done. In the end, she too accepted her death as an adventure.

In my sixty-seventh year, my sister Beth will call, and tell me, "When Mom fell six or seven months ago, they discovered lung cancer on the X-rays. Mom talked it over with the doctors and decided she'd take the six months they said she'd have—without surgery, chemo, or radiation."

Mom told Beth but also told her to tell no one. Mom said, "I will tell them when they need to know." Beth paused and then said, "We are admitting Mom to the hospital. You should come."

With a three-hour time change in my favor, I arrived there by 10:00 a.m. the next day. They had just finished draining her lungs. Beth brought me up to date. She found a nice nursing home up the coast in Carlsbad that will take her and has arranged for hospice care. We will we transfer her tomorrow.

The first day in the nursing home, Mom told each of her children to come at a particular time each day. She wanted time alone with each of us. I drew the early morning shift. I was to be there at 6:30 a.m. I got up early, leaving enough time to stop at Pannikin's where Mom used to walk for coffee when she and Wayne lived in Encinitas. Large, half decaf, with lots of cream.

She was awake, waiting for me when I arrived the next morning. While she was in the hospital, they had put her on a ventilator while they drained her lungs, and her throat was still raw. Hot coffee hurts, so I went to the nurse's station to get a glass of crushed ice for her to doctor the coffee. We talked.

That first morning, Mom said, "You have known me longer than anyone alive, except my sister Dorothy. You and I share memories no one else has." That morning, Mom reminded me I was still a work in progress. We also talked about Wayne and his death two decades earlier.

It occurred to me this was a conversation Wayne and I never had. He and I were never able to bridge the moats of emotional privacy, self-sufficiency, and pride that we both sheltered behind. The closest we had was the week before he died. I flew to San Diego to help Mom. Wayne was home from the hospital and mostly bedridden. I brought him a framed poster of the Boeing F4B4, a Navy biplane fighter from the early 1930s. The poster was called *Scaring the Cows*, and show two aircraft flying low over a pasture. These were the glory airplanes of his childhood. I hung it next to his bed. He said, "Thank you." Without looking away from the picture, he said: "Mike, take care of your mom."

But now, Mom and I were sharing the memories we had of him, each from our own perspective. We talked of what he did for each of us, and for all of us, and the immense hole his death tore in our lives. I told her I could never shed a tear for him. She said, "Mike, it's okay to cry. It's good for you." I nodded, but thought: *I don't do grief.*

That morning the routine was as natural as if we had been doing it for years. Every morning, I would get the coffee, stop at the nurses' station for ice, and we would have an hour-and-a-half together. We talked about the years we were together alone, while Wayne was in Caltech, and then off to post-war Europe. The years when we wondered about the ants, Raggedy Andy, and all the rest.

Mom never gave up being a devout Catholic. One morning, she looked like she had been crying. When I asked how she was doing, she took a deep breath and said, "Oh, Michael, I am afraid I am going to hell."

I could not believe what I was hearing. I reached back to my catechism days. "No. You have confessed and received absolution. You are forgiven."

She did not look comforted. I grasped at straws.

"Mom, you have lived a good life filled with love and compassion for others. If you don't make it into heaven, there's no hope for the rest of us. . . . If that's the way God is, He is going to be lonely up there. It will just be Him and all the dogs."

She laughed.

Later, I took our family's former priest aside and told him. He and Mom talked. She moved past her doubts—and her fear.

Every morning when we were having our coffee together, the hospice doctor stopped by. On about the third morning, he asked if she wanted morphine. I sat there feeling like a little boy listening to the adults talk.

Mom, said, "Not yet."

The next morning, he said, "I know you are in pain. Why not take a little something now?"

215

She explained, "My family and friends are coming. I don't want to be drugged when they get here. I want to be here for them. I have things I want to tell them, things I want to say. I want to say good-bye."

Several days later, when the doctor asked yet again, she relented, "Okay. They are all here and I have talked to each of them. I am ready. I could use some morphine now."

Fifteen minutes after I left her the next morning, Mom took a deep breath and—did not take the next.

I SHARE her last week with you here because I am astounded at the gifts she gave and the lessons I absorbed from her in my childhood, lessons that made possible my decision to stay on the line in July 1967—gifts that will come to my rescue in future uncounted days and weeks.

THE NORTH VIETNAMESE have left Dick Hartman on his ridge as bait for two days hoping to lure us into another rescue effort. Their patience runs out. Late on July 22, 1967, the word comes down. Hanoi announced it has taken Lt.Cmdr. Richard Danner Hartman prisoner. We knew this was coming, but it sucks. We know that being a POW at the hands of the North Vietnamese is physical and psychological torture, solitary confinement, and starvation rations of pumpkin rinds and fish heads. But at least he is alive.

We will get him back. When this war finally ends, we'll be there to welcome him home.

Bud Edney is recommended for a Silver Star for his efforts to rescue Hartman. Bud refuses to let the recommendation be submitted.

The North Vietnamese will release the POWs in 1973. Dick Hartman is not among them. The released POWs are sure he was never brought to the Hanoi Hilton. Finally, on March 5, 1974, the North Vietnamese return Dick Hartman's remains. The North Vietnamese send a copy of his death certificate. It is dated within twenty hours of Hartman's capture. The place and cause of his death are left blank. As lonely and forlorn a death as I can imagine.

In my seventies, I will think of Dick Hartman often, remembering him as a quiet man, serious and steady. Blond, with a thin face and deep-set eyes. Wiry, with a diamond-hard core. I don't think I ever saw him have a drink. He chose not to play in all our reindeer games. He just did what he did, leaving the rest of us to it. A good man.

He and his family deserved better, even from our enemy.[12]

IN '67, I ASSUME I am the only one who accepts the fact he will not live to see the end of the cruise. It's not as if my squadronmates ever talked about it—or ever will. Conversations about our emotions are not on the agenda. If one of us accidently trips over an emotion, he invariably jumps up and quickly moves off to another subject, slightly embarrassed, hoping no one noticed. If any of us happen to notice, we pretend we don't and hurry past.

Over the course of the cruise, I hear lots of rationalizations, said only half in jest. One of my squadronmates says, and hopes to believe, "I am invisible. If they can't see me, they can't shoot me down." Another claims, "I am too good a pilot to get shot down."

No one is invisible. No one is "too good."

Fifty years later, I will discover I was not the only one who understood we were dead men flying. During the second decade of the next century, I will hear Don Purdy say:

"It was pretty bad starting in July of '67. . . . By August, you didn't have to be a math whiz to figure out none of us were going to survive. . . . Strange as it seems, once you accepted that, it was like all the worry was gone, and yeah, we aren't going to make it out, but, *okay, I accept it.* I mean, it was to that point."

Part IV

WARRIOR

Lady Jessie with a heavy bomb load.
She carries a 2,000# Mk 84 on the centerline, 1,000# Mk 83s on the
inner wing-stations, and 500# Mark 82s on the outer wing-stations).

CHAPTER 17

END OF ROUND ONE

Mule dismounting.

CHURCHILL famously said: "Nothing in life is so exhilarating as to be shot at without result." He was right about that. There is nothing to match the feeling of walking back down the flight deck after a hot mission. The fact that I do not expect to live does not diminish the immense feeling joy that comes with beating the odds one more time.

Fifty years on, I will miss the rush of bomb release and bending the bird back skyward until my vision closes down to a thirty-degree aperture and, as soon as the nose is above the horizon, momentarily easing the Gs and snapping into a sixty-degree bank before pulling it back to six- or seven-Gs while craning my neck around to see my bomb fall, then off the Gs again for a maximum-deflection roll into a ninety-degree bank in the opposite direction.

Having a chance to shoot back makes the experience even better.

One day, Rock Hodges was flying a flak-suppression mission in support of an Alfa Strike. As he arrived over the target seconds ahead of the main body, his aircraft was surrounded by flak bursts. They miss. Rock's laconic voice came across the strike frequency as he rolled in on the flak site, *"Nice shooting, soldiers. Now, watch this."*

I know exactly how Rock felt in that moment.

But they don't always miss. July isn't done killing us.

ON JULY 25 the bell tolls for Lt.Cmdr. Don Davis of the Saints. Don is an "old guy." He is thirty-two when he dies. In 1997, after two failed searches, they will recover bone fragments at a crash sight. They find enough to positively identify Don's remains. What they recovered are buried with full honors at Arlington National Cemetery.[13]

On July 28, the bell tolls twice. We lose one of our tankers, a KA-3B Whale, in an operational accident while flying to Cubi in heavy rain. First one, then the second engine flames out. A-3s are not equipped with ejection seats. Only the pilot is found and rescued. The other two in the crew, Ensign Bruce Patterson and AE2 Charles Handy, are both listed as killed in action. I have no trouble walking past their deaths. I am already so distanced that I barely hear the bell.

The next day, July 29, I fly with Dick on an Alfa Strike. Afterward, I'm done for the day and head to my stateroom to take a nap. C-10 bolts in, "Mule! Get up! *Forrestal* is burning. It's just like *Victory at Sea.*" He grabs his camera and heads out, banging up the ladder. I drag myself out of the rack and follow at an ever-increasing distance. When I emerge from the island, *Forrestal* is maybe a half mile off on our starboard quarter. There is a tower of ugly black smoke looming several thousand feet above the ship.

Ordinarily the three carriers on Yankee Station are out of sight of each other from the deck, but once launched, we often see one or both of the others steaming in their assigned boxes as we climb and the horizon stretches. The captain of *Oriskany* has closed on *Forrestal* to render aid.

Forrestal is nearly dead in the water. The landing area, packed with aircraft ready for a launch, is a roiling inferno of smoke and flames. *Forrestal*'s captain has slowed to a crawl to avoid fanning the flames and pointed her into the wind to keep the smoke off the deck. The *O Boat* is also just creeping along, maintaining station on *Forrestal*.

I see one, two, maybe three explosions, the shock waves visible as they rip out through the boiling smoke and flame, the noise following a second later. A helo is approaching our bow, swooping around to land. There is another helo outbound from us, almost to *Forrestal*. The helo that lands on our bow is swarmed by corpsmen and stretcher bearers as it touches down. They off-load casualties, putting most in Stokes litters (A stretcher made of wire netting into which an adult can be placed.)

The casualties are hurried onto the forward deck elevator and dropped to the hangar deck with medics already rigging IVs. Then, they are taken from the hangar deck directly to the fo'c'sle for triage and emergency treatment. Those needing surgery are carried aft and below to the sickbay.

There is a chain of sailors acting as a human conveyor belt moving OBAs and canisters of firefighting foam from the port deck edge to an area next to where the helos are landing. As soon as the wounded are unloaded, the OBAs and foam canisters are hurriedly tossed in the helo for the return trip to *Forrestal*.

After about ten minutes, Marines and the Master-at-Arms' Mates come along confiscating film from all the cameras and telling the owners, "Next time we take the cameras." C-10 grumbles but disappears below, returning empty-handed.

I watch as sailors on *Forrestal's* flight deck forward of the fire push one and then a second perfectly good RA-5 Vigilante over the side. The Vigilante is the most expensive carrier aircraft in the Navy's inventory, but *Forrestal's* crew needs the space for the helicopters to land.

The fire erupted on the flight deck during engine start before a launch. The rear half of the deck was full of fueled and armed aircraft, some with their engines running. A Zuni air-to-ground rocket on the wing of an F-4 was ignited by an electrical fault in the F-4. The rocket roared out of its launcher, flashing across the deck. It hit the centerline drop tank of an A-4 on the port deck edge. The rocket went through the drop tank. Two-thousand pounds of jet fuel gushed onto the deck in a widening pool. It only took a second for the spilled fuel to erupt in flame. In a matter of moments, the burning fuel quickly spread, enveloping several other A-4s in a raging fire.

Lt.Cmdr. John McCain is the pilot in the A-4 parked next to the one hit by the rocket. His is a familiar name to us because his father is Admiral John McCain, Commander in Chief Pacific (CincPac) in Hawaii. John's name will become familiar to us all for other reasons in the years to come. Finding himself in the midst of burning jet fuel, John unstraps, unplugs, opens the canopy, and stands on the ejection seat. There is fire on both sides and underneath his cockpit. He climbs out of the cockpit over the windscreen onto the nose, steps out on the refueling probe like a tightrope, runs to the end, and jumps as far as he can. Momentarily clear of the fire, he runs forward for the Island. It isn't long before the bombs on John's A-4 begin to cook off. The burning jet fuel under the adjoining aircraft soon set their centerline tanks afire. Seconds later their bombs begin exploding.

As the fire pushes aft, many are trapped with no escape. They jump into the sponsons in search of a route to the hangar deck, where they can work their way forward to safety beneath the fire. The bombs blow holes in the flight deck, and the fire spreads to the hangar deck, trapping men on the back edge of the flight deck and fantail (the open stern behind and below the flight deck). Their only option is to jump. It's forty feet from the fantail, and sixty from the flight deck to the water. I watch them going off, heads erect, hands over their groins, legs crossed, just as I was taught on the thirty-foot tower at the swimming pool in Pre-Flight. I can see splashes in the tepid wake as they hit the water. *Forrestal's* escorting destroyer is no longer trailing in its wake. It is close alongside *Forrestal* to lend the weight of its fire hoses to fighting the fire. The destroyer Captain has laid her so close aboard *Forrestal* that it is completely obscured by the smoke of the fire.

The Chinese "fishing" junks with all the high-tech aerials and antennae that infest Yankee Station have moved in like hyenas sniffing after a wounded lion. They are trying to pick up sailors bobbing in *Forrestal's* wake. The SAR helos arrive. Unlike our angels, they are armed. I can see them hovering over one junk after another. At least two junks are dead in the water when the SAR helos move on; the other junks get the message, come about, and haul off toward China. The SAR helos begin hoisting sailors from the water, taking them back to *Forrestal* to join in fighting the fire.

I remember the exhausting half hour I spent on the nozzle in the fire pan during our firefighting training. *Thank God it's their turn.*

When the fire is over, *Forrestal's* butcher bill is 134 dead and 161 injured, many with terrible burns. After the fire, *Forrestal* goes back to the States for repairs. Two A-4 pilots from *Forrestal* will volunteer to transfer to *Oriskany*, as replacement pilots. Lt.Cmdr. John McCain joins our sister squadron, the Saints; Lt.Cmdr. John Donahue comes to us. Father John is a combat-experienced pilot who steps in to replace Dick Hartman. Father John is an easygoing guy who fits in quickly. I like him, am comfortable flying with him, and leave it at that. At the end of the '67 cruise, he is combat-limited and leaves us.

ONCE I ACCEPT my death, it is easier to sleep at night and go hard at every mission. It is harder, however, to write home. I am not sure how or if I should tell my wife and family.

I write nothing to my wife about anything beyond the bubble of today and never anything about the dying and losses, which does not leave much to talk about that won't scare the shit out of her. The death notice telegrams fly faster than our letters. She will know about our losses long before my letters arrive. That is why she stays at Lemoore and doesn't "go home" to Indiana. She stays where she is plugged in to the wives' network.

Most of my letters are written during the line periods and when we go to and from. I don't write much during the four or five days we are in port between line periods. I am mostly drunk doing things she doesn't need to know about. The only time I remember writing about our "plans for the future" is a letter about our twelve-day R&R period halfway through the cruise.

I have accepted the fact that I will never see home again. She is my home. If she comes, and we spend time together, I am afraid I will lose my edge—afraid I'll look ahead—afraid that I might not be able to accept death again when the R&R is over—afraid that when I go back to combat, I will not be able to handle it. In an odd way, in order to accept my death, I have had to accept that home is dead to me. It's as if Death already stands between us. I cannot remember what I tell her about why she shouldn't come.

I think, *I am doing her a favor.* No use in getting her all geared up to see me. It will just be that much harder when she answers the door and finds the base commanding officer and chaplain standing there.

In the next century, I will realize this was just a rationalization. My motives were all about me, about me being able to do what I have to do. I understand that the letter must have been a cruel blow to her. If any of the other guys wrote similar letters, there weren't many of them. It rained wives when we docked for our R&R in-port period.

About the same time, I write a "Don't Grieve for Me" letter to Wayne. I tell him I know that what I am doing is the most important thing I will ever accomplish in my life and that I am proud to be counted among my squadronmates. I know he will understand. He is plugged in to what is going on through his Navy friends. He knows about every one of our losses. I leave it for him to decide whether he should show my letter to my mother now or "later" but ask him not to show it to my wife until "after." I don't know if he shows it to Mom, but he eventually writes and says he shared part of the letter with a friend in Congress, who put it in the Congressional Record.

At the time, I thought Wayne was trying to stem the rising tide of dissent to the war. In retrospect, I realize it was more like the time on the beach when I was five or six, and he helped me try to defend my sandcastle against the rising tide with a sand wall. Wayne's letter was an attempt to push back against death, trying to give his son some faint thread of immortality.

I never write a similar letter to my wife. She is from a devotedly civilian family, and I am certain she will not understand. I probably underestimated her. Young or not, ready or not, she was a Navy wife, living among a community of Navy wives. As my mother discovered a generation earlier, they are a tough and supportive breed with a collective wisdom passed from generation to generation, from war to war, from loss to loss.

Sometimes, it is hard keeping home at bay. One day during mail call, Don Purdy is in the ready room reading a letter from his wife.

"Holy shit! NO! That can't be true!"

We all perk up.

"We agreed, no kids until after this was done."

Don's goes on. We are laughing and congratulating Don. He's not having it.

"She is not pregnant. It's a Goddamn figment of her imagination!"

As the weeks go by, we never pass up an opportunity to ask how the "figment" is doing in our most solicitous tones. Sets him off every time.

Writing this now knowing Don too had accepted the certainty of his death, I finally understand why he was so upset.

DURING ONE MISSION, we hear a call over the emergency guard channel:

"Mayday! Mayday! Mayday! This is Hot Rod 2, Hot Rod 1, 3, and 4 just got shot down!"

Hot Rod is an Air Force call sign, probably an F-105 squadron. In that instant, Hot Rod 2 has become an orphan, suddenly alone in a very dangerous neighborhood. I feel for the poor son of a bitch.

Assuming he too isn't shot down moments later, it is almost impossible to imagine how vulnerable he must feel. He cannot do what the survival instinct in every cell of his body is screaming for him to dump the nose, roll into a high-G 180-degree turn, kick in the afterburner, and get the hell out of there. His duty is to stay on scene, mark the locations of not one but three pilots, establish contact, assess the chances of rescue for each, and confirm the physical condition of each. The women in their lives will want to know if they are wives or widows.

There is no second call from Hot Rod 2.

THE WORD comes down: because of *Forrestal's* departure, our line period will be extended three weeks to allow time for another carrier to arrive from the States. Most of us receive the news with a shrug. I know I did. However, I soon realize that the carefully husbanded fifth of liquor in my stateroom safe will not last until the end of our extended line period. I am not the only one with this problem.

Navy regulations prohibit alcoholic beverages, other than the doc's medicinal brandy and the chaplains' communion wine, on all its ships. In 1967, this regulation has long since become the subject of the original "don't-ask-don't-tell" policy. Every pilot who chooses to has a stash. As long as we are discreet and not drunk on duty, no effort is made to discover our stash or interfere with its enjoyment.

Within days, the word quietly circulates that we are sending an aircraft to Cubi for an engine overhaul. The pilot will pick up a repaired aircraft and fly it back. It has been arranged to load the outgoing aircraft with a blivit, which will be transferred to the returning aircraft. The pilot will take our cash and orders for any liquid refreshment we might want. I order an extra fifth. The aircraft is launched. The pilot is admonished not to tarry in completing the mission.

Vultures' Row, is a small porch high on the island with a view of the flight deck. It is a favorite hangout for sailors who are off-duty and who would like to watch the show. When the "special flight" is in the air heading back, Vultures Row is packed with pilots. I watch on the closed-circuit TV in our ready room with many of my squadronmates.

The aircraft lands and taxis out of the arresting gear. When the aircraft stops just clear of the foul-deck line, we watch Chief Mac trot out, duck under the wing, and hold his hand under the blivit. I notice a stream of liquid draining into his hand. He holds his hand up to his nose, sniffs, licks his hand, and comes out from under the bird. He looks up at Vultures' Row, shakes his head, and gives thumbs-down.

The cargo netting installed in the nose of the blivit to keep the load from slamming forward on landing has failed. Every bottle in the load is smashed. Only a few cans survive. I remember Coleridge's line from the *Rime of Ancient Mariner*, "Water, water everywhere and not a drop to drink."

I decide, I will start keeping a spare bottle against the slings and arrows of outrageous fortune. Generations will come and go before I hear the term "self-medication."

INTELLIGENCE THINKS it has found the location of a major North Vietnamese air defense headquarters, if not *the* air defense headquarters. We will hit it and hit it hard. If the intelligence is accurate, generals being generals, no matter whose army, it means the target will be well defended. The headquarters is in a place called Van Nhue (pronounced by us as "Van-Newie"). It is nondescript and located in a featureless area of rice paddies and small villages about five miles south and east of Hanoi. It is on the target list for July 31. Our ops officer, Bob Arnold, is leading the strike. He decides to fly in straight at it in the hopes the North Vietnamese will think we are going into Hanoi and leave us alone so as not to draw attention to their hidden headquarters. Nope. They start shooting the shit out of us as soon as we are in range.

The target is hidden and hard to find amongst all the small villages. Between the flak and the difficulty finding the target, our bombing is less than effective. Charley Zuhowski is an F-8 pilot in VF-111 flying TARCAP for the strike. He is hit and has to eject. There is no chance of a rescue.

Charley will not be released until March 14, 1973, having endured 2053 days as a prisoner of the North Vietnamese. I cannot imagine.

July is finally over.

AUGUST STARTS a little better. Death may not take a holiday but is no longer working overtime. On August 2, we find a ferry used by the North Vietnamese to do a run-around of a bridge we dropped earlier. As I am in my bomb run, the needle ball at the bottom of the instrument panel catches my notice for some reason. It is not part of my normal scan in a bomb run; this time it just registers for some reason. What I see is the ball jammed up against the right-hand corner of its little tube. I am in a hard skid. I jam my foot onto the right rudder pedal and move the ball back to center. The bomb line on my bombsight skews left. I make a quick correction to get it back on the target. I get good hits. A little long but dead-on center. *What the hell?*

Now the North Vietnamese have a downed bridge *and* a sunken ferry. I feel good. Next, the North Vietnamese will probably try a pontoon bridge, up after dark, down before light, hiding the pontoons along the little river through the daylight hours, like a moth hiding from the birds.

Once we are feet-wet, I think about what happened. Bombing in a skid explains my left-right problems. *"But I always trim the aircraft after takeoff—jets aren't supposed to need rudder?"* I tell/ask someone. "Oh, yeah. When you get up above four-hundred knots in the dive run, the centerline drop tank tends to kick off a quarter of an inch or so to one side or the other. I always check the needle-ball about a third of the way down the pipe." *Maybe I am one of the 2 percent who never get the word.* I build the ball into my bomb-run scan. My bombing becomes better. A lot better.

On August 4, 1967, three years to the day after the Tonkin Gulf incident, the Saints lose Lt.j.g. Ralph Bisz to a SAM. No ejection, no chute, no beeper, no radio call. Ralph is listed as a POW, just in case. I stuff my emotions into a box. I think:

I am beginning to grow emotional calluses.

I also think, *This can't be right—or good. But, what the hell, we are all going to go down. The order doesn't seem too important.*

I hope Ralph's family and friends will forgive me. I can still see Ralph, young and full of life. I know how devastating his loss must be for them. It's just that—if I was to keep on doing what we did—I could not allow myself to feel.

Ralph's remains will be returned in June 2008. Even then, I do not, cannot, will not grieve his loss.

ON AUGUST 7, I fly my first night-combat mission. The weather is not too shiny. It is a dark night with multiple cloud layers. The mission is okay, but the landing gets interesting. I get two hook-skip bolters. When I come off the angle deck after the second bolter, I am down to less than eight-hundred pounds of fuel.

The Air Boss bingos me to the tanker. Its holding pattern is in the dark abyss between cloud decks. CCA gives me a vector. I climb through the lowest cloud deck. When I pop up out of the cloud deck, my fuel gauge shows two-hundred pounds of fuel. The gauge is not reliable below two-hundred pounds. I look up and see the tanker's light about a mile off at my two o'clock and a thousand feet above me. *I might make it.*

Because of the loss of depth perception, a night rendezvous is done slowly. Vertigo be damned—I don't have the time and come barreling in. I don't stop on his wing to establish a parade position but slide directly into trail behind the buddy tanker with the speed-brakes out and the throttle at idle in a thirty-degree angle of bank. Against all odds, I manage to stop the relative motion in all three dimensions. I push the throttle up, level my wings, and put my right foot in the basket on my first try. The fuel begins to flow. Deep breath.

Thank you, Dick Perry.

A few minutes later the green transfer light blinks to red. The tanker pilot says, "**That's fifteen-hundred pounds.**" I pull a little power off to back away and disconnect from the basket. I glance at my fuel gauge. It shows thirteen-hundred pounds.

Holy shit, I just ran out of gas while refueling.

I thank the tanker pilot, call approach control, and get a vector to let down below the undercast and re-enter the bolter pattern. My next pass is a trap.

ONE NIGHT, I am lying in the bunk trying to find sleep. My mind throws up *Navajo sheepdogs*. Somewhere, sometime, I heard about Navajo sheepdogs. Although called sheepdogs, they don't herd sheep. They protect the sheep.

The puppies are raised within the flocks, not in the home with the family. The Navajo intentionally minimize human contact with the puppies to ensure they bond with the sheep, not people. The dogs grow up thinking they are sheep, sheep with teeth that aren't used for grazing. Teeth that predators understand and fear. The mixed-breed dogs are attentive, protective, and trustworthy. They effectively protect the flocks from predators, including their canine cousins: coyotes.

That's us. A breed apart, born into every generation to protect the others.

NOT LONG AFTER Van Nhue, Dick and I are on another strike just north of Haiphong. The target is across the river from downtown Haiphong, on the north side of the Câm River. The same flat and featureless land as Van Nhue, but the target is almost on the riverbank, and we can use the built-up area across from Haiphong and the shape of the river to find and orient our approach to the target.

Instead of going out back across the flat area to the north or south across the city, Dick and most of the other section leaders elect to hang a half left off the target, fly south to the river, then another left and go out east down the river at very low level. This will take us past the "neutral" ships anchored nose to tail out in the river like circus elephants as they wait to unload. Not only will the ships provide a shield against someone shooting from the far side of the river, but the nearside gunners are probably under orders not to shoot up their friendly suppliers. It is also possible that, even where the ships are not a factor, the gunners on either bank will be reluctant to shoot for fear of hitting their comrades or civilians on the other shore.

We pull off the target, get to thirty-five-hundred feet, and jink to the riverbank, then a diving-hard turn to the left, onto the river running downstream to the Tonkin Gulf. This will only work if we stay very low and very fast. Dick is going out at forty feet; I am doing my best to stay below thirty (and above zero). As we flash by the deck of the merchant ships at eye level, I see guys in deck chairs with refreshments watching the show in all their neutral splendor. *Assholes.*

One of our guys, who can be a bit feisty at the best of times, decides that a little audience participation is in order. He pitches up into a Chandelle—a hard climbing then descending turn of 180 degrees—diving back on a ship sporting the Union Jack. We may have only forty rounds per gun, but that's a lot if you are the target, especially if you are a civilian who thinks he is enjoying a spectator sport while protected by international law. Lawn chairs and refreshments are sent flying, as the merchant seamen scatter like cockroaches when the kitchen light is turned on.

Back on the ship, a cone of silence descends over us all. Not that anyone asks the JOs. The CAG and A-4 COs absorb the heat, denying any knowledge of anything like that happening, promising with great sincerity that nothing like that will ever happen again. I am sure Skipper Mow has a quiet word with the someone who didn't do it.

If there are any repercussions from our allies, they are absorbed somewhere in the State Department, the White House, and the Pentagon.

ON AUGUST 4, our failure to obliterate the Van Nhue headquarters, comes back to haunt us. Van Nhue is back on our target list. Bob Arnold asks to lead the second strike. He sees it as a piece of unfinished business. Bob gets the nod. I can't imagine anyone else argued too hard for a chance to lead us against this target. For whatever reason, Bob is the only double-dipper. All the other Ghost Riders who were on the first strike get to sit this one out. It is within the overlapping range circles of a half dozen or more active SAM sites. Their color-coded flak plot looks like someone spilled a big bag of M&Ms on the map. This time, Bob decides we will go feet-wet east of Haiphong and then loop around to come at the target from the north and west.

Because of our losses, the Ghost Riders and Saints can only muster twelve strike aircraft between them for the mission. Dick Perry and I are the second section in a division on the far left of the strike group. I am number four and have everybody in front of me to my right. We go feet-dry at Cat Ba Island northeast of Haiphong. I hear what even I can identify as the slow rhythms of long-range search radars long before we go feet-dry.

Eventually our arc around Haiphong brings us onto a southwesterly heading, maybe twenty miles from the target. As always, I look ahead trying to find and fix the target in my mind. This time, I can't do it. There are no landmarks that let me superimpose the map of the target's location that I have memorized over the ground laid out before me. The fact that I can't locate the target on the ground is annoying but doesn't bother me much. Finding the target is the strike leader's job, and after him the division leaders', and after him, Dick's job as section leader. Besides, I will recognize it from the aerial photographs when we get close to the roll-in.

In the minute it takes us to close from twenty miles to fifteen, the ALQ jammer starts giving me the pulse-rate signatures of a whole bevy of SAM acquisition radars. I can't sort them out, but it's clear a lot of missile sites are teeing us up as we come in. I know what happens next.

I am not too edgy—I have done this before. We'll get a missile or two, make it through the flak, hit the target, and get out.

"Missile launch!
Twelve o'clock
this side of the river!"
a new voice
"Missile launch!
Two o'clock – thirteen miles!"
I see both launches
both are edging right
not a threat—to us
My warbler sings
voices crowd the radio
"Shotgun"—a Shrike is in the air
"Magic One, warb . . ."
"Old Salt Three, war . . ."
"Sundowner Two, warbler"
calls for breaks come fast

two more Shrikes are launched
crowding each other off the air
"Missile launch!
twelve o'clock at eleven miles"
I see it.
it's coming our way
I watch Dick, thumb on radio
"Missile launch!
Ten o'clock – ten miles"
I keep my eyes on the missile at twelve o'clock
I open my mouth to call the break
Someone transmits over my call,
"Magic Stone Three, break!"
Dick snaps left, rolling past vertical
condensation vapor trailing from both wings
he puts on the Gs
I follow
staying inside his turn
down and away
I stretch against the Gs
to look over the right canopy rail
trying to keep the missile in sight
it's past in a flash
detonating behind us
no break in my warbler
looking for the missile from ten o'clock
Dick reverses his turn
gets his nose above the horizon
climbing back to the formation
Dick's voice
"Magic Four – break left!"
Shit!
he's rolling fast to half inverted
I need a full deflection roll to follow
I never see the missile
the warbler doesn't stop

There must be another missile
I look but can't find it
I am beyond scared
I am in a full-blown panic
Dick recovers again
movement to my left
a missile
ten o'clock, high and close
I key the mic
"Magic Three, break right!"
I am rolling as I make the call
Dick is coming
the missile tries to follow
WHOOMP!
Jesus fucking Christ!
close—but a miss
we are down in the weeds
no warbler—*Finally!*
We are now below one-thousand feet
lost in the ground clutter
too low for the missiles to see us
Dick starts to climb back up to ten-thousand feet
I start to hear the crickets
I look up
no strike group
in one glance I see
at least three missiles in profile
half a dozen orange smears
lots of sections—all dodging
most below five-thousand feet
some climbing
some flying off at odd angles
Dick's voice
"Magic Four – do you see the target?"
I look, miles of rice paddies
at this altitude I can't even see the ground

where I think it must be
no diving A-4s
no smoke from bombs
"Negative."
"Jettison your bombs."
Thank God!
I see Dick's bombs salvo off
I look down, rice paddies
I salvo my bombs
Dick edges up to thirty-five-hundred feet
above effective small arms' fire
heading southeast
jinking like hell
I am scanning, looking for missiles
I think, *MiGs?*
pulling back to the right
twisting to see behind us
scanning up and down
checking the sun
nothing
reversing
twisting to the other side
nothing
Missiles?
I wipe the sky back to our right
but see nothing
silence
We're clear
my right leg is hopping
I hold up my left hand: shaking
heart race-horsing

They beat us. Dick and I did not get to the target. They broke up the strike group. I am pissed. Angry like you cannot imagine. Pounding the glare shield angry. Jerking the aircraft around like it is my enemy

237

rather than my lover kind of angry. Angry at them. Angry at us. Angry at me.

What the hell just happened?

I try to piece the fragments together. I count at least a dozen SAMs in the flashes of my memory.

Somewhere in the melee, "Marvelous" Marv Reynolds of VA-163 takes a hit. He makes it back to feet-wet and even lands it aboard the *O Boat*. The next time his aircraft leaves the ship, it is dangling from a crane at the carrier pier in Cubi Point.

After we recover and debrief, Dick says, "We were below a thousand feet, neither of us knows where the target is; there is no strike group left. The odds are too high against us. Better to go home and come back another day."

The bomb damage assessment (BDA) photos provided by the "Photo Beanies" shows that someone put some bombs on the target. The AIs decide the target suffered "major damage." I am astounded but grateful. Maybe there will not be a third visit to Van Nhue. Another good reason not to think about yesterday and tomorrow.

When the AIs finish screening the pilot reports for bullshit, adrenaline-fueled confusion, paranoia, wishful thinking, and consult the electronic intelligence, they opine that seventeen SAMs were fired against the twelve-strike aircraft.

This will be the only time that the air defenses break up our strike group. On other strikes, we certainly take some hits, but the group makes it to the target, and we deliver our payloads. Which is not to say that Van Nhue is the only target we have to hit more than once. But, more often than not, second and third strikes are necessary because the North Vietnamese repair the road, runway, bridge, etc. They are good at filling in bomb craters, but every guy with a shovel up north, isn't carrying an AK-47 south of the DMZ.

The second go at Van Nhue has a long tail. From that day on, it is all I can do to press the warbler self-test button during the preflight test of our ALQ. It's like touching metal when you know you will get a static electrical shock. It has to be done, but I flinch and get a jolt of adrenaline every time.

WE FINISH the first line period. Only four more to go. Between July 14 and August 7, I have flown twenty-three missions, one of them noncombat. I have become habituated to the pace, but God knows I feel years older. I have learned from each mission. I have become good at what we do. I am able to stay ahead of the aircraft, dealing with the changing threats almost instantaneously. I am comfortable in the strike group or on armed recces. Most of the time I know what Dick is going to do before he does it. I can find and hold a target from two miles up while looking away for threats. My bombing and lookout doctrines are better. I am alive to the threats, but I am not intimidated. Death is just another bully. It does not scare me.

During the day, when I am not flying, I dump the memories of everything except the lessons learned. I mostly look for things to laugh about. Every evening during the ready-room movies I do my best to go out-of-body. After the movie, I read tomorrow's flight schedule, put that information away, get in my bunk, and go somewhere inside a book. I get to sleep most nights.

I think, *I am a made warrior.* I am wrong, but for now we are done being shot at for a week or so.

We secure from flight ops on August 7 and head east for six days at the navy base in Subic Bay. The next morning, as we sail toward the Philippines, we hold a memorial service for all the people we lost and for those on *Forrestal*. I don't want to go. I don't want to put on my undress whites and go stand at parade on the flight deck. "Memorial" means remembering. I don't do remember. It's not like I will ever forget. But I have closed those doors behind me and don't want to reopen them. Memories are for the living, not dead men flying.

I remember thinking, *Hell, we don't have any bodies. The guests of honor won't be there. Why should I.*

But I go. I spend the entire service practicing not feeling. Standing there I think about the memorial service we will have after the second line period—and the one after the third—and the two after that, wondering, *Which will be the one when my name gets read out?*

EN ROUTE to Subic, the aircraft division works nonstop on corrosion control. There will be no liberty for them until every spot of corrosion on every aircraft has been ground off, primed, and repainted. No liberty for their division officer either.

About 1400 on the second afternoon in-port, Chief Mac is satisfied. I change into civies, throw my dopp kit and a couple of changes of clothes in a small bag, and follow the sailors down the gangway. I head for the Cubi Point BOQ. C-10 beat feet down the gangway as soon as we docked and was able to get a two-man room. He held the bed for me. We will bunk ashore together just to get a break from the ship. That night we "jump the ditch," slang for crossing the bridge over the open sewer that divides the base from the city of Olongapo.

I have four days left. Olongapo is as wild a city as you can imagine. Most of the city is off-limits to military personnel, but the possibilities are limitless inside the "on-limits" portion of town. I drink a lot and go to bed with my first prostitute. I don't remember her name, or the sex, but she worked out of the U&I Club, a squadron favorite for those of us who "jump the ditch." I have a bout of Catholic guilt but not much or for long. The built-up hormonal demand for sex is a good release. I feel marital guilt a little more acutely, but I am not going to be seeing my wife again, so, somehow, it seems less of a betrayal to her.

I don't defend what I did, or the logic of my rationalization; but that is what happened and how I felt.

There is one woman at the U&I Club who I do not forget, Mama-san. Tiny, ancient, the dictionary definition of "wizened." She sits at a table on the back edge of the club where she can see the whole room. Someone says I should go talk to her. So, walking back from a beer dump in the head, I stop at her table. I ask if I can join her. She invites me to sit down with a melodic Filipino accent but does not ask me to buy her a drink. I offer. She cackles, shaking her head no.

When I sit down with her, I assume she is part of the decorations, kept on as atmosphere. Maybe a kind of mascot, welcome out of affection and habit. I ask her when she came to U&I Club. She tells me she was "still a girl." She remembers the American fleet and sailors back to what must have been the early 1900s.

"What was the club like back then?"

"Just thatch on poles. No walls."

"Did it have a dance floor?"

Slightly offended, "Oh, yes. Board floor, and a bar with stools over there," pointing to the wall opposite the current bar. "Tables around the edge."

"A board floor all over?"

"No, just for dancing."

Mama-san has lived through a giant slice of Philippine and U.S. naval history. She was already the madam in charge of the bar girls when the Japanese came after Pearl Harbor.

I ask, "Did the club stay open during the Japanese occupation?"

Another laugh. "Oh, yes. Very busy. But we all like the Americans better."

She rounds this out with a number of reasons for their preference, some having to do with size, and all recited with a cackle, well calculated to play to the pride of young American men. This is patter. Delivered as a well-practiced line like a joke a comedian has used too long. Polished, but all the enthusiasm has long since worn away.

I enjoy sitting with her. She is engaging, witty, and way ahead of a drunk nugget JO. She suggests I might enjoy this one or that one of her young ladies, giving a short, lurid, and detailed description of their charms and skills. After a while she just gives up.

I know that she and the club not only survived the Japanese invasion and occupation, and the liberation by the United States Army; they also successfully negotiated the perils of independence and the Huk[14] insurgency that followed World War II. There is so much more I'd like to ask, but I am too shy to keep the conversation going. *I should have brought C-10 over.*

During the growing silences, I notice she is constantly watching the room. She is working. Even while she talks, her eyes never leave the room for more than a few seconds. During her patter, she sees something she does not like. She hisses. Even over the noise of the music and general hubbub a waiter hears and appears, a short burst of Tagalog, and he is dispatched to deliver the message. *Great scan. Great situational awareness.*

I later wonder if she had seen (and serviced) Teddy Roosevelt's Great White Fleet on its around-the-world tour. I don't know if it even stopped at Subic Bay or if so in what year, but Mama-san seemed to me to be someone who has seen it all, sitting at her table in the back of the U&I Club. A living memory of incredible depth. Now ignored, I get up and go back to our table. Whenever I come back to the U&I, she is there. She laughs when she sees me.

She will be long gone by now. I hope she had an easy death surrounded by people who loved her.

ONE NIGHT, we are enjoying a squadron party in the Subic Bay Officers' Club. At some point during the festivities at our table, C-10 gets up and says, "Watch this."

He walks across the room to where the officers of a destroyer are having a formal dinner hosted by their captain. C-10 approaches their quiet, decorous table. Watching, we witness what happens in pantomime. C-10 introduces himself to the destroyer captain sitting at the head of the table. There are a few minutes of polite chit-chat. We see C-10 reach down and finger the corner of the tablecloth. A quick comment to the captain.

The captain pushes back in his chair. He appears uncertain, even reluctant. C-10 keeps talking. Finally, he nods at C-10. The captain rises and moves his chair back from the table. C-10 stands at the head of the table. He speaks to the seated officers. They all lean back and put their hands in their laps.

With great aplomb, C-10 reaches down, taking the end of the table-cloth in a careful two-handed grip. Crouching, he pauses, concentrating. He takes a deep breath. The entire dining room has noticed. Everyone is silently watching.

With an explosive yell, C-10 violently uncoils his body, jerking the cloth down the long axis of the table as hard as he can.

The cloth comes mostly off the table. So does almost everything on it—much of it landing in the officers' laps. C-10 stands there holding the tablecloth, a look of surprise on his cherubic face. Bemused, he hands the captain the tail of the tablecloth and walks back to our table.

"What the hell did you say to him?"

"I began by telling him how cool I thought destroyers were, the 'greyhounds of the sea.' I bullshit him a bit and mention that I was a magician in civilian life. I tell him my signature trick was the ability to whip a tablecloth out from under a fully set table so quickly everything stays perfectly in place on the table. I admit that it really isn't magic at all. Just a matter of physics: friction, inertia, speed, and, of course, hundreds of hours practicing to develop instantaneous acceleration and the ability to maintain a precisely horizontal pull on the cloth."

"Really? You were a magician?"

C-10 laughs. "Of course not."

"So, what the hell did you say when you dumped their dinners in their laps?"

"I said, 'Damn. It's been a long time. I must be rusty.'"

CHAPTER 18

ROUND TWO

C-10, Gary Kirk, and Mule after a mission.

August 18

OUR BREAK is over. We sail back to Yankee Station for the second line period. It starts with a run of good luck. We are flying three Alfa Strikes a day. Same type of targets, including return visits to targets that need more attention or have been repaired while we were frolicking in the Philippines. We begin a run of two or three missions a day against targets in Haiphong. The defenses are still voracious for our blood; the flak is no less thick or accurate; the missiles still as active; but we all make it back. No losses!

There is a learning curve for everything.

A couple of days into this routine, we are flying against Haiphong yet again. Everything is the same, except: No SAMs. The SAM's Fan Song radars are up; even the guidance radars set off a chorus of warblers. But no missiles are launched. Later the same day we go again. Same thing. No missiles!? Next morning same thing. The word comes down, perhaps based on the empirical evidence alone, or perhaps helped by some intelligence, we are told, "They are out of SAMs."

What are we waiting for? Let's get 'em while the getting is good.

Our political masters choose this moment to declare a two- or three-day bombing pause as a negotiating ploy in Paris.

I begin to think my arithmetic is off. *Maybe July was just the steep part of the learning curve.* I am confident I can dodge any missile—if I see it in time.

My resurgent optimism, the bombing pause, and the North Vietnamese's missile shortage are all short-lived. We are launched against a resupplied enemy who are anxious to make up for missed opportunities.

Press on.

THE AIR WING is short on pilots and planes. The pipeline provides both slowly. It is not until the second line period that we get two JO must-pumps to replace Duthie and Barry. Being a must pump is tough at the best of times. I am blissfully unaware of it, but in the fleet, our air wing is becoming known as "Bloody Sixteen." This has to increase our replacements' anxiety levels by several orders of magnitude. For us, the new faces in the ready room are disconcerting but not nearly as bad as the empty seats. Although they are welcome, most of us will keep a safe emotional distance.

I think Rob Woods is the first replacement pilot to join the Ghost Riders. He is a U.S. Naval Academy graduate, stocky, blond with a broad grin. If he ever caused anyone a problem while he was with us, I never heard of it. I fly with Rob during the '67 cruise and again during the '68 cruise. A good man in the ready room, in a fight, and on liberty.

I never saw or spoke with Rob after I left the Ghost Riders. I have since been told he survived his next cruise and stayed in the navy, but his career came off the tracks when he refused a posting back to an A-4 squadron at a time when the A-4s were being phased out and replaced by the A-7 Corsair II. The squadrons that did not transition to A-7s were dead-ends, doomed to extinction, like the Spads before them. I also learned that, by this time, Rob had another problem. Like Bo Jangles, he "drinks a bit" and left three wives in his wake. Sounds like many men I will sit with in PTSD groups. Rob died young. All three of his ex-wives attended his funeral and spoke fondly and well of Rob. I can't think of a better tribute to a good man who wrestled with demons.

NOT LONG after Rob joins us, another new face appears in the ready room, Mike Williams. He seems young to my eyes but must be close to my age. Green as grass but in a hurry to get started. He quickly picks up the nickname "Willy." He is small, with a gymnast's build, very earnest and anxious to learn, wants to fit in, please, and excel. He is also basically a happy person—if intense and a little edgy, but the Buddha himself might be a little on edge if he were thrown straight into Bloody Sixteen as a must-pump.

I don't remember who was assigned as Willy's primary flight leader, but the system of dedicated pairs is fraying at the edges because of our losses. I fly with Willy on my wing several times.

One day, I am scheduled to lead a section of flak suppressors in support of an Alfa Strike, with Willy as my wingman. During the briefing the strike leader designates two sites close to the roll-in point he wants us to suppress. I tell Willy to hit one of them and that I will take the other. I tell Willy, we need to get in and get out before the strike leader to avoid getting tangled up in the strike group's bombing runs. Willy and I will make simultaneous runs dropping all our bombs on our flak sites, pull off, rejoin, and get out.

Photograph taken by an A-4 at the top of the bomb run during an Alfa Strike on Phuong Dinh railway bypass bridges on September 10, 1967, by CVW-16. There is a flak site in the top-left center of the picture. Note the two other bypass bridges to the left.

We follow the Iron Hand out front of the Strike Group. We both make our runs. As I pull off, I am looking for Willy to join up with me so we can get out of Dodge. I don't see him. I ask his location from the target. He tells me. I head that way. I am astounded to hear Willy call,

"Magic Six is in to strafe."

I look up and see him rolling in on a six-gun 37mm site that is lit up, all six barrels pulsing like strobe lights. Willy is just starting his dive, flying through a fog of grey 37mm bursts. A flash of anger.

Shit! He's going to get himself killed.

I key the mic: "MAGIC SIX, ABORT! ABORT! ABORT!"

He does, joins up, and we go out at thirty-five-hundred feet, dancing for all we are worth.

When we are back in the ready room, we sit in the back, out of the way.

I ask him, "How many guns do we have on the A-4?"

"Two."

"What caliber?"

"20mm."

"How much ammo per gun?"

"Forty and thirty-eight."

"How many guns did the flak site you were going to strafe have?"

"Six."

"What caliber?"

"37mm."

"How much ammo per gun did they have?"

"I don't know—lots."

"How many guns were you going to aim at in your run?"

"One."

I pause to let him think it over, keeping it as calm as my adrenaline-high will allow and do what Dick has done for me. I commend his courage, but suggest he needs to be brave *and* smart. We don't want or need reckless risk-taking. I remind him we are expected to make one run on one flak site, giving it all our bombs. We did that. We each made one flak sight duck for cover, while the strike bombers were at the roll-in. We might even have killed or wounded a couple of gunners or damaged a gun or two. Once the bombs are away, our job is to get safely out so we can come back on the next mission.

"We don't make second runs. Second runs in that environment will get you killed—and you especially don't need to pick a fight when you are outgunned and outnumbered." I point out that the easiest shot any flak gunner has is an aircraft diving on him. Just put the gun sight a little above the cockpit and keep shooting—the pilot will fly into it.

He says, "Thanks."

I think, *Thank you, Dick Perry.*

As I said, I like Willy and do my best to bring him up to speed, but I am careful to keep the emotional firewall between us. I am sure I am not the only one. This is not something I can explain to him but hope he knows we are just protecting ourselves, not rejecting him.

Woody Knapp, Robin Wood, and author.

A little later, Forrest Woodrow Knapp shows up. "Hi. I'm Woody." He has dark hair, is quieter than many of us, and a teetotaler, but Woody enjoys the Reindeer games. Stocky, well-muscled. I look at him and think, *Maybe a wrestler.* Turns out he played football for Yale. I am impressed. Although John Davis went to Brown, we don't see many Ivy League types in naval aviation, especially from classes graduating in the second half of the 1960s.

Woody quickly establishes a reputation in the squadron as a good stick and reliable wingman.

A MONTH or so after the Great SAM Drought, we have our own logistical glitch. We run out of the Shrike anti-radar missiles we depend on to suppress the SAMs. This is not good news. Deny Weichman puts his combat experience, tactical talent, and love of a practical joke together and comes up with a solution.

We have a number of training Shrikes on board. God knows why we have them, or how Wuff knows about them, but we do and he does. The training Shrike looks like a normal Shrike but has no warhead. What they do have is the seeker head that detects the SAM guidance radar and relays that information to the cockpit and the aircraft's bombing computer we use to locate the SAM sites and launch the Shrikes. Good for practicing on the electronic training range in California. Not much use over North Vietnam—until now.

The Shrikes leave a distinctive white smoke trail when launched. We know the North Vietnamese have a guy, maybe several, sitting on the roof of the radar trailers with binoculars. Their job is to stomp on the roof whenever they see a Shrike lofted in their direction. When they stomp, the operators inside shut down their guidance radars until the Shrike runs out of hang time and crashes.

Wuff's idea is to put a training Shrike on the outboard station of one wing and a four-pack of Zuni high-velocity rockets on the other. The Zuni is unguided, but it leaves a smoke trail when launched. The Zuni's smoke trail is smaller and doesn't last as long as that left by a Shrike, but it might fool the guy with the binoculars. We load the two wing-stations with Mk 82 bombs. When the SAM shooters turn on their guidance radars, we can use the training Shrike to locate the missile battery and loft a Zuni at it. No chance of getting anywhere near the SAM site, but if the guy on the trailer goes stomp, they'll shut down. Better yet, we'll have four Zunis and can repeat the trick at least four times on the same mission. The frosting on Wuff's cake is that we can follow-up with the four Mark 82s, something that can do more than scare them.

Wuff gets first dibs on the faux Shrike gambit. It works! They shut down the guidance radars. It continues to work long enough for us to get an emergency shipment of Shrikes airlifted out from the factory. Ha, ha, ha, Uncle Ho!

ON THE MORNING of August 29, Dick and I are part of an Alfa Strike to Hanoi. We are flying strike bombers. We are about twelve miles from the target when a missile is called. I can't find it. I keep searching as the clock in my head winds down. I am getting frantic,

251

There!
one o'clock low
I wrench the stick hard right and back
WHAM!
The explosion slams into the bottom of my aircraft
the plane is thrown over on its back
I'm dead!—No—I'm okay!
I'm inverted—Gs on—nose way below the horizon
Off the Gs
stick forward then left
she rolls upright
520 knots
60° nose down
Passing through 8,000 feet
Gs on—*tenderly*
The nose rises
She's flying.

I whip my head around, looking up for other aircraft. Nothing—no one in sight.

I'm alone.

I look toward the target and see the strike group. So far no one has missed me. Good wingmen are heard but not seen. I zoom climb, instinctively hurrying back to rejoin, like a minnow who suddenly finds itself alone and darts back to the school.

I put my head back on its swivel, stealing glances to take stock: no holes in me; engine's running; gauges normal. I check what I can see of the aircraft outside the cockpit. There's a softball-size hole in the left wing out near the tip, beyond the wing tank. The left aileron works, so it missed the hydraulic control lines, or at least one of them. No other holes I can see. But the hole tells me the beam spray caught me.

When the SAM, or any rocket or missile with a fragmentation warhead goes off, the frags (shrapnel) are blown outward to the side in a circle. The outward push of the warhead's explosives combines with the movement of the missile, so the frags expand outward forming an expanding circle of lethality as they move forward. This is called the "beam spray." The big hole in my wing is from a piece of the missile

252

that mixed in with the frags. I know the bottom of my aircraft has to be perforated—but, *So far, so good.* No signs of serious trouble. It's good to be Irish.

As friend after friend got shot down, crashed, or just disappeared, I have wondered what I would do when it was my turn to be hit. Now, I will find out. I've been well and truly hit, but the bird is still flying, and the engine is strong.

Suck it up—Press on.

It takes agonizingly long minutes to catch up. When I finally rejoin Dick and the strike group, I check the fuel. Lower than I expect—too low? I check the mirrors for streaming fuel. Nothing.

Do your job—jink and look for threats.

Check the fuel gauge again.

I am losing fuel. Time to head for the water—No, we're almost there.

I stay with it. We deliver the bombs and head out. I can see the gulf in the distance. I think I'll have enough fuel. I tell Dick, "I've been hit. Losing fuel but will make feet-wet." No need to call the wet-wing tanker to come in and meet me.

Feet-wet; Dick checks me out. "Lots of holes underneath. A little fuel vaporizing out of the bottom of the fuselage." The drop tank is holed but long since empty.

Thank God for the roll rate. If I hadn't gotten the wing up, I would have taken the beam spray in the cockpit instead of the drop tank.

On the way back to the carrier, I rehearse the ejection sequence in case I catch fire. A-4s don't burn long before they explode. The NATOPS Manual says: "If you have a fire, eject." I decide there may be no time to reach up with both hands to pull the face curtain handle above my head, so I will use the alternate handle between my legs. I fly with my left hand on the secondary ejection handle.

I need a cigarette—well, maybe not on this flight.

I get a little fuel from the duty tanker overhead. I am told to wait until last.

I sure could use a cigarette about now.

Someone once told me that a fuel leak in the fuselage puddles in the bottom of the aircraft's belly and will splash up on the engine during an arrested landing and ignite.

Okay. There's no NATOPS *emergency procedure for a fire in the arresting gear. So, make one up:*
> *Report the fire*
> *Shut down the engine*
> *Unplug my radio*
> *Unplug the oxygen hose*
> *Drop one side (the right by habit) of my mask so I can breathe*
> *Release the lap belts*
> *Pop the canopy*
> *Stand on the seat*
> *foot on the starboard canopy rail.*
> *jump down to the deck.*
> *Get the hell away from the aircraft before it goes* BOOM!

I run through my mental checklist several times.

Okay. Got it—now, focus on the landing.

When I call the ball, I am also to report any unexpended ordnance, so the Air Boss can warn the deck crew that a bomb or rocket may come bounding up the deck when I catch a wire or, worse, hit the ramp—both things that have been known to happen.

I decide to be witty just to show I am Zen with my problem. When I call the ball and give my fuel state, I add, "One *expended* SAM on board." I get a laconic "Roger ball" from the LSO. No sense of humor.

I fly a good pass. The hook catches a wire, slamming me forward in the harness. A hundred and twenty knots (138 miles per hour) to zero in about 110 feet. Violent but normal. Every arrested landing is a survivable crash. As the gear drags me to a stop—WHOOMPH! A low-order detonation behind me. Smoke and flames flash out of both intakes, enveloping the cockpit on either side—then are immediately swallowed back down the intakes. The fire warning light on my instrument panel starts to flash.

I thumb the mic, "Magic 408, in the gear. Fire. Fire. Fire." I leave the hook down, jerk the throttle around the horn to shut down the engine, and start unplugging and unstrapping. No more flames from the intakes. I pop the canopy. I stand on the seat facing right toward the island and safety. Left hand on the canopy bow, left foot on the canopy rail.

Ready to jump, I look down. Chief Mac is standing there, holding out both arms, "Jump! I'll catch you!" He weighs maybe a 150 pounds after Sunday dinner. Geared up, I weigh north of 190 pounds. It's about 10 feet from the canopy rail to the deck.

I'll crush him.

I turn around and jump out the port side. The weight of my flight gear drives me to my knees. I get to my feet, spin around, duck under the nose behind the nose landing gear, rise up like a sprinter coming out of the blocks. I look at Chief Mac as I go past, and yell, "Let's get out of here!"

Head down, arms pumping, I am two strides toward my decidedly unimpressive top speed afoot, when I look up. I see the fire/rescue guy. He wears a suit of aluminized, fireproof cloth, complete with a hood. The hood has only a small eye-slit covered with reflective glass. His vision is limited at best. He is lumbering forward holding a ten-foot metal pipe like a medieval knight late for the joust. The tip of the pipe is cut like a hypodermic needle and is razor sharp. His job is to jam the metal pipe through the aluminum skin of the aircraft. The aft end of the pipe is connected to a fire hose. Once jammed into the aircraft, he will pull the trigger on the nozzle and pump fire-retardant foam into the fuselage to smother the fire.

After he lances the bird, he must clamber up on the burning aircraft and get the pilot out—not an easy job on an A-4. Not a safe job on any burning aircraft.

I have made the second half of his job unnecessary, but here he comes running into danger to save me. The problem is that his lance is pointed at my chest.

What a stupid way to die.

I dodge left, nearly knocking Chief Mac off his feet, laughing all the way to the island.

Alive again.

I HAVE TIME for a quick lunch and a couple cigarettes before we head off for the AI spaces to brief for the next go—this is one I don't want to miss. It will be Dick Perry's first time as leader of an Alfa Strike—a big step for him. Most strike groups are led by the CAG, a squadron CO, XO, or ops officer. Dick isn't even senior enough to be a department head. It is a tremendous vote of confidence by the Skipper and CAG—a sign of great expectations.

The target is in Haiphong. I am proud to be on his wing, but it feels odd to be number two with the whole strike group spread out behind us on Dick's other wing. It goes well from briefing to recovery. We put bombs on the target and everyone comes back. A great day for Batman.

That night, I go to find the aircraft I flew that morning. She is done for. They have parked her back aft in a dark corner of the hangar deck. She will be used as a spare parts bin. I am told they counted 114 holes in her and the drop tank.

I feel a touch of regret for her fate. She brought me home, only to perish at our hands as the victim of mechanical triage. I slide my hand over the side of her nose. *Thank you.* I also send a silent *Thanks* to the people at Douglas who built this to ugh little bird.

Dick "Batman" Perry.

When we get to Cubi at the end of the line period, they will strip her of everything useful and her carcass will be hoisted over the side by a crane to be shipped home in the hold of a freighter.

ON AUGUST 30, Dick and I are back in the pack, toting bombs to the target on another Alfa Strike. Nothing exceptional happens. After the movie that night, I check the schedule. Dick and I are scheduled to fly strike bombers on two Alfa Strikes tomorrow. Time for bed.

Our first mission on August 31 is yet another strike into Haiphong. Dick will lead our division. It is so routine that years later I won't remember any details of the brief, other than the target is in Haiphong—or any of the rest of the ritual and routine of manning up, preflight, starting the engine, launching off the cat, rendezvous, going feet-dry, or anything else until we are about ten miles out. It is just another trip downtown.

We are on the left wing of the strike group. The group is not as large as it was in July. We are still short of aircraft. I am on Dick's right wing so I am between him and the division on our right. As usual, John Davis and S-10 are the second section in our division. They are on Dick's left, so S-10, out on John's left wing, is tail end Charlie in the strike group. He will be the last bomber to make his run on the target.

A missile launch is called. Someone else calls a second launch from a different site. My warbler sings out. Someone, maybe Dick or John, calls the warbler. I see the first launch but not the second. The first missile veers off toward the far side of the strike group.

Ignore it.

I start looking for the second missile. I am hopped up on adrenaline, way up, but not panicked. I am not particularly scared at this point. My focus is on finding the damned missile. Time slowing. Every fiber alert. Every sense stretching out. I am jinking right,

There!
one clock low,
Close!
"Magics, break now!"

257

I keep going right
rolling well past vertical
pulling hard
I glance back over the left canopy rail as it rises above the horizon
a snapshot memory:
Dick and John, going hard left, pulling away
condensation streaming off their wing tips
disappearing beneath my upturned belly
I look back to my right
WHOMP!
the blast rocks my aircraft
I recover
reversing back
and up
I'm okay
engine's okay
control's okay
can't see any holes
All good
Close—but a miss
I look for the other three
"Magic One, I'm hit"
Dick's hit
I climb
turning back to the strike group's course
expecting to see them
coming back up from my left
no joy
nothing
look up, nothing
twist my body left looking behind
up and down
roll right and look under me
reverse back to the left
looking over my shoulder
I call

"Magic Two, no joy."
John answers,
"We are with him, Magic Two.
Headed feet-wet."
I roll right
looking east out to the horizon
"Magic Two, no joy."
John's voice, "Magic Two, stay with the strike group."
"Roger"
I roll back to the left.
I'm a half mile behind
and below the nearest Old Salts
I am bending the throttle forward
against the stop
I give up a little altitude for more speed
I am the lone minnow
I want back in the group
John calls a radio switch to the SAR channel
I switch with them
when I join the nearest Old Salt division
I switch back to strike channel
and tell their leader I am aboard as their number five
I get a double click of a mic
switch back to the SAR channel

I hear Dick calling feet-wet.
Great!

(silence)

John's voice,
"Magic One, EJECT, EJECT, EJECT!"

(silence)

"Magic One has a Good chute."

I breathe again
Great
He's feet-wet,
out with a good chute.
Big Mother will get him.
brandy with the flight surgeon
and a story to tell
I see the strike lead roll in
switch back to the strike channel
look down and find the target
Focus on the run
I'm tail-end charley
in and off and out
I switch back to the SAR channel

(silence)

It's over—they got him.
switch to the ship's approach control channel
Dick may already be there
enjoying the brandy
Can't wait to hear his story

Feet-wet, I check in with Red Crown as a solo
and fly back to the ship
"Signal Charlie"
I enter the break
land
out of the gear
taxi forward
park it forward
they tie my bird down
I shut her down
I note the rundown time of the engine,
unstrap, unplug, grab my helmet bag,
kneeboard off, in the bag, pat the instrument glare shield,

a silent *Thank you* to the bird
climb down
the plane captain is there.
"Check her for holes.
I had a close one"
walking aft toward the island and the escalator
still up on adrenaline
enjoying the post-mission high
I see the skipper, Doug Mow

Doug's walking up the deck toward the bow. Pilots do not walk forward during a recovery. All the pedestrian traffic is going aft to the island to get off the deck. I don't think this, but I know it's wrong.

The skipper walks straight at me. At four feet he stops.

"Mike, Dick didn't make it."
Didn't make it?
Didn't make it?
Didn't make it?

No

Time holds its breath

My brain shouts
NO!

Damn it

He had a good chute

I start to walk
the skipper walks beside me
silent

I debrief in Air Intelligence and then head back to the ready room. There's a small crowd standing around John Davis and S-10. John is telling the story. I stand behind the group still in my flight gear— listening. After the missile detonated, Dick continued his hard-turn left for 270 degrees, rolling out eastbound behind the strike group toward the water.

John Davis

That's why I couldn't find him. When I am looking for them to my left, they have already crossed behind and below me to my right.

Dick cleaned his wings of bombs and bomb racks and went out at high speed, pulling ahead of John and S-10 who were still dragging their bombs and racks along.

Didn't know that

As Dick approached the coast, his aircraft started to burn. John had him in sight, called for Dick to eject—*Heard that.*

Dick stayed with it until he crossed the beach going feet-wet at about ten-thousand feet. His aircraft did a roll to the right. As it rolled back upright through wings level, he ejected. In the same instant, his aircraft exploded. Dick had a good chute.

Heard that, too.

John and S-10 were there in moments. Dick was still descending in the chute. They orbited him. S-10 called, "Shouldn't Dick have come up on his survival radio by now?"

Didn't hear that.

John did a close, slow, flyby.

Oh shit. Here it comes.

John says,

"Dick was hanging limp in the chute."

He didn't release the chute as his feet entered the water. The parachute canopy settled over him like a giant shroud. Dick didn't swim out from under the chute.

The rule is they will not send a SAR helo into an area under fire from the beach until they have eyes on a live pilot. When the SAR helo arrived in the area, John and S-10 had not seen Dick since he entered the water. They sent the helo in anyway. The helo was taking fire from the beach, but the pilot put it into a hover next to the submerged chute.

The para-rescue swimmer went in. He dove down under the canopy, grabbed the shrouds, and pulled. There was weight. He hand-lined the body up. There was a fist-sized hole in Dick's chest.

Dick's body was tangled in the shroud lines. The fire from the beach was getting more accurate. The helo pilot pulls his swimmer. The SAR was abandoned—leaving Dick's body still hooked to the parachute.

I remember thinking,

The right thing to do.

But I hate that we left him there.

I am dead inside. There is nothing there. Nothing. No feelings. Just cold emptiness in my gut. Hollow.

Dick is gone.

I can't listen to anymore. I have to get out. I go to the head.

When I come back to the ready room. Someone is saying that the other SAM, or maybe a third SAM, bags both Al Stafford and Dave Cary from the Saints. I know nothing about it. I may have heard something on the strike channel, but if so, it is gone from my memory.

I was too busy dodging our missile and too worried about Dick and rejoining the strike group.

Al Stafford was a lieutenant commander. I only knew him by sight and name. He was well thought of by his squadronmates. Dave Cary was his wingman. I don't know if I ever met Dave. Both Dave and Al survive their missile and ejections. Both are captured.

Bad luck for them, but at least they're alive.

Both come home after almost six years of captivity in the hands of the North Vietnamese.[15]

JOHN'S ACCOUNT is cut short. Dick, John, S-10, and I are scheduled for another Alfa Strike at noon. I assume John Davis will lead our division, and I will fly a solo number three behind S-10. It is time to head to the AI spaces. Doug Mow comes to the three of us. He will fly as our division lead in Dick's place. I will fly as his wingman.

Douglas Mow,
Commanding Officer VA-164 (1967)

Doug Mow is stocky, a bull of a man with a beard so thick he has to shave twice a day to "pass inspection." He is the epitome of a naval officer through and through. Throughout this cruise, he has been rock steady under fire and leading the squadron. His constant thought is for those he leads. No matter the situation, he treats his subordinates with calm courtesy. He was, as my father would say, "a good man."

I grab my kneeboard and join the gaggle heading to AI. I find a seat. Still hollowed out, I mechanically write what I need to know on my kneeboard. We go back to the ready room for the division brief. We are sitting in the back of the ready room in a small circle. John, S-10, myself, and, in Dick's place, Doug Mow. I feel nothing. I watch the pre-mission rituals play out—shutting out the last mission.

The skipper says something . . . .

I sob

NO!
Deep breath. Holding it.
Don't do it!

I struggle for control
Tightening my chest
Holding my breath
Swearing at myself
Biting the inside of my right cheek
tasting the blood
Choking off the next sob
I exhale slowly

Sob

I fight it again
but I can't stop it
the sobs keep coming

The skipper says, "Mike, it's okay

Go down to your stateroom
I will send the doc"

"No, Skipper,
I can do this
Just give me a minute
I'll be okay"

"It's okay, Mike
Go to your stateroom
Wait there"
I go

By the time Doc Farhenbruck gets to my stateroom, I have pushed it all down. Nailed it shut. No more sobbing. It's only about 1100 hours. There is still time.

I should fly the mission.

"Doc, I'm okay. I can fly the mission."

Doc says, "No. You sit this one out." He has two of the little bottles of brandy. He takes the top off one and hands it to me. "Drink this."

I stare at the little bottle.

This is wrong. I didn't eject—Dick should be drinking the Doc's brandy, not me.

"But, I . . ."

Doc says, "Drink it."

I do.

He hands me the other. "Have this one, too."

I drink it. He produces a syringe I have not seen.

He's going to put me out.

"Roll up your sleeve." I give up and roll the sleeve.

He gives me the shot and says, "You'd better lie down."

I climb onto my upper bunk. He sits down in the metal chair at the little desk built into the dresser I share with Don Purdy. I look at him sitting below me, arms on his knees, head down. I close my eyes.

I OPEN my eyes. Doc is gone. My watch says it's five o'clock. C-10 and S-10 are in their bunks. It's 5:00 a.m.—tomorrow. I need to go to the head. I climb down.

I don't remember showering and shaving or even getting out of my camos and changing my underwear. I must have done my ablutions. I wouldn't have gone through the day unshaven. Maybe I did. I don't know.

Reliving this while writing this book, I wonder who flew in my place. I never thanked him.

Dick's death drives me to the bottom, forcing me down to where no emotions can find their way out. I leave his loss there and come back to now, to the place where Dick is not, to retake my place in the line.

I need to check the flight schedule.

Later I will not remember seeing anyone in the Ready Room, but there had to be a couple of maintenance guys in the back doing the paperwork and the talker and SDO up front. I remember going up to the SDO's desk and checking the schedule. I am on the first mission—with somebody who is not Dick Perry

Hungry.

I go to the wardroom and eat. I can't taste it. Not even the bacon. Back in the ready room before the AI brief, no one says anything to me. I fly the mission—but later I will not remember with whom, or where we went, or what happened.

I AM BLINDSIDED by Dick's death. Years later, I will read T.E. Lawrence's *SEVEN PILLARS OF WISDOM*. There I find words that send me back to August 31, 1967.

We had learned that there were pangs too sharp, griefs too deep, ecstasies too high for our finite selves to register. When emotion reached this pitch, the mind choked; and memory went white till the circumstances were humdrum once more.

Yes. Exactly.

Living with the whiteout blizzards in my memory was something I had done and would continue to do for the long years that came after. They hid the places I only went when a flashback involuntarily jerked me back to those moments.

Somehow, even though I accepted the certainty of my own death, it never occurred to me that Dick might die before me. I have no memory of ever anticipating or thinking about his death before Doug Mow met me on the flight deck. Maybe I thought Death would save the best for last. Maybe it hit me so hard because I assumed he had survived the ejection and had been rescued. But, whatever the reason, when the moment came, I was not prepared. In that moment on the flight deck with Doug, I had no defenses. His words flooded me with loss and pain that swept away all my defenses.

AS I WAIT to brief for my mission, it is clear:
I cannot go through this again. I will not let it happen.
I am hard—but not hard enough. If I am to function, I have to make myself emotionally bulletproof. The solution is obvious—don't care. If I don't care, I won't hurt. So, I make it my business to not care.

The only problem is I already care too much about C-10, Purdy, S-10, Duter, and Duthie. Duthie is back in the States—safe, but the odds are at least one or two of the others will die before me.

I DON'T REMEMBER anyone ever saying Dick's name again during the rest of the cruise. Maybe they just didn't talk about him while I was around. Maybe they did, but I just wouldn't hear it. I did write about the fact of his loss in letters to my wife and parents. I don't remember, but I wrote it in another letter—I think—I hope—I must have written to his widow, Margot, and son, Steve. The chaplain must have said his name during the memorial service at the end of the line period while we headed to port, but I don't remember hearing it. Once again, I did not want to go but could not fail to show up. I just stood there in my whites—numb.

I WILL NOT, cannot think about, much less grieve Dick's loss for decades. Nor will I grieve for anyone else. Decades later, I will understand that grief delayed is grief denied.

Part V

A SPACE BEYOND

    The soldiers who stepped over the dead bodies of their comrades entered a space beyond life and death.

—Eiji Yoshikawa

CHAPTER 19
PRESSING ON

Going Downtown.
Iron Hand with a max load of four Shrikes

O N SEPTEMBER FIRST, I get up, swallow hard, and push on. By October first, I am well on the way to becoming one hard son of a bitch. I remember thinking, *If they can get Dick, they can get anyone—including me.* My arithmetic looks good again, but I don't give a shit.

I am ruthless with myself. There is *nothing* outside of the bubble, not when I am briefing, debriefing, eating, horsing around, watching a movie, writing home, or trying to sleep—and never when I am flying. I fight by my friends' sides. I laugh with them, watch them go, step past their bodies, and, when the moment comes, I will die among my friends who will carry on as if I had never been—all within the bubble of the eternal present.

I work hard at this. I shrink my emotional universe down to our ready room. Down to those who sailed under the Golden Gate with me. They are important. It is too late not to love them, but it is not too late to walk past their deaths without pause. For a while, I force myself to imagine each of their deaths, trying to train myself to not care. I am in the space beyond. Fear lives in the future. I have no future. Grief lives in the past. I have no past. I will not care, will not feel the pain. Nothing that can happen, can touch me.

There is no room for "then" or "next" in the bubble. There is only "now." In the bubble, there is no room for "good" and "bad." Everything is or is not. The bubble defines the temporal boundaries of everything I allow to be real. I either die or I live to the next instant, carrying my bubble with me.

I WILL HAVE almost no memories of the rest of the line period. On September 11, I make a note in my flight log, "Na Tin Bridge" and draw a star next to the name. I am sure when I made the entry immediately after landing, thinking: *I'll never forget this one.*

I was wrong. I can't remember the mission. I assume I hit the damn thing. The records show that, between August 31 when we lost Dick Perry and the end of the second line period, the Saints lost an A-4 and the fighters lost two F-8s, all to operational accidents. All three pilots were recovered. None of which I remember.

WHAT HAPPENED yesterday, the last mission, an hour ago, a moment ago are all gone, beyond remorse or recall. I have no time or energy to waste on them, nor on what might have been. Nor any to waste on the maybes of the next minute, hour, or day.

There are things I must do now for what comes next. I have to preflight the bird because I will fly it off the bow, but right now, I am only preflighting the bird. I will deal with the catapult when the cat officer touches the deck, I deal with the flak when we go feet-dry, with the missile when the warbler sings. I will deal with the landing when I call the ball.

I barely noticed as I stepped in to the place outside life and death.

> So it is for the rest of the day
> and two, long cruises
>
> We fly together
> fight together
>
> surf the adrenaline highs together
> drink together
>
> bitch together
> laugh together
>
> living together
> while we can
>
> We keep faith
> each with the other
>
> we bear the losses
> swallow our fears
>
> and surrender

our hopes

never asking another
to shoulder our load

We fly back into the fray
day after day

Time to grieve
a luxury denied

for the strangers
we never knew

ready to come
whenever we flew

There at our call
risking their all

to save us from death
if it took their last breath

Nor even a moment
for those at our side

who gave their best
but died

Never a moment
for each or all

never a pause
to honor their fall

taking all who died,
hiding them deep inside

Storing the bitter ocean of grief away
to drink, on some far-off day

DENIED GRIEF, I am filled to overflowing with anger. Cold, hard, implacable anger is good. It is the only emotion I allow myself. The only one compatible with combat. It is my one emotional luxury, but I find it hard to keep it turned toward the enemy. Not letting the anger boil over onto friendlies becomes a struggle. Some idiot is always lifting the lid and letting it out.

Sitting on a bar stool next to a lieutenant commander from the Saints, both drinking beer, both getting drunk. Shooting the shit. I say something. He misunderstands and gets insulting. I know he misunderstands and tell him to get the beer out of his ears—and repeat what I said. Angry, he hears only his misunderstanding. I tell him to get fucked. He tells me to shut up. I am trying to decide whether I should punch him off his bar stool or invite him out back when C-10 appears between us. "Let's go, Mule. We are moving on."

Another night, I am sitting in the Cubi O Club bar when pilots off another carrier swarm in. They are fresh from stateside, headed for their first line period. Some nugget JOs from one of their A-4 squadrons take the stools next to me. Beers ordered; the guy next to me introduces himself.

I tell him my name ". . . from the Ghost Riders."

"Aren't you guys from Bloody Sixteen?"

First time I've heard "Bloody Sixteen," "What's that?"

"Bloody Sixteen, off *Oriskany*. Aren't you the guys that are losing all the pilots?"

"Yeah."

"How come you are losing all those guys?"

The anger rises, leaking out between the seams. "'Cause they shoot a lot. We are doing three Alfas a day."

"How do you handle the missiles?"

I tell him.

"Shit, no wonder they are bagging you. If anyone gets a warbler, our whole strike group goes into an evasion maneuver."

I swivel on the stool to face him. "You'll never get to the fucking target. You might as well jettison the bombs over the gulf and never go feet-wet. You'll be plenty safe that way."

He swivels to face me. "Fuck you."

His buddies intervene, and they take him to a table. He tosses me a parting "Asshole" thrown over his shoulder. I just sit there. *Good fucking luck to you buddy.*

He was probably born within twelve months of me, but I feel decades older.

Later in the cruise, I will almost kill myself and come back boiling with rage that I spill all over an enlisted man. Within two years, I will take a tire iron out of the trunk to teach another driver some manners.

I AM AN ORPHAN in the squadron. I don't have a flight leader, but there are no section leaders who need a wingman. That's fine with me, but I am the fifth at a bridge table. I go to the skipper. I tell him, "I want to fly Iron Hand missions. That way I won't need a flight leader." Iron Hands fly as a single A-4 with an F-8 wingman as escort. I have an unspoken reason. It will give me the opportunity to kill SAM operators—something I want to do.

Up to now, the targets have been things. Now there are people who are my targets. The SAM operators are experienced and good at what they do. Every one I can kill will be replaced by someone who isn't as good. Besides, it's a place to put my anger. Maybe it will wash away some of the guilt I feel for not seeing the missile that killed Dick sooner, and for not being there when he died.

When I ask, the skipper pauses. I know he is thinking that will mean I am a section leader for the F-8 escort. We both know I am awfully junior and inexperienced to be leading anybody anywhere. He has to remember me sitting across from him sobbing.

After a moment, he nods and says, "Okay. Tell Ops and Schedules I said it is okay."

I fly a bunch of Iron Hand missions. The Shrike is hard to deliver accurately. I work at getting off a good shot. But, good or bad, the missile operators just turn off the radar. That helps the strike group because the enemy can't guide the SAMs with the radars shut down—when they do, any missiles the site has in the air go ballistic, harmless, wasted. Even if the missile shooters don't see the Shrike launch and leave the radar on, the Shrike is unlikely to kill them. It just shreds the radar antenna, which thoughtful operators ensure is no longer near their trailer.

When we head to downtown Hanoi or Haiphong where we know we will stir up a hornet's nest of SAMs, we often carry four Shrikes to try and keep them shut down a few minutes longer. Otherwise, the normal Iron Hand load is a Shrike on each outboard wing-station and two Mark 82 five-hundred-pounders on both of the two-inboard wing-stations or maybe two Zuni packs with four rockets each. Bombs and Zunis kill operators.

If you zero out your bombsight when using the Shrike launch computer, the pipper will point at the missile site when the Shrike needles are centered-up on the cockpit display. It's eight to ten miles out, so you can't see the missile battery, but you know it is *right there*—I memorize enough landmarks and the general pattern of the ground to find the area where the pipper is pointing. I then concentrate on the needles, pitch up, and deliver the Shrike, rolling inverted as soon as it is gone, put the pipper back on the place it was pointing and start a long, jinking descent to ten-thousand feet to gain speed as I fly to it. Once in the neighborhood, the pattern of the typical missile battery is usually easy to spot.

Our tactics put the Iron Hand and his F-8 escort above and on either end of the strike group. When we move out ahead of the strike group to engage the missile batteries, we stand out like a couple of sore thumbs. The couple of minutes it takes to cover the ten miles to the site seem like hours.

Someone, Rock Hodges I think, calls the follow-up attack on a missile site a "rhino hunt." An apt description. When the North Vietnamese turn their radars back on after the Shrike is down, they will see my F-8 escort and me coming at them. They or one of the interlocking sites are likely to take a shot at us. The missile shooters must want to kill the Iron Hand pilots for the same reasons I want to kill them. If another site launches a missile at me, and I have a Shrike left, I try to get off a quick shot before I have to evade. I will then try to put my bombs on their heads. Seems fair.

Because the SA-2 cannot be guided until the booster stage falls off, once we are within a couple of miles, the missile site we are attacking cannot shoot at us. But its neighbors can. And every SAM site is surrounded by flak batteries for close-in defense against rhino hunters. If the MiGs are up, they might see the two of us as a juicy target, but that's my fighter escort's worry and hope.

Classic Soviet style SAM site. Four of the revetments have launchers. Reloads will be hidden the adjoining village.

When I find the site, I still have to find the trailer where the operators are. Traditionally, they put it in the middle of the site, but now they often have moved it out to the side and camouflaged it, just like a spider hiding from birds in the daylight. But it has to be connected by cables to every launcher, so it's not far. When I find it, I will have my chance. One time, I see the crew running from the trailer to a slit trench. I aim for the trench.

I only get one pass, so it better be good. A second pass is worth your life in that environment. I am homicidal—not suicidal.

ONE DAY, our strike group is headed north up the interior plain toward Big D Island on the way to Hanoi. Red Crown issues a MiG warning. The F-8 pilots perk up. I'm sure they all have erections at the mere thought of a MiG engagement.

This kind of opportunity is rare for them. The MiGs generally leave the Navy alone, especially air wings with F-8s, preferring to try their luck against Air Force strikes with the box formation dictated by their ECM gear. As our strike goes in, an Air Force strike is headed outbound on an opposite course off to our right.

Someone on the edge of our strike group reports: "There's a parachute about a half mile east. Got smoke over here. Looks like a downed aircraft."

All of our practice in Nevada comes into play. Strike lead organizes a SAR effort. He names a SAR commander, details A-4s to provide close air support, and F-8s as fighter cover. The rest of the strike group continues on to the target. Over on the SAR channel the dialogue runs something like this.

"The parachute is green? You ever seen a green parachute?"

"It's got to be an Air Force chute."

"The Air Force has green chutes?"

"Apparently."

"Does that chute look small to you?"

"Yeah, kind of."

"Okay. That's what I thought."

The pilot under the chute lands about a klick (kilometer) south of a village. The A-4s swoop in, trying to raise his survival radio on the guard frequency.

"Air Force pilot eight miles south of Big D Island, this is Navy jet, Old Salt 306, on guard. Respond. We gotcha partner."

The pilot looks up and begins to run north.

"Air Force pilot south of Big D Island, Negative Air Force. Don't go north. Run west. Go left. Run toward the karst . . . . Negative, Air Force, turn left!"

The sprinting pilot doesn't swerve. Despite increasingly desperate pleas, he runs straight into the village. In the village the pilot is surrounded and taken inside a building.

Shit. Must have lost his radio during the ejection.

Turns out that little green parachutes are used by the Vietnamese People's Air Force. The sprinting pilot flew a MiG. We don't know what happened to his MiG. No one on our side claims credit for shooting him down. You can be pretty sure if anyone had a credible claim, he would make it. Painting a red star on your aircraft is *tres chic*. I hope the North Vietnamese AAA gunners shot down one of their own, but it is probably an operational accident—the MiG just quit on him as he was trailing the outgoing Air Force strike hoping to catch a straggler.

I hope the Air Force appreciates the gesture. I know they will enjoy the joke on us. The rancher outside NAS Fallon would probably just shake his head.

THE SECOND LINE PERIOD ENDS on September 15. We leave Yankee Station and head northeast to the U.S. Navy base at Sasebo, Japan.

While in Sasebo, I sit down with a call girl in a "Sailor Town" bar. Not particularly attractive, at least to my Western eyes, she is quiet and speaks good English. I am still just hollowed out, still being as hard as I can make myself. But I am not being shot at and need to fill the hours.

I ask her name. "Midori."

"I am Mule."

I ask her where she is from. Somewhere north of Tokyo. She asks me.

I say, "Mostly everywhere. My family moved a lot."

She says, "Very un-Japanese."

I laugh. "Very American."

We slip into a conversation. I spend the night buying her drinks and talking about whatever thoughts wander through the moment while I am at her table. I am happy to just be with someone who doesn't know or care about airplanes and the Vietnam War. Maybe I simply want to be with someone who doesn't much know or care about me. A couple of hours later, it is time to go back to the ship. I leave her a large tip to make up for the lack of a sex wage.

I come back the next night.

I ask her, "Does 'Midori' have a meaning or is it just a name?"

"It means, green, like the color."

"I've never known someone named Green. Is that your real name or just one you use at work?"

"Oh, no. It is my name. Mule is an animal, isn't it?"

"Yes. A cross between a donkey and a horse."

"Why are you named Mule?"

"I don't know. Maybe I look like a mule."

She laughs with her hand in front of her mouth. At the end of the night, I walk her home but don't go in. She tells me tomorrow is her night off. Maybe I would like to come visit her at home. She will cook dinner.

"Yes. Of course."

Even by shipboard standards, her two-room apartment is tiny. Midori lives with her younger sister, who is still in high school. The sister is introduced. Her English is schoolish. She is very shy and formally polite in the Japanese style. She sits on the couch and does homework. Midori and I sit at the little Formica table. Midori offers me tea. After a while, she gets up to cook dinner. Clear soup, some noodles with a piece or two of vegetables. We just talk until it is clear that her sister needs to go to bed. I slip several ten-thousand-yen notes under my placemat and take my leave.

It is a good and relatively sober in-port period. Before I leave her for the last time, I draw a stylized wave and write, "Green is the color of this man's wave." She takes the gift and thanks me. I was and am grateful to her for the time we spent together, talking about nothing important to anyone, not even us.

ONE AFTERNOON, my three bunkies and I are killing time waiting for sunset. We wander into the base exchange. The toy department has Cox ready-to-fly control-line model airplanes. Someone says, "Hey, let's get one and fly it on the flight deck." "Good idea." I buy a replica of a P-40 with the Flying Tigers' teeth on the cowl because it looks cool. A wiser head picks a trainer model held together with rubber bands and designed to survive multiple crashes. While we are in the checkout line one of us asks, "Any of you guys ever fly one of these before?" "No's" all around. Shrugs all around. What the hell. We are all flying jets on and off carriers. We can fly anything, much less a model airplane.

The Great Model Airplane Air Show and Crash Fest before the laughter.
(Inky, S-10 (with the trainer), and Mule.)

We decide the carrier deck may draw some heat from authority, so we opt for the quay alongside the carrier. I crash the P-40 twice within ten feet of lift off. Someone else tries it. Crash and it is done. On to the trainer.

There are a number of spectators, mostly sailors who are enjoying our inability to master the plastic toys. As crash succeeds crash, despite all the expert advice we are giving each other, our embarrassment turns to laughter. No matter how violent the crash, the pilot always walks away uninjured.

Money well spent.

After nine or ten crashes, something other than a rubber band breaks. We decide it is still theoretically flyable. But in our hands, it proves just as unflyable with missing pieces as it was whole. Two more tries, and the trainer is a write-off.

MEANWHILE, Woody Knapp, our new guy, has caught a train to Tokyo and checked into a hotel. Later that day, he is standing outside the hotel trying to communicate with a cabby, when a young woman named Jodi introduces herself and offers to help. She speaks English with an empire accent—and Japanese. Woody thanks her for her help, admitting he is "out of his depth" in Tokyo. The lady has time on her hands and offers to go along and keep Woody out of trouble. She is an entertainer and booking agent for bands appearing in USO shows in South Vietnam. She is in Tokyo taking a break from the war zone. They spend three days together. Their time out of time together becomes something more than just a moment of distraction, at least for Woody.

Then time runs out. Woody has to go back to the ship.

Woody will write Jodi. It takes a while for his letters to travel across the Pacific to the fleet post office in San Francisco and then back to Jodi in Japan, so it is a conversation in slow motion. Near the end of October, she will receive a letter from Woody asking if she will marry him when he is finished with Vietnam. She had an unhappy marriage that ended badly and promised herself to never remarry. She mails him a letter saying, "It would never work." In the end, she may have waited too long—or maybe just long enough.[16]

WHILE WOODY is falling in love, and while I spend time with Midori, Rock Hodges convinces a couple of JOs to forgo the Officers' Club and "Sailor Town" long enough join him on a "cultural" excursion to ground zero of the atomic bomb blast at Nagasaki.

David "Rock" Hodges

As luck would have it, Rock and the others arrive while the local Communist Party is holding a demonstration against the United States. A group of protestors confronts the four young Americans with close-cropped haircuts. One or more speak passable English and begin giving Rock and friends what-for. It doesn't take long to exhaust Rock's patience. He points at the memorial and says, "You need to remember: We did it before. We can do it again."

Thinking, *Rock is picking a fight with about two-hundred angry young men*, the other three drag Rock away while smiling for all they are worth at the Japanese protestors.

I like Rock. He is a bit of a zealot; other than that, he is what I hope to become, especially after Dick dies. When it comes to courage and duty, he is hard and steadfast. He is, however, worried about becoming a POW. Because he had been a Strategic Air Command pilot, he knows a lot of secrets. If he is captured, the North Vietnamese and their Soviet allies will do some opposition research and are likely to find out what he did before the Navy. When they do, they will put the screws to him until he breaks. They will do almost anything for his kind of information.

Rock's bottom line is: "I am not going to be a POW."

UNFORTUNATELY, a few do not measure up to Rock's example. We have one pilot, not a JO, who is determined to survive the cruise at all costs. He takes to dropping his bombs from nine- or ten-thousand feet. He just dips the nose and pickles the bombs off, letting gravity do its thing. I first hear about this from the JOs who fly with or near him. Not long after that, I fly as his wingman on a road recce mission. We are bombing a tiny little bridge with no AAA defenses and not a chirp out of any SAM sites. He rolls in at eleven-thousand and is out of his dive by ten.

Rock is an early witness of this behavior. He keeps the title, but makes up new lyrics for the popular song "Yellow Bird," first popularized by Harry Belafonte. The lyrics make it clear that someone's A-4E is a high-flying bird. Whenever the dip bomber comes into the ready room, Rock starts humming "Yellow Bird." I think, *There goes a promising career*—but the dip bomber seems never to notice.

Our sister squadron, the Saints, has a different version of the same problem. A lieutenant commander downs his bird, declaring it unfit to fly for some reason or another—several missions in a row. Maintenance cannot replicate his down gripes. (Maintenance issues that must be corrected before the aircraft can be flown.)

The Saints skipper, Magnolia, is informed.

The next time the pilot is scheduled for a mission, he downs the aircraft. Magnolia appears beside the airplane, gesturing for him to get out. Magnolia climbs into the cockpit. Checks the bird out, gives a thumbs-up, flies the mission. The officer in question is on the next COD flight off the ship. I never see or hear of the pilot again. Such things happen, but they are rare. Out of both our squadrons, these were the only two who tried to fake their way through it. I don't count Barry Wood. He had the courage to turn in his wings and went on to re-prove his courage in Swift Boats.

We leave Sasebo and sail for Yankee Station on October 1, 1967. Four days later we are back at it.

CHAPTER 20

APOGEE

Mule and Sam Holmes.

OUR THIRD line period starts October 5, 1967. I am ascendant and triumphant. Every moment is a gift. I look forward to strapping the aircraft on my back. Rock, Lamay, Davis, Kirk, and Chuck are still minor gods, but I have earned my place alongside them, trusting and trusted. A brotherhood more than worth my life.

I am the whole package. The passing instants of near death, the reverberating toll of the bell for others when Death takes his due, I have survived them all and thrived. Living in the moment, flushing the minute, the mission, the day behind me as I go has become second nature. I have learned what Death has to teach the living.

Decades later someone will say to me, "The bubble may have protected you from pain, but . . . dive deeper into how you dealt with your feelings. . . ." He misses the point. In the bubble there is no "deeper." There are no feelings. Such things have been banished from my world. My feelings are ephemera: the sound of laughter, the smell of food, the burn of alcohol on the throat, threat, the copper taste of fear, the need for a cigarette, the slow motion of adrenaline highs, grunting and straining against the Gs, anger, and euphoria followed by lethargy as the adrenaline melts away in my head. I inhabit the space outside life and death—a place most have never been. I am in a strange land, but I am no longer a stranger there.

I am proud of who I have become. I am self-contained. My own man. All the illusions and self-deceit have been burned away. I owe no apology to anyone for anything I do. I am a warrior. I have become Mule. This is a life worth living, a life worth losing.

ON THE FIRST DAY of the third line period, Dave Matheny, an F-8 pilot from VF-111, is hit flying escort during a mission attacking a pontoon bridge. Dave has to eject over land in a place where there can be no SAR. He becomes a POW. Not a Ghost Rider, he passed through my bubble only occasionally.

Two days later, Rock Hodges is flying Iron Hand on a strike against railroad yards south of Hanoi. A SAM site lights up. While Rock maneuvers to get it in the crosshairs of his Shrike, a second site launches two SAMs at Rock. He doesn't see them coming. The first misses. The second nails his aircraft. He calls:

"Pouncer One has flamed out."

Rock is over a populated area where a rescue is impossible. His aircraft rolls inverted. The nose pulls down. He impacts the ground at a steep angle. No ejection, no chute, no beeper.

I know there are other possibilities, other interpretations, other ways you might want to think it happened, but:

Rock always said he would not be a POW, and he won't.

An hour or so after we learn of Rock's death, I find myself alone walking from the ready room to one of the aircraft division shops. A sob comes out of nowhere.

No! Not this time.

I clench my teeth on my inner cheek and exchanged loss for anger. I never break stride. Twenty feet later, I am under control.

I am proud of my hardened warrior soul. But there is a cost. I do not cry again for decades. Somewhere I go from "I will not grieve," to "I cannot grieve."

In the mid-1980s, my father's death will come and go without a sob or a tear. When Brother Death brushes past, I just get hard and hollow inside and push on. Half a decade into the next century, I will spend two days of the Memorial Day weekend, binge watching the *Band of Brothers* miniseries on PBS—trying to cry, trying to get past the first sob. I can't do it.

We list Rock as missing in action (MIA) because of the possibility he survived the crash. We do this if we cannot confirm the death to avoid the barest possibility of listing someone KIA who is in fact a POW. Beyond the family problems of someone returning "from the dead" after the war, we know that the North Vietnamese confronted one POW listed as KIA with a copy of his hometown newspaper that reported his death and the memorial service held by his family. They used it as leverage against the man, saying, "No one will ever know you are alive unless we tell them, and we will not tell them unless you . . . ."

Being MIA also means his family will continue to receive his full pay until such time as he is formally declared KIA. We make sure his family is aware of what happened and why he is listed as MIA.

Rock's remains will come home on April 16, 1999. He will be buried in Arlington National Cemetery. God bless you, Rock.

ALTHOUGH I HAVE accepted my death as inevitable, until now I have ignored the fact that I might not be killed outright when I am shot down. Rock made it impossible for me to ignore the possibility any longer.

I might survive—as a prisoner of war.

I know that means years of torture, maltreatment, and malnutrition—years of unrelenting pressure to disgrace myself by doing what they want. I fear I may not be able to hold out.

Rock had the right idea.

But, do I—will I have Rock's courage? Or will I eject, hoping for rescue, telling myself that I can swallow a bullet if I have to? I can see myself, procrastinating my way into the Hanoi Hilton.

Plan B

My sanity
has always been
like the balloon on a string,

a gift
from my parents
when I was a little boy.

I had to
concentrate
on holding the string.

If I let my mind wander,
even for a moment,
it would slip through my fingers,

bobbing, up
and away,

out of reach

before I could
snatch it back.

Gone forever.

Later, when I must think
about such things
it is clear

I am more afraid
of being a prisoner
than of dying

Death means no more
threat, pain, fear,
or failure.

So, plan A
is death
not capture.

But, can I?
Will I?
Maybe not.

In training, they told us
about the POWs in Korea
who went crazy.

Broken beyond repair,
any usefulness gone,
they were left alone.

And so, if I can't pull the trigger,
Plan B is: Let go of the string.

But my luck holds.
That is a hell
I never have to visit,

and here I am,
still clutching
the string.

Meanwhile, in the bunk below me, Don Purdy, father of the unborn figment of his wife's imagination, has also decided he does not want to be a POW. He, however, has a different plan A.

DON'S PLAN will require help.

Don: "If I have to eject feet-dry, I want any of you who are in the neighborhood to fly over and snag my chute on your refueling probe."

Chorus: "You're crazy."

Don: "No, it'll work. Fly in slow just below the canopy and snag a bunch of shroud lines."

Chorus: "So, we are supposed to drag the open canopy behind us. We'll stall out."

Don: "No, you have enough power; the canopy will collapse and tear itself into rags."

Chorus: "What if the canopy blankets the cockpit?"

Don: "That's why you were trained for blind flying under the hood. Just head for the nearest SAR destroyer. Use the TACAN, you don't need to see."

Chorus: "So, what the hell do we do with you when we get there, assuming you haven't been roasted to a crisp in our exhaust?"

Don: "I'll be all right. You just have the Whale meet us at five-thousand feet over the SAR destroyer. Slow it down to 120 knots. Tell the Whale pilot to blow the escape hatch on the cockpit roof and fly in trail behind you. He can come up under me and have one of his crew pull me inside. I'll use the quick disconnects on my harness as soon as

I'm inside. We throw the shroud lines out the hatch and—*voilà!* I am saved."

Chorus: "Sure, you're safe. But how the hell do I land on the carrier dragging your parachute behind me?"

Don: "You don't. That would be crazy. You are over the SAR destroyer—eject. They'll pick you up."

Chorus: "You are crazy."

Don: "No, it'll work. Trust me on this."

As the years go by, I will realize this is one of Don's better ideas.

COMING OFF A MISSION, I find an Air Force pilot standing in our ready room wearing his light gray flight suit. An Air Force officer in our ready room is almost as big an anomaly as a man from Mars in our living room.

Captain Sam Holmes is a Tactical Air Command (TAC) pilot. He flew F-100 Super Sabers with one of the first, if not the first, Air Force detachment sent to South Vietnam. Originally designed as an air superiority fighter, by the 1960s the F-100 has been relegated to the role of fighter bomber, which, in an Air Force dominated by the Strategic Air Command (SAC) generals, was decidedly *déclassé*. In the Air Force, tactical air was the redheaded stepchild. Vietnam changes the Air Force's perspective—slightly.

Sam is wiry, with a nose someone flattened for him and a fighter-pilot attitude. I'm told Sam and others come to us because the Air Force is worried about its kill ratio against the MiGs in Vietnam, which is nowhere near the 13:1 ratio it enjoyed in Korea. Worse yet, the Air Force's MiG kill ratio is lower than the Navy's.

Although Sam is sent to discover why the fighters' kill ratio is what it is, something gets lost in the translation. He ends up in the A-4 RAG rather than the F-4 RAG or, even better from Sam's point of view, the F-8 RAG. Sam is a single-seat-gunfighter kind of fighter pilot. But the bottom line is that we fly missions over North Vietnam. That is where the MiGs live, and he is determined to shoot down a MiG.

TO HIS CREDIT, Sam never once says anything about being disappointed at being sent off to war in an "attack" aircraft dedicated *solely* to delivering air-to-ground weapons. Nor does he complain that the A-4 has only two, not four, 20mm cannons. He was undoubtedly dismayed to discover those two cannons are notoriously inaccurate. I can't imagine what he thought when he learned that the A-4's 20mm ammo cans were removed to make room for electronic gear, leaving us with only forty rounds per gun. And, just to make sure no one in an A-4 is ever tempted to think he is flying an air superiority-fighter, it has a bombsight—not a fighter's lead-computing gunsight. To make it worse, he joins an air wing that includes two squadrons of F-8 Crusaders, the "last of the gunfighters."

Sam's bad luck is my good luck. I will be his wingman. The first thing Sam says to me is, "If we see a MiG, I am going to get him. Do your best to stay with me."

He is dead serious. Unfortunately, the MiGs seem to prefer not to tangle with the Navy, especially the air wings protected by F-8s. Sam might have had a better chance if he had flown Iron Hand missions, but I don't think he was trained on the Shrike system in the RAG. If Sam did fly Iron Hand, I would love to have been there when Sam told his F-8 pilot escort, "If we see a MiG, I am going to get it. Try to stay with me." The fates are unkind. Sam will never get his MiG. Sam lost people in his first deployment to Vietnam and comes to us with the combat veteran's emotional distance built in. We never develop a close personal bond, but that is fine with me. We work well together, or at least we do from my perspective. I never feel uncomfortable flying with Sam. He is as good a pilot as we have, a warrior through and through, and fun to be around.

The bottom line is that I'll go anywhere with him and trust my back to him anytime, anyplace. My Irish luck is still holding.

Robin Wood and I carry Sam Holmes across the flight deck. I have no idea why.

I GET LETTERS. My wife writes often, especially at first. I try to write something every other day—or so. My folks write and so do my sisters every now and then. Every week, I get an envelope from my sister Ginger. Still in high school, she is the quiet sister, the thinker, with a devilish sense of humor. She and I both like the newspaper comic strips. Ginger knows that *BC* by Johnny Hart in collaboration with Brent Parker and *The Wizard of Id* by Johnny Hart are my favorites. Each envelope has a week's worth of both—twelve little coupon-sized strips of comics—and the two big strips in color from the Sunday paper. I read them. Enjoy them. A leak in the dam I have built against thoughts of home and before. The strips are not memories of home but something from home. Each a slender filament connecting me, a luxury I allow myself for a moment, then stow them all in the desk drawer I claim as mine. At some point, I take them out and glue them in a spiral-bound red notebook, writing "BC etc." on the cover with a marker.

I keep the notebook. It is one of my life treasures. Just holding it will always make me feel better. Sometimes when things are bad, I will sit and read a few strips at random, laugh, and say a silent "thank you" to Ginger.

CHAPTER 21

UNLEASHED

Survivor Bias
The Ghost Rider pilots, October 1967.

Flight pay is the retirement pay you'll never live to collect.
—Naval aviation aphorism

N O MATTER what you fly or where you go, Brother Death is on the wind. The air wing has a detachment of E-1B Tracer aircraft from the Sea Bats of VAW-111. The Tracers are the carrier's early warning and electronic surveillance aircraft. On October 8, one of their airborne controllers, Lt.j.g. Wayne Armstrong, is ashore in Cubi. He runs into a friend who is an F-4 Phantom driver from USS *Coral Sea*. His buddy offers Armstrong a ride in the back seat of his Phantom just for the fun of it. They run fun into trouble, and both have to eject. Only Armstrong's friend, the pilot, survives.

The same day, one of our Tracers leaves Chu Lai in South Vietnam to return to the ship. They take off in a rainstorm so thick it blinds their radars. They crash into Monkey Mountain (Son Tra) near Da Nang. The bell tolls for all five aboard: Lt.j.g.s Andrew Zissu, Norman Roggow and Donald Wolfe, ATC Roland Robert Pineau, and Seaman Raul Guerra, a Navy journalist along for the ride.

Six young men from our air wing die in one day. None of their deaths test my equilibrium. Emotional calluses.

Alfa Strike by CVW-16 on Kien An airfield 8 October 1967.
Note the section leader with bombs rippling off in upper left.

OCTOBER EIGHTH is memorable for another reason. We are unleashed against Kien An, North Vietnam's secondary fighter airfield. I am not on the strike. I am flying the SDO desk. They get some bombs on the runways, hangars, and revetments and come away with no losses. We know it is only a matter of time before we will be sent against their main fighter base, Phuc Yen (pronounced Fook-yen by us). It seems to me this is also clear to the North Vietnamese. Our leaders are adept at telegraphing the punch.

The next day, C-10 manages to get himself shot down a second time. Once again, he makes it to the water before the aircraft quits on him. He ejects. This time, he is rescued the old school way: by a whaleboat off a destroyer. More brandy. Hurt, but not so bad he can't fly the next day. He was right. It is a long fucking war—and getting longer, but I am not spooked by Death's proximity. Near misses are just misses.

IN THE TRAINING COMMAND, a flight instructor told me "Flying at night is just like flying during the day, except it is dark." In October 1967, I fly two-night missions with Sam Holmes. They are both unremarkable—except it is dark.

After even a brief exposure to white light, it takes at least thirty minutes for a person's eyes to fully dark-adapt. When scheduled for a night mission, pilots must spend at least one hour out of the white lights that illuminate most spaces on the ship. Because red light does not ruin dark adaptation, the ready rooms, AI spaces, the flight deck, adjoining heads, and all the ladders and passageways that interconnect them are restricted to red lighting before and during night flight operations. If for any reason we must go into white light, we wear goggles with red lenses. The red lights create their own atmosphere. For me, it is a bit like a thick fog on the beach. Quiet, closed in, and slightly eerie.

Mood lighting aside, the best thing about night ops is breakfast. They start serving breakfast two hours before flight ops, whatever the clock says. I like breakfast on the ship. Just walking into the service line, the smell of unlimited bacon and sausage, white toast drenched in melted butter and buried in sugar and cinnamon, hash browns by the pound, and the pervasive smell of Navy coffee is heaven.

During the AI briefing, the meteorologist tells us the predicted surface winds in our operating areas will be from the east at five knots. *Add a westerly one mill offset on the bombsight.* We will have a high, thin overcast at fifteen-thousand feet. The moon is a waning crescent. What moon there is will set by the time we recover. There will be no Air Force birds in-country during our mission, but one of the big deck carriers will have some of the all-weather A-6 Intruders going in at low level ahead of us. They will be egressing while we are going feet-dry.

This is not my first night combat mission. Dick and I flew a few night missions before he was killed so I knew the drill. Over the beach, no one shows any running lights. With sections assigned adjoining recce areas, Dick explained there is a gentleman's agreement, "No one ventures too close to their area boundaries. Nevertheless, keep your eyes dilated and open. People get lost and wander about." I nodded, thinking, *not to mention me.*

We are told there will be some friendly PT boats operating along the coast south of our area. "They are out hunting junks and motorized barges trying to sneak south. Please do not bomb them or reveal their location with a flare."

The AI tells us truck traffic has been reported on one of the secondary roads in our recce area during the last several nights, and there is a truck convoy north of us they expect will move down into our area tonight. The AI also mentions a couple of bridges that have been dropped recently and at least one ferry known to be operating in our area. Dropped bridges and ferries can lead to trucks backed up at a river crossing.

I mark each prospect on my chart in black marker, having learned by painful experience in the training command that all the red on my charts and kneeboard became invisible in the soft red glow of cockpit lights. After the briefing, I plot and write the bearing and distance from Red Crown of each area of interest on my chart so I can use its TACAN to find them.

We are told about the active flak and missile sites. *No missiles tonight, please.* We are warned about a flak trap operating in our area. They have a dozen sets of headlights mounted on poles they set out on a road to look like a truck convoy. They surrounded the lights with mobile flak batteries and wait for us to notice them. "If you see a convoy that is parked with their lights on, be careful."

They tell us where the ship expects to be for recovery. Not too much different from the briefing for a day mission. Less traffic, but—it *is* dark.

Back in the ready room, we stop at the maintenance desk to get our aircraft assignment for the mission. Sam will fly AH 409, and I draw AH 404. Sam goes through the management and use of navigation lights (red on the port wing tip, green on the starboard, and white on the tail, with the red rotating strobes on the top and bottom of the fuselage midship). We test them on the deck before taxiing, keeping them on only for a couple of seconds.

Dick taught me to put down my helmet's sun visor while we test the navigation lights to protect my night vision as best I can. "But, remember to tighten the set screw down when you put it back up. You don't want it falling down at the end of the cat stroke." Dick would always remind me to go slowly on the taxi. He'd say: "Remember, everyone out there is working in the dark."

When on the cat, we turn the navigation lights on to signal we are ready to launch instead of saluting the cat officer. When the aircraft on the cat in front of me turns on his lights, his white taillight will be feet away at eye level. Dick's solution, "Don't look. Close your eyes." But—I love watching the bird go down the cat track into the darkness and always watch with one eye.

We will leave our lights on after the launch to avoid a mid-air and so we can find each other to join up after launch. Sam gives me a bearing, distance, and altitude on the carrier's TACAN where he will start a left-hand orbit and wait for me. A couple of miles before we reach our coast-in point, he will flash his lights as a signal for me to drop a mile behind him and a thousand feet above his altitude. When I am in position, we will turn the lights off.

At night the section leader has to tell his wingman every time he changes heading, speed, or altitude. We use a simple code in case the flak gunners are listening. When he calls a turn, I will continue on course for fifteen seconds on the clock before turning to the new heading. In theory, that will keep me one mile directly behind him. The reality is more like a room full of kids with sticks wearing blindfolds, all trying to whack the pinata at the same time.

Sam lays out the general route he plans to fly, checking out the AI's "hot spots" in our area and everything in between. Against the chance we lose communications, he establishes an emergency rendezvous point five miles offshore from the mouth of the largest river in our recce area. The five miles is so we can safely turn on our lights and find each other.

We review the procedures for using our flares. Whoever is going to illuminate a suspected target will fly over it at twenty-five-hundred feet. The gunners will hear us coming and so have some idea of where we are. When we drop a flare, its arming lanyard leaves a small shower of sparks as it ignites the flare's ten-second fuse. At that moment, the gunners will have a fix on our location, altitude, and course—so, as soon as the flare is away, we change all three before the cannon shells can arrive.

We both carry flares on the outboard starboard wing-station. Tonight, we will carry seven Mk 81 bombs (two-hundred-and-fifty pounders), instead of five of our usual Mk 82s (five-hundred-pounders). I think of the Mk 81s as glorified firecrackers and much prefer the Mk 82s. To kill a truck with a Mk 81, you pretty much have to hit it. A Mk 82 should do the job if it lands within fifty feet of the truck. However, we can carry seven Mk 81s, instead of five Mk 82s. We will drop two bombs per pickle with a short interval between them to stretch the kill radius a bit. The seventh Mk 81 on the outboard wing-station opposite the flares will go on the fourth pickle.

We use a thirty-degree dive-bombing run at night instead of our standard forty-five degrees. Rolling in at ten thousand feet, we accelerate to 450 knots, speed-brakes out, power back to 85 percent, pickle at four-thousand feet instead of six thousand, and pull out no lower than three thousand feet. The shallower dive angle decreases both the rate of descent and the Gs necessary to pull out, both calculated to reduce vertigo. The low release also means I have only a thousand feet to bottom the dive with a five-hundred-foot cushion above the flare. Flying into the light below the flare will get you killed.

For me, flying at night is like driving in the first snowstorm of winter. I have to constantly remind myself that slow and easy does it.

Thirty-degree dive or not, I can expect vertigo if I jack the plane up and around pulling out after bomb release.

Preflighting the aircraft with a red flashlight beam is different. Hydraulic fluid is red and invisible except for the reflected shine. When we do the post-start checks and are taxing, the plane captains and yellow shirts all have two flashlights with opaque cones screwed on the front that give off a dim yellow glow, making all their hand signals both visible and measurably cooler than in the daylight.

Some of the guys I fly with think the night catapult shot is the scariest thing we do. Zero to 140 knots in nothing flat, straight into a wall of darkness, no horizon, sixty feet over the water, instruments bouncing all over the place, often night blinded by the afterburner of an F-8 on the catapult in front of you. A sure prescription for vertigo.

Landings can be worse. I remember someone, Purdy I think, who came into the ready room after a night mission in bad weather still hyped up on adrenaline.

"Sweet Jesus, what a landing. When I look up at a quarter-mile, the carrier is in a forty-degree left bank! I think it's going to capsize. It doesn't. It just sits there." Standing in the ready room, he mimes holding the stick in his right hand and the throttle in his left and leans far to the left, balancing on one leg saying, "So I put the aircraft in a forty-degree left bank and land it on that sucker."

He almost falls over trying to simulate a forty-degree bank.

I quickly learn to live with the moment at the end of the cat when everything is an unknown. Maybe I have had enough day cat shots to know I will catch the stick, and the confidence to do nothing until the VSI settles down—trusting that it will fly.

For me, the stress of a night cat shot isn't a patch on night carrier landings. Sam Holmes has the same attitude. He feels that, day or night, if the plane doesn't fly off the cat, it is somebody else's fault. If he makes the save, good on him. If not, too bad—*but* not his fault. On the other hand, if he screws up a landing, *his mistake* kills him. How embarrassing. I agree, but must add that the stress of a cat shot is over much more quickly than that of the landings. The vertical speed indicator is the first instrument to settle down when you go off the front end. Once you know you have a positive rate of climb, all the rest are mere details. If not . . . eject.

By comparison, the landing is a long, drawn-out affair. The landing approach gets progressively more demanding, critical, and dangerous the closer you get to the ramp. It is more likely that you will know you are in trouble before the crash. Of course, when you finally hit the ramp, it is also likely to be over pretty quickly.

However, in October 1967, I am not yet fully Zen with the night cat shot. I still hold my breath as I go off the bow, blind with no references outside the cockpit and everything inside dancing.

FINALLY, IT is my turn. I find myself on the catapult watching the cat officer signal his deck edge shooters to tension the cat, pulling my aircraft forward, straining against the hold-back fitting. The cat officer twirls a wand above his head. I push it up to full power, checking all the engine instruments. My brain clicks in. Thoughts become actions.

Scan the engine instruments
She is turning and burning sweet
wipe the cockpit with the stick
peering out to watch the controls respond
check the engine gauges and flap indicator one more time
back straight
head against the rest
right elbow in my gut to catch the stick
left fist in a death grip on the throttle and hold-back bar
turn on the navigation lights by flicking the switch on the throttle with
my little finger
Eyes darting between the VSI and attitude gyro
In the corner of my eye, the cat officer's wand touches the deck
A deep breath
the interminable one-second delay
The bird squats
WHAM!
Hurtling down the cat into the black velvet wall
eyes glued to the VSI

> when the cat bridle falls away
> the acceleration sags and
> the nose pitches up
> catch the stick
> hold six degrees up by feel
> VSI settles
> needle above level
> *I'm climbing*
> the gyro settles
> Five degrees – stick back a notch
> angle of attack indicator – *okay*
> Roll left to clear the air for the guy behind me.
> Check the angle of attack and airspeed
> gear up
> flaps up
> accelerate to 250 knots as I climb
> passing through one-thousand feet
> I reverse my turn
> vertigo whispers *Gently, gently*
> crossing back in front of the carrier
> *Go find Sam.*

I find Sam, rendezvous, and join up. He rolls out on a heading to bring us to our coast-in point. Approaching the dark line of the coast, he checks us out with Red Crown, then tells me, "Magic 404, go tactical." I double click an acknowledgment and switch the stick to my left hand, reaching down with my right without taking my eyes off of the lead's aircraft. I find the radio channel selector by feel. I have memorized all the settings and turn it counterclockwise, counting the clicks, until I get to the squadron's tactical channel. With my left hand back on the throttle I key the mic, "Magic 404's up." A double click acknowledges.

About seven or eight miles out, Sam lets down to 3500 feet. As he levels off, he blinks his lights. I climb to 4500 feet and bank left until I am thirty degrees off his course, hold it there long enough for him to get a half mile ahead of me, then roll right, turning until I am heading thirty degrees to the right of his course and hold it there. As I approach his flight path, I roll left, ending up directly behind him at what I think is about a mile. I call, "Magic 404's aboard." He gives me a double click, and his lights wink out. I turn off my lights.

Less than a minute later, Sam calls a change of course. I wait ten seconds and follow suit. Sam checks us out with Red Crown. "Magic 404, master-arm on." "Click–click." I switch to left hand on the stick and reach down to the bottom-center of the instrument panel, find the master-arming switch by feel, pull it out, then up. I risk vertigo and gently lower my head to glance down and double-check the individual arming switches, making sure I have stations one, three, and five off Don't want to be dropping the [do-not-drop] drop tank, or an unintentional flare. With stations two and four hot, one pickle equals one bomb from both with a short interval that should give me a fifty-foot spread.

Sam finds the first downed bridge in the dark. He does a couple of orbits, as I hold off in my own orbit. "Nothing, I'm rolling out on two five zero." I wait fifteen seconds, add thirty degrees and follow. Fifteen minutes and three course changes later, we are heading roughly north by northwest. At my two o'clock, I see a "Christmas tree" formed by a cone of flak tracers converging at about my altitude about four or five miles north. I key my mic,

"Magic 409, are you the tree topper west of Vinh?"

"Negative."

Two minutes later, another tree of flak erupts at my eight o'clock. Before I can ask,

"Magic 404, that's me. I'm climbing to base plus two and coming left to zero niner zero."

"Shit. I've overrun him."

I crank it around and head northwest toward the tree. I turn too hard and have some vertigo. I am trying to reorient myself to him. *He's behind me to my left, turning into me and climbing.* I push up the power to stay above him. I stop my turn and hold my course for an interminable ten seconds flying toward the flak and then start a wide turn to my right hoping I will tuck in behind him. How far behind him is anyone's guess.

"Magic 409's clear. Coming right to one five zero and going to base minus 3500." I wait fifteen seconds; on the unwarranted assumption I am something close to a mile behind him.

Another turn or two later, Sam says, "Orbiting left. Over the river." I start a right orbit. I have the river—well, *a* river—about a quarter mile to my right. Sam calls, "Magic 404, there's no ferry, but I think we have some trucks lined up waiting north of the river. I'll make the flare run heading one niner zero, off right. You make the bomb run heading one two zero. Off left."

I answer, "Roger," and begin a climb to ten-thousand feet while he sets up for the flare run. I draw a mental diagram of his flare run and my bomb run in relation to the target but can only guess where the target is until the flare goes off.

"Flare's away."

I don't see the sparks.

Where is he?

Ten long seconds later, the flare erupts at my ten o'clock at two miles. *Wrong damn river, but not as bad as I thought.* Thumb the mic button, "Magic 409, I am two miles southeast climbing through base plus five."

I get a double click.

It takes an agony of time to get to the perch. I can see four trucks lined up single file at the riverbank. No sign of life. The drivers must have headed for the woods as soon as the flare went off. No flack, but there will be automatic weapons with the convoy. "Magic 404 is in." I roll in on the bomb run. My inner ears and stomach are arguing with my brain. *Focus, focus, focus.*

My run is shallow but otherwise pretty good. Ball centered, on speed. *Delay the drop three hundred feet.* Tracers from two and five o'clock chase me. They appear to be two dual mounted 12.7mm heavy-machine guns, one on each side of the river. One pickle. Two little bumps as the bombs are kicked off the racks. I pull off hard enough to avoid going below the flare despite my low release. I hold wings level until my nose is 15 degrees above the horizon, unload the Gs, and wait half a second to give my inner ear a chance before rolling left. "Magic 404's off left."

Out of habit, I twist in my seat to see the hits. A mistake. My head spins. Two flashes. I'm close enough to damage the last truck—maybe, but no secondary explosion or fire.

A Mk 82 would have killed it.

I hear my father's voice, *It's a poor workman that blames his tools.*

I turn back and almost fall off the ejection seat. *Don't be throwing your head around, you idiot.* I focus on the instruments trying to let my inner ears catch up.

"Magic 409's in. Off right." Sam's first bomb catches the truck nearest the water. The second is long and in the river. A small fire on the lead truck. I'm almost back to ten-thousand feet. Calm down. Slow and steady.

"Magic 404's in, heading one five zero, off right." A good run, but my bombs are short and right.

As I pull off, the flare gutters out. It is amazing how dark it is after looking into the pool of white light. My turn to drop a flare. I stop my turn and back off the power, descending to 2500 feet. I circle around to the northeast for the flare run.

I change my armament switch settings making sure station five is "hot" and the others are not. They know we'll come with another flare. I will make my flare run about thirty degrees off Sam's just so they can't go to school on us. Double-check my armament switch settings. "Magic 404 in for a flare, heading two-two-zero, off left." At this altitude, I am well within range of their machine guns, but they are shooting at my noise, and the tracers are behind me as I get to the target. I trigger the flare, climb, turning harder than I should in the dark, as the tracers whip around to catch up with me, curving like water from a hose. Vertigo sucks, but it's better than dead.

Sam is sitting on the perch waiting when the flare lights off. "Magic 409 in, one five zero, off right." I'm surprised to see five bomb flashes. His bomb stick falls across the second truck but is at a shallow angle and takes out the third truck as well. He calls off and tells me to drop my remaining bombs.

I am at a good roll-in. I change my armament switches so station five is off and stations one, two, and four are hot. "Magic 404 is in, one seven zero, off right." I have a good run. Two of my three bombs straddle the last truck, killing it. No "maybe" this time. I am rewarded with a small fire but no secondary explosions.

Time to go home. Sam heads out to feet-wet at five-thousand feet. I am somewhere behind him at six-thousand. As I cross the beach I hear, "Red Crown, Magic Stone 409, feet-wet with two." I reach down and turn the master-arming switch off. Thirty seconds later, I see his lights come on. He is at my one o'clock at about three-quarters of a mile. "Magic 404. Tallyho. I'm at your seven o'clock at a klick." *Not bad. Better.* Sam starts a gentle left turn to help me join up. I close about half the distance before turning my lights on. Rendezvousing at night can be dicey. You lose depth perception in the dark. This makes closure rates hard to estimate, but I take it slow and slide into place with no drama. We have time to kill, so we climb and throttle back to max conserve to save fuel.

I know this all sounds like I was lost most of the time, and I was. Over time, I will get better at playing follow the leader in the dark. But the night hops, were always iffy, at least those I am involved in. Still and all, every now then we manage to whack the piñata.

THIS MISSION is over—except for the getting back aboard part. We use carrier-controlled approaches (CCAs) for all night landings and in bad weather. A CCA starts at ten-thousand feet or more, several miles behind the carrier. At the assigned time and position, we will make a standard "jet penetration," plunging down as we close the distance on the carrier. Approach control monitors us during the penetration, but only to make sure we maintain separation from the aircraft ahead and behind us in the pattern. When we get in-close we will be passed onto final approach control and are talked onto the glide slope. With good visibility like tonight, we are brought to a point where we are a mile and a quarter behind the carrier and on glide slope at six-hundred feet. In poor visibility they can bring us down to a quarter mile, and two hundred feet.

When we check in, *Oriskany*'s approach control gives Sam a bearing, distance, altitude, and approach time. Mine is on the same bearing, a mile farther out, a thousand feet higher, and a minute later. Approach control is stacking all the aircraft on a long slant behind the ship, oriented on the expected recovery course. I acknowledge the controller's instructions and give him my fuel state.

Our job now is to conserve fuel while flying a left-hand racetrack pattern starting precisely at the assigned bearing, distance, altitude, and time. The turns at each end of the racetrack are to be made at the "standard rate" (i.e., one minute to complete the 180 degrees). We fly a two-minute outbound leg. The leg back is a little longer because the ship and its TACAN are moving away from us, dragging our start points along with it. The only thing left for me to do is to adjust the length of the straight legs so I will be at the start bearing and distance at precisely my assigned time. If I am more than ten seconds off either way, I have to announce my sin so the controllers can do whatever is necessary to keep me from crowding the man in front or behind me in the pattern. Everyone on the approach frequency can hear my confession. Embarrassing. Better to be on time.

Dead on time, I start the jet penetration. Speed brakes out, power down to hold my speed at 250 knots, coming down at four-thousand feet per minute. Once I establish my descent, I look out where the carrier must be. The sea is an infinite depth of black on black. I sweep the engine instruments one last time and then focus solely on my flight instrument scan.

My brain and eyes fall into the well-worn groove. I start with a glance at the attitude gyro that gives me my flight attitude relative to the invisible horizon; then, on to the TACAN telling me my heading and the direction and distance to the ship, the airspeed indicator; the vertical speed indicator (VSI) that tells me my rate of descent; and then back to the Gyro to start over. I don't look at each so much as sweep past, my brain registering only that the dial or needle is where it should be. I must maintain the scan through all that happens over the next few minutes.

At 5,000 feet, I push up the power and raise the nose to slow the rate of descent to 2,000 feet per minute, maintaining 250 knots. Approaching 1,200 feet, I retract the speed brakes and add power to level off.

At 10 miles, approach control slows me to 150 knots. I pull the power back and put out the speed-brakes, retrimming the aircraft as I slow. Time for flaps. I put them down full by feel while continuing my scan. A couple of seconds later, I make sure they are fully down by breaking my scan long enough to glance at the flap indicator. When I slow to 150 knots, I reach for the landing gear handle, recognizing it by the little tire on the end of the handle. I put my left hand back on the throttle and push the power up to hold the speed against the added drag, retrimming the nose up, hold the speed. A minute later, I glance over to check the gear indicators for three little tire symbols indicating all three legs of the landing gear are down and locked. I reach over to make sure the tailhook handle is in the down position, throw my weight forward to make sure my harness is locked.

At six miles the approach controller calls again, "Magic Stone 404, switch to final approach."

"Magic Stone 404, roger." Switch hands on the stick, find the radio channel nob, count the clicks. Glance at the fuel state. "Final approach, Magic 404, 2.1, three unexpended flares."

"Roger, Magic 404, Do not acknowledge any further transmissions (i.e., "Shut up and listen"), if you do not receive a transmission for more than ten seconds, execute a missed approach (i.e., the assumption is that one of us has a radio failure).

I am responsible for keeping my aircraft on speed. He will feed me lineup and glide slope prompts. I like to keep a couple of knots in hand until I get in close. Less risk of a stall. At three miles, I hear, "Magic 409, approaching glide slope."

I risk a glance up. I'm close enough to see the centerline and drop lights. The drop lights are on a pole hanging down off the flight deck from the ramp centerline. From the air, they and the centerline lights make a straight line if you are on lineup. If you are off to either side, it makes an angle with the centerline lights; to correct your line up, just turn into the angle. Simple and effective, even for the dyslexic among us.

The green datum lights are just visible. The ship itself is invisible, a darker shade of black.

Get back on the instruments.

The controller starts his chant. The controller continues to talk me down with a constant patter, making ever-smaller corrections as I get closer. At a mile and a quarter from the ship, he tells me to look up from the instruments and call the ball.

Head out of cockpit. I see the datum lights, ball, and centerline drop lights floating on a pool of dark nothingness. I shift to my landing scan:

Meatball—angle of attack—lineup . . .

"Magic 404, Ball, 1.8, three flares on board."

. . . meatball—angle of attack—lineup—meatball . . .

"Roger ball. A little power, come left."

a familiar voice

Tom Lamay's the LSO tonight

. . . (*add a little power*), line up (*slide left*),

meatball (*rising, take a little off*),

angle of attack (*okay*),

line up (*come a little left*), meatball (*okay*) . . .

crawling the power back to avoid going high,

Lamay is quiet, so he's happy

in close now,

angle of attack—(*okay*)

line up—(*okay*)

meatball sinking

(*burble—bump the power*)

line up—(*okay*)

meatball climbing

(*power bump out*)

WHAM

full power—speed-brakes in,

body slamming into the shoulder harness

full stop

. . .

hook up

throttle to idle

find the yellow shirt's wands

power on, right brake

hurry across the foul deck line

. . .
Alive again

Back to the ready room, light a cigarette, shuck the gear, deep drag, and stub the cigarette out. Off to AI by way of the nearest head. Debrief. Back to the ready room. Lamay comes by, looks at me, "OK-3." A perfect pass.

Time for second breakfast.

AS LUCK WOULD have it, I fly two missions on October 14 and one on October 16, but I don't fly on October 15—the day my self-calculated "use by" date expires. If my increasingly dubious math is right, the life expectancies of all the surviving A-4 and F-8 pilots expired on October 15, 1967. All the remaining Ghost Riders, Saints, Hunters, and Sun Downers are officially on borrowed time.

I am not sure, but think the fifteenth was our stand-down day—the twenty-four-hour break in flight operations at the middle of the line period. If so, none of us flew. Maybe Death was over the beach looking for me but couldn't find me because I was drunk in my bunk.

OCTOBER 18 is not a good day. John Barr, our maintenance officer, launches as an Iron Hand in support of a raid on Haiphong. John is a senior lieutenant commander, fourth in the chain of command behind the ops officer and the XO. John is a serious man who has a serious job. As the aircraft division officer, I report directly to John, but any interactions we have are all business. If he thinks I have a problem, he calmly tells me and expects me to solve it. "Aye, aye, sir."

John goes rhino hunting. In his dive-bombing run on the missile site, he is hit by antiaircraft artillery. His A-4 explodes. No parachute. No beeper. No call on his survival radio. We assume he is dead, but report him as MIA—just in case.

John is the Ghost Riders' fifth casualty. He was flying AH-406, the original "*Lady Jessie.*" It is the eighth aircraft we lose. We have now lost a quarter of the pilots and more than half of the planes we came with.

There is no lesson for me to learn in John's death. Getting hit while holding steady in a bomb run is a risk we all must take. John's luck just ran out.

I walk past his death. Not feeling has become autonomic.

RICHARD WOYNARSKI, "Ski" to his buddies, is one of the men in the squadron's aircraft division. He is from New York. A jet engine mechanic, he is on the flight deck maintenance gang that services aircraft and performs minor repairs between mission cycles. A tire on one of the squadron's aircraft blows on landing. Richard is sent from the flight deck down to the hangar deck to get a new tire. They need it *now*. They need to change the tire before they tow the aircraft aft to be fueled and re-armed for the next launch.

Richard hustles to the hangar deck and gets a tire out of stores. The tires have multi-ply steel belts and are built to be inflated to extremely high pressure. The steel belts and high pressure are necessary to withstand the impacts of carrier landings. The compressed air to inflate the tires is taken from the ship's high-pressure air supply on the hangar deck. To avoid over-inflation, there is a pressure-reduction fitting that lowers the air pressure to a few pounds over the tire's rated inflation pressure. If overinflated, the tires literally explode like a mortar round laced with shrapnel.

There is a steel safety cage to contain any such explosion. The cage is to be used when inflating the tires, but it is hard to get the tire in and out of the cage, and it is hard to hook the pressure-reduction valve on the tire inside the cage. Even when properly hooked up, it takes longer to inflate the tire using the reduction valve.

The guys in the shop had complained about the poor design of the safety cage, but nothing was done, so they stopped using it when in a hurry. I knew none of this. But I should have. It was my job to know about such problems. I should have tried to get or build a better cage and insisted they use the old one until it was replaced.

Pressed for time to get the aircraft back up for the next launch, Richard does not use the safety cage and pressure-reduction valve. He stands over the tire and uses the air hose connected directly to the ship's high-pressure air system. He misjudges it. The tire explodes. The wheel rim comes off the deck and hits him on the forehead just below the hairline. Richard dies instantly. He was twenty-one years old.

I get the word in the ready room shortly after it happens. By the time I get to the hangar deck, his body has been taken away, but his flesh and brains are still splattered on the safety cage he didn't use.

SIXTY YEARS LATER I will still see it. Still smell it. I felt nauseous 1967. I feel sick feel writing about it in 2020.

Richard died because he knew we were depending on him to get the new tire ready and up to the flight deck in time to get the plane up for the next launch. He died because I didn't know about, much less do something about, the problems with the safety cage. He died because I did not know they weren't using the cage and reduction valve.

I didn't know Ski personally, but I wish now that I did. I wish I had a chance to tell him how sorry I am that I let him down. In the next century, his death will bother me still. My sense of shame and guilt will not diminish. In 1967, I feel no remorse. Remorse is for the past. I have no past. The best I could do for Ski was make sure it wouldn't happen to any of his buddies.

It will be five decades and more before my remorse breaks through.

TWO DAYS LATER, Denny Earl, a JO from the Saints, takes a AAA shell through the cockpit. The shell does not explode, but the dud warhead takes off his big toe and continues on to shatter the bones in his other leg. He is bleeding heavily.

There is little Denny can do about that, but the aircraft is still flying, under control, and not on fire. Denny heads feet-wet.

Doc Adeeb, our air wing flight surgeon is listening to the radio chatter. He comes up and tells Denny to manually inflate his G-suit. It will act as a partial tourniquet to staunch the blood flow. It slows but does not stop his blood loss.

Ordinarily, Denny would have to wait to land last, but he will bleed out before then. While he is still en route to the carrier, they check the tanking assets in the air and decide to take the risk of a deck crash and land him first. They order an emergency pull forward to get him a ready deck. But, even then, Denny must wait while they finish rigging the crash barrier for him.

The twenty-foot-high crash barrier is a curtain of heavy nylon straps that run vertically between two steel cables stretched across the deck. The cables are attached to retractable poles on either side of the flight deck. The whole idea is that you land into the barrier. It is used when an aircraft cannot get its hook down to catch the arresting gear or when the pilot needs to land on the first pass. A pilot like Denny. They also recalibrate the optical landing system to make the one-wire (that closest to the ramp) the target wire, instead of the normal three-wire.

Denny waits, the shock wears off. He takes to pounding the canopy with his left hand to help distract him from the pain in his shattered leg. Finally, the deck is ready, and the barrier is rigged. Denny is cleared to land.

Denny Earl in the barrier

Denny flies a good approach. He snags an arresting gear cable, which slows him considerably before he hits the crash barrier. Nevertheless, his aircraft is entangled in a mass of nylon straps.

They race out and pull him from the cockpit. He is almost dead. They put tourniquets on both legs and start an IV, lift him into a Stokes litter, run him onto the deck edge elevator, and drop to the hangar deck. From there, they carry him down two more decks to the sick bay.

I like Denny. He has his head screwed on straight and is mostly cheerful. He has a great smile and wears it often. I am glad he survives

No. Don't do that. If you feel good when he is saved, you will hurt when he is lost. He's alive for now. Leave it at that.

It's not long before they call for blood. C-10 and I both share Denny's blood type. We head down to sick bay. There are a lot of sailors lined up to give blood. C-10 and I assert our privilege as officers to jump the line. We can see corpsmen taking full-pint bags of blood from the guys on gurneys in front of us, hurrying across to the surgical area, flipping them upside down, hanging them on a pole, and hooking them up to Denny. He is on an operating table surrounded by a lot of people in scrubs.

A corpsman comes up and throws us out of the line. Rules are, if you give blood, they are required to ground you for twenty-four hours, and pilots are in short supply right now. C-10 and I go away grumbling.

Denny survives and recovers. He goes on to serve twenty years as a Naval Aviator. After retirement he is hired as a contractor to fly a civilian aircraft equipped with a military radar to train back-seaters. He does this for more than another twenty years.

ON OCTOBER 21, one of our KA-3B Whales is taking off from the airfield at NAS Cubi Point at Subic Bay in the Philippines. They are using JATO (jet-assisted take-off, pronounced "jay-toe") to get the bird airborne with a full load of fuel on a short runway. The JATO bottles are small solid rocket motors that can be bolted onto both sides of aircraft to give them extra thrust on takeoff. The trick is to have them all fire at the same time. If not, the power of the rockets on the one side will skew the aircraft toward the side of the failed rocket. About halfway down the runway, a JATO bottle on the right side explodes. The aircraft swerves right. The pilot has about 140 knots and manages to stagger into the air as he goes off the right edge of the runway. Moments later, the Whale's right engine fails. They crash land in the bay. The cockpit disintegrates on impact. All four crew members are thrown clear. All four survive. Dumb luck. This time dumb good luck, with an assist from a pilot who flew it until it fell apart around him.

THE NEXT DAY, Jim Dooley's aircraft is hit by a missile during a raid on Haiphong. Jim is a JO with the Saints. He comes off the target streaming fuel. He heads for the water. He makes it feet-wet. About a mile offshore, his aircraft noses down. It impacts the water at about a thirty-degree angle. There is no chute or beeper. The SAR comes back empty-handed. Jim is listed as MIA.

Jim passes out of my bubble. Another name to not forget. Another one of us to not think about.

Others have hope. Fifty years on you can find entries on the internet by those who wore his MIA bracelet, sending messages of hope for him. In the neverland between the living and the dead, the Navy bureaucracy promotes him first to lieutenant, then to lieutenant commander. In 1973, the promotions stop—his status is changed to KIA [Killed in Action]. He was twenty-four when shot down.

October is proving to be a long, hard month on both sides of the Pacific. One night, in an all-pilots meeting, Doug Mow says, "Listen up. You have to keep your letters home positive. It's tough for the wives back home. They never know from one moment to the next whether you are dead or alive."

Sam Holmes pipes up, "Skipper, I can't help but think it's a lot easier to be a live widow than a dead husband." I laugh so hard my stomach hurts. I am not alone.

October 23

AFTER THE MOVIE, I check tomorrow's flight schedule. I am scheduled for two missions: one against the Haiphong railroad yards (again), the other against a target in Hanoi. Notwithstanding a daily double of Hanoi and Haiphong, I will miss the big strike of the day. Tomorrow is the day we practiced for when we scared the bejeebers out of the rancher in his little blue airplane near Yuma.

We are finally unleashed against Phuc Yen, the Vietnamese People's Air Force main jet base about twelve miles north of Hanoi. It was built to provide fighter defenses for Hanoi. They have operated MiGs from it against us for most of the war but it has never been on the White House's target list. Now it is.

Everyone wants in. Phuc Yen will be hit with a series of attacks involving the Navy, Marines out of South Vietnam, and Air Force squadrons out of Thailand and South Vietnam. It is a rare honor for any target to draw the attention of all three services on a single day. The airfield is well defended by flak and SAMs, and you have to believe the MiGs will come up to defend their base. This strike is going to be as dangerous as it is overdue. That is not a coincidence.

October 24

The next morning, I am on the first go. We hit a railroad yard. I won't remember it. We go in, bomb it, and get out. I am also on the second go, this time against the Haiphong rail yards. Skip Foulks of the Saints is almost out at about sixty-five-hundred feet when he is hit by AAA. His engine quits, but he has enough speed to carry him to feet-wet, where he ejects. Skip is recovered with no serious injuries. I feel good about his rescue. I like Skip. Decades later, I will learn he told his friends he wouldn't survive the cruise. Another member of the "No Hope Club" with Don Purdy and me.

While we are hitting Haiphong, the first strike against Phuc Yen is underway. The Navy's honors for the first mission fall to USS *Coral Sea*. That night, we learn she lost two F-4 Phantoms and all four of their aircrew as the price of admission.

We get a slice of the pie on the last strike of the day, but I am done. Two combat missions a day is our limit. Deny Weichman leads the four Ghost Rider Iron Hands, each with their own F-8 escort. Wuff designs the overall plan, but each Iron Hand operates independently in the target area. They do not lack for business. The strike is met by more than two dozen SAMs. Wuff takes out one site, is hit by AAA, but stays in the game. He engages and destroys a second site, taking another flak hit in the process. His bird gets him back and aboard. He will be awarded the Silver Star for his valor that morning.

That night, I take my ritual peek at tomorrow's flight schedule. We will hit Phuc Yen three times. I scan down the schedule for my name. *Bingo.* I am scheduled as section lead of strike bombers! I can't believe it. It is only a week into my third line period, and I am leading a section —not someone's wingman. Three months ago, I was a combat virgin, clinging wide-eyed to Dick Perry's wing. Tomorrow I will be responsible for my wingman, for getting us to the roll-in at the target and out again to feet-wet and safety. It is our turn at bat, and I am in the lineup.

I do my best to maintain my cool, but I'm so excited I turn and step away before realizing I probably ought to look at the rest of the schedule. I turn back.

Holy shit! I am flying Iron Hand against Phuc Yen on my second mission.

I don't sleep much that night—rehearsing tomorrow morning's section brief, trying to articulate everything I learned from Dick about being a section leader. I realize that is a mistake and go to sleep.

October 25

The next morning, I am as ready as I am going to get. Confidence in each other is important. My wingman needs to know I have confidence in him. I tell myself: *Calm, matter of fact, keep it brief. Don't tell him things he already knows.*

He doesn't run screaming from the ready room during my briefing. So far, so good. We fly the mission, dodge the SAMs, drop our bombs. I get my wingman back feet-wet safely and then to the break over the ship. He is on his own for the landing.

I land, taxi forward, we go to the AI's. I give them my version of what happened and what we did, then the AI turns to my wingman,

"Anything to add?"

"Nope."

Back to the ready room. I do a short debrief. I have ten minutes or so. Smoke as many cigarettes as I can while drinking a Coke and eating a candy bar.

Time to get my head back in the game for the Iron Hand. The mission is special because the Saints will be using their new precision weapon, the AGM-62 Walleye, a television glide bomb.

The rituals begin: AI, brief the escort, suit up, man aircraft, start, launch, rendezvous, feet-dry, run in to the target—all flow through my bubble.

Time to sprint out in front of the strike group. The SAMs' search radars are up. I acquire one in my sector, track it. Other sites start launching SAMs, but my warbler is quiet.

I wait for my site to turn on its guidance radars and launch. Sure enough, it comes up just as a missile roars off in a cloud of dust. I am ready. I center the needles, pitch up, and shoot a Shrike at the site.

Cutting the runways at Phuc Yen. Note the hangar on the right

There are a lot of SAMs in the air. As soon as I recover from my launch maneuver for the first Shrike, I switch to the Shrike on my other wing and acquire a second site. I track it and pitch up to launch my second Shrike. Out of Shrikes, I follow the second in to deliver my four Mark 82s. I hit the site but do not get a direct hit on the command trailer.

The hangar at Phuc Yen moments after being hit by a TV-guided Walleye delivered by John "Fritz" Schroeder of VA-163, who took this picture just as his Walleye hit. There were ten MiGs on the base when it was attacked. All were destroyed.

Pulling off, I look back. My escort is right there, covering my six. Time to get feet-wet. No MiGs bother us.

Our strike on Phuc Yen costs the Saints. They lose Jeff Krommenhoek, a JO. He is twenty-six. Jeff is listed as MIA, just in case what we know must have happened did not.

Unlike Dick Hartman, the North Vietnamese never acknowledge having captured him. A decade later, his status will be changed to KIA.

IN NOVEMBER 1967, it will be decided that another strike is necessary on Phuc Yen. The Air Force goes in, preceded by four F-105s Wild Weasels, their version of our Iron Hand. Two of the Wild Weasels are shot down by MiGs, and several of the strike group are lost to SAMs. An F-8 escort is a blessing the Wild Weasels are denied. You've got to love our F-8 pilots.

October 26

THE NEXT DAY, *Oriskany* flies two strikes against another high-value target: the Hanoi Thermal Power Plant. We are going to turn the lights off in Hanoi. We will hit it twice. I am on the first strike.

The power plant is deep inside the city, as "downtown" as you can get. The missiles are up in force. The missiles and flak come thick and fast. The strike is a welter of events racing by with no time to do more than react as the perceptions flood in. Even the time-slowing effect of adrenaline is swamped by the speed of events.

John McCain is flying a strike bomber. Flak blows the right wing off his aircraft. With all the lift gone on the right side, the aircraft snaps into a violent roll to the right, generating high lateral Gs in the cockpit. Inside the wildly rolling aircraft, just reaching the ejection handle is a struggle. John finds the handle. The rigid, vertical posture for a safe ejection is impossible. Nor can he slow the aircraft. Out he goes. A good chute, but the opening shock of the canopy in the high-speed airstream is vicious. Both of John's arms gyrate in the wind. He is knocked unconscious. He lands in a small lake in downtown Hanoi. The water revives him. He has a badly broken leg and is unable to use either arm.

Magnolia, the Saints' skipper, circles back into the maelstrom trying to raise John on his survival radio. All this is happening while I am still evading a missile. It is chaotic—as bad as the second Van Nhue mission in August. This time I do not panic; the strike group holds together, and we hit the target. We have learned a lot since August. But the tuition has been god-awful expensive.

THE NORTH VIETNAMESE drag John McCain from the lake into the midst of an angry, armed mob. He is stripped of his clothes, clubbed with a rifle butt on his injured shoulder, then bayoneted in the leg. The soldiers calm the crowd down long enough to take some pictures before John is thrown in the back of a truck and taken to prison.

John is dumped in a cell, his injuries left untreated—until they find out his father is Commander in Chief of the Pacific Fleet. Then they send him to a first-class hospital. They offer him an early release. John McCain refuses. He tells him he will walk out with all the rest of the POWs. He tells them exactly what he will tell the world if they release him early.

The North Vietnamese are not pleased. His treatment goes from kid gloves to the worst they can deliver. He does not break. He is awarded the Silver Star, the fourth-highest medal awarded for valor by the United States. The citation for his Silver Star reads:

> The President of the United States of America takes pleasure in presenting the Silver Star to Commander John Sidney McCain III, . . . for conspicuous gallantry and intrepidity while interned as a Prisoner of War in North Vietnam. In October 1968, his captors, completely ignoring international agreements, subjected him to extreme mental and physical cruelties in an attempt to obtain military information and false confessions for propaganda purposes. Through his resistance to those brutalities, he contributed significantly toward the eventual abandonment of harsh treatment by the North Vietnamese, which was attracting international attention. By his determination, courage, resourcefulness, and devotion to duty, he reflected great credit upon himself and upheld the highest traditions of the Naval Service and the United States Armed Forces.

In 1981, I will be practicing law in Phoenix. One morning, my partner Jon Kyl will come by and ask me if I knew a guy named John McCain. "Yeah. I was there when he got shot down." Jon told me

McCain is moving [or has just moved] to Arizona, and he was having lunch with him, would I like to join them? "Sure."

Jon Kyl is active in the Republican Party. He wants to get to know John. I'm not political or affiliated with any party, but I knew and respected what John endured as a POW. It turns out I like John McCain. Over the following year or so, I will volunteer to work in his first run for Congress with a little money and shoe leather canvassing door to door. A few years later, I will leave Arizona for Maine.

I am in Maine in July 2015 when Trump famously says, "He's not a war hero. He's a war hero because he was captured. I like people that weren't captured." Over and above the fact that John McCain was captured when he fell unconscious and severely wounded into the North Vietnamese laps, he earned the Silver Star for what he endured and did as a prisoner. Beyond its departure from reality, the criticism lies poorly in the mouth of a man who hid from the war and the draft. All that stored-up anger at the way the Vietnam veterans have been treated boiled up and over again. I was done with Donald Trump, bone spurs and all.

DURING OUR second strike against the thermal power plant on October 26, Charley Rice, from VF-162, is flying his F-8 when his aircraft is blown in half. He manages to eject. Chuck Nelson is watching and takes the picture. It shows half of Charley's airplane still in midair. Charley survives the explosion, manages to eject, is captured, survives, and will be returned in 1973.

Meanwhile, *Coral Sea* has launched another strike on Phuc Yen. They lose an A-4 flown by Cmdr. Verlyne Daniels, who survived the ejection to become a POW.

Charley Rice's F-8 after the SAM hit.

I fly one mission on October 27, two on the 30th, and two on the 31st. The first mission on the 31st is at night. The sequence of the flights tells me we were flying midnight to noon. Half night, half day, with a "pinky" wedged between the two at dawn. Not my favorite schedule, but it gets me breakfast for at least two and sometimes for all three meals.

The second mission I fly on the 31st is an Iron Hand mission on the early morning launch. I punish a SAM site. A good way to end a bad month.

October has run out of days. It has been a long war unto itself.

WE DON'T SEE MANY PEOPLE on the ground. The ranges are too great, and most people are ducking for cover when we are about. Not only do I see few people, but I rarely think of them. I know they are there, but I usually have other things on my mind. At the time, I give little thought to those who happen to be where I am putting my ordnance.

That will come later—after. In the decades that make up the aftermath of my life, I will feel remorse for killing and maiming those who were uninvolved but had the bad luck to be in the wrong place at the wrong time. It will be even later before I will think about the truck drivers, barge operators, and others who worked on or around the things I was trying to destroy.

But, in 1967, I do think about and look for the missile operators and flak gunners. Them I want to kill. Even so, I rarely see them sitting behind the flashing muzzles of their cannons or crowding in a slit trench when we drive them off their guns or outside the missile command trailer.

There are, however, a few times when I am aware of individuals on the ground. And I will remember them all.

I fly Sam Holmes' wing on a mission into Hanoi. The strike group goes feet-dry well south and loops around to attack from the south-west. We will exit west, south of Thud Ridge, then bear left and south out of the heart of the air defenses, before making the run east back to the Tonkin Gulf. Sam says that once clear of the target area he will drop down and go out low, under the SAM envelope, until we get to the mountains, then climb to five-thousand feet. Fine with me. I have a thing about missiles up the tailpipe. Besides, I like flat-hatting (slang for flying very low and fast for fun).

The missiles are up, and the flak is thick on the run into the target. There is the normal split-second chaos at the roll-in, as I find the target and focus on the bomb run. Coming off the target, I put on the Gs and pump out some chaff, following Sam as he bends it hard coming off target. We jink our way out of the immediate target area, and then Sam dives for the deck and we start our runout. We've put bombs on the target. Our sole mission now is to get the hell out of Dodge.

Anything under a thousand feet should keep us below the missile envelope, but it puts us in more jeopardy from the flak and smack in the sweet spot for automatic weapons. If you are going out low, you have to go out very low and very fast.

By going out at fifty feet, we shrink the local horizon for the gunners down to the tops of the nearest hedgerows, trees, and buildings. If we go fast enough, they can't hear us coming until we are on top of them, and we will flash across their sight line before they can react and bring their weapons to bear. At least, that's the theory.

Sam is down under fifty feet and pushing four-hundred knots (460 mph). I am below him at twenty feet with room to maneuver inside his turns.

My adrenaline is in full flood. I am always worried about what is behind us, but this low and fast there is damn little time to look. No jinking now. That, too, seems unnatural, but straight-line speed is everything. We are bending the throttles over the stops.

Seconds drag, but in clock time we are soon out of the urban area and deep into the countryside. I am on Sam's left. We are hopping over trees and bushes and then pushing it down again to put them behind and between us and anyone with a gun. The rice paddies flash by. I am focused on my front but still thinking about the threats on either side and behind. That's my job, but I dare not do more than glance away from the trees and hedgerows racing at me. I look ahead for the hills every time we pop over something. Once we get to them, we'll be outside the SAMs range and can climb above the effective range of small arms and children throwing rocks. Time crawls. The hills stay stubbornly distant. We pop up over another row of trees lining a paddy. Push the nose down, aware of the ground. It's too easy to misjudge the dip and smack a paddy.

I level at twenty feet and focus on the next obstacle—there in front of me, frozen in my memory, is the figure of a small man in black pajama bottoms rolled up to his knees, no shirt, a conical-straw hat on his head, face turned toward me, running from right to left in shin-deep water for all he is worth. Even the splashing water is frozen in my memory. I know he is running for his life; sure we are going to kill him. He doesn't know he and I are both running for our lives. In that instant the thought flashes, *Only I know he will survive the encounter.* I roar over him before he can take another stride.

Years later, I will watch *Monty Python and the Holy Grail* and hear the command, "Run away. Run away." I laugh. *Been there, done that.* I will think of the running farmer from time to time and wonder what he tells his grandchildren about the moment our lives intersected.

November 1

October, with all its grinding losses, may be over, but the line period has two more days to go, and I am not on the flight schedule. The skipper takes me aside. I am too far ahead in the number of combat missions I have flown. I must look dismayed. He adds, "It's not fair to others" (i.e., someone is complaining).

Skipper Mow, Woody Knapp, Mike Williams, and Roger Duter.

I am off the flight schedule until further notice. I argue. I have done no more than fly the schedule. I've been lucky. No down (unflyable) aircraft, and sometimes I get launched as a spare. I don't take myself off the schedule to fly an aircraft to Cubi Point for an engine change. It's not fair to me. The skipper just shakes his head. I point out that he has flown even more missions than I. Mistake.

"I am the commanding officer. I am expected to fly more missions. You're done for a while."

"Aye, aye, sir." I walk away feeling hard done by.

Safely out of his earshot, I resort to the ritual incantation of Yeoman Berry: "Shit, piss, fuck, damn. Why is everyone always picking on me?!"

WESTERN UNION DELIVERS a telegram in New York on November 3, 1967.[17]

```
Washington, D. C. 3 November 1967

REPORT DELIVERY
DO NOT PHONE

I deeply regret to confirm on behalf of
the United States Navy that your son,
LT.J.G. Frederick Woodrow Knapp,
6936605/1310, USN was killed in action on
2 November 1967 while on an armed
reconnaissance mission over North
Vietnam. His aircraft rolled in at 9000
feet in a 30-degree rocket dive and was
observed to impact with the ground. No
parachute was observed nor was an
emergency beeper signal heard. There was
light anti-aircraft artillery in the
target area. It is with further regret
that I must advise you that your son's
remains were not recovered. Your son died
while serving his country. I extend to
you my sincere sympathy in your great
loss. A letter from his commanding
officer setting forth the circumstances
of death will follow. If I can assist you
please write or telegraph the Chief of
Naval Personnel, Department of the Navy,
Washington, D. C. 20730. My personal
representative can be reached by
```

telephone at Oxford 42746 during working
hours and Oxford 42768 after working
hours.

Vice Admiral B. J. Semmes, Jr., Chief of
Naval Personnel
  (DEATH - No Remains - Primary
  & Secondary)

What the telegram doesn't say is that it was a night mission. His section leader saw Woody make his run. He watched as Woody flew under the flare and straight into the ground. There was no ejection. We don't know why Woody flew into the ground. Maybe he fixated on the target, easy to do at night with rockets. Maybe he was killed by small arms fire when he flew below the flare.

Nor do we know if he ever got the letter from Jodi declining his marriage proposal.

Whatever the cause, whether he got the letter or not, Woody is gone. I liked Woody as much as I let myself like anyone and am sorry to see him go so soon. At this point in the cruise, I am feeling old and think of Woody as young, almost a kid, even though we are both twenty-four years old on the day he dies.

Woody's death marks the end of our third line period. Two more to go.

After the war, a source from a village near Woody's crash site reported that the people of the village removed the body of the pilot from the wreckage and buried him nearby. Later, an official of the North Vietnamese government will surrender Woody's Geneva Convention card. His remains will be returned to his family in May of 1982.

AT THE END of flight ops, we leave the line and point the bow toward Yokosuka, home of a U.S. Navy base at the mouth of Tokyo Bay.

Tom Lamay, our senior LSO comes to me in the Ready Room. He says: "You have earned a Top Ten Award from the LSOs based on your cumulative carrier-landing scores. Congratulations." Tom hands me the patch depicting the original mirror and ball optical landing system with a centered ball, with the words "Top Ten–CAG 16–USS *Oriskany*." I go down to the parachute riggers and ask them to sew it on my flight jacket. Later, I ask Tom for a second patch and mail it with a thank you note to the admiral, who gave me the extra chance to CarQual in the F-9. Given the way our first cruise was going, I wonder if he still thought he had done me a favor.

En route to Japan, the inevitable, unavoidable memorial service is interminable. Another out-of-body experience in un-dress whites.

On November 6, we dock at Yokosuka. We will be here until November 15, but at least half the pilots must be in the immediate area at all times in case of an emergency sortie, so pilot leave is split into two shifts. My three bunkies and I all opt for the second shift. When our turn comes, we get on the train and head for Tokyo. We get a good view of Mount Fuji and the immense Buddha at Kamakura as we roll by.

We rent rooms in a small traditional Japanese inn someone recommended. It is about a forty-minute taxi ride from the Sanno, a U.S. officers' club in downtown Tokyo. The Sanno is the epicenter of our inebriated sojourn in Tokyo. I remember having Mongolian barbecue cooked over a wok in the Sanno's garden on the first night. Good eats.

I WAKE UP. *Where am I?* I am lying on my back. *I don't sleep on my back.* I start to roll on my side. Nausea—*Don't move.*

I wake up again. Still on my back. Open my eyes. A familiar jumble of ducts, pipes, and conduit. *It's the overhead. I'm in my bunk.* With some effort I remember leaving the ship—being on the train going—to Tokyo. I become aware of noise. Vibrations. The ship's engines. *We are at sea.* I lift my right arm—look at my watch. *12:10—midnight or noon?*

Slowly, I recover episodic memories of the preceding five days, most them in the early morning when we hire two taxis to take us back to the Sanno. We got the drivers to race by promising them the winner would get a big tip. One driver drove half a block on the sidewalk to get around some blocked traffic.

Other than the taxi rides, I remember wandering around with C-10 looking for a party on the nineteenth story of a hotel down the block from the Sanno. We had a bottle of champagne C-10 bought at the Sanno bar. We wandered about listening at doors. Nothing. "Maybe it is on the eighteenth floor." More ears to doors. After the seventeenth floor, we quit and . . . I don't know what happened after that.

I have a vague memory that one night, or maybe one afternoon, some rear echelon Army guy, a major I think, joined our table. Or, maybe, we joined his. He was staying at the Sanno and running a tab. An hour or so later he face-planted on the table. Passed out. No problem—he became our honored financial host for the rest of our party. That's about it. I have lost most of five days.

I am not the only one trying to piece together those days in Tokyo. The Army major is trying to figure out his enormous bar tab at the Sanno.

For my part, I have never blacked out before. *Maybe I should cut back on the drinking.* I make a deal with myself: *I can drink, but I will not get drunk—except on stand-down days. But, if I ever get drunk any other time, I will quit drinking altogether.* For the next fifty years, I will believe I keep that bargain.

The Army major has a different approach.

A few days later, a fat manila envelope arrives on the ship addressed to the air wing commander. Exhibit A is the major's bar tab. The envelope also contains witness statements, our names, and all kinds of supporting evidence. Turns out the Army major is a JAG officer or head of the military police, or something else with access to all the forensic resources he needed. Skipper Mow calls us together. We pony up the required amount.

CHAPTER 22

THE FOURTH LINE PERIOD

USS Oriskany *recovering aircraft.*
An F-8 on a bolter is about to fly off the angled deck.

O N NOVEMBER 19, we leave Yokosuka and head south to
Yankee Station for the fourth line period. I am gently reminded that I am still off the flight schedule, so I will be
doing extra shifts as the squadron duty officer and standing Pri-Fly
watches. However, I will be scheduled as a spare pilot on some
missions, so there is hope.

We conduct flight ops on the way out to Yankee Station to shake
out the rust. I get to fly because it is not a combat mission. *Whoopee.* As
I am being shuttled into line for the starboard cat, someone ahead of
me calls on the radio saying he got "a hard shot" on the starboard
catapult. My ears perk. The A-4 ahead of me bangs off. He calls, "The
cat shot was abnormally hard."

I'm next. *Yup.* I call back and say something is wrong with the
catapult. Lt. Ed Van Orden's F-8 is behind me in line ready for launch
on the starboard cat.

F-8 on the starboard cat, 1967

When I recover and walk into the ready room, they are rerunning
the video of Ed's launch over and over on the closed-circuit TV. When
the cat was fired, the bridle that connected his aircraft to the catapult
shuttle broke, or maybe the right bridle hook on his aircraft failed, I

can't remember which. Either way, the catapult transferred enough energy to break the hold-back and got the plane moving forty or forty-five miles per hour. Ed was accelerating because he was at full power, but he was never going to fly by the time he ran out of deck. Because the failure was on the right side, he came out angling left across the deck. Ed got off the power and on the brakes. He skidded across the deck toward the bow at the end of the left catapult.

The plane was going slower and slower, but the edge was getting closer. When he reached the edge, he was going less than ten miles per hour—but it was clear he was going to skid over the bow. As his nose wheel dropped over the edge, he ejected—the canopy flew off, and the seat fired—up and out.

The F-8's ejection seat is older than the A-4's and not as capable. The seat could not save him on a zero-altitude ejection going so slow, but he was on the flight deck, sixty feet above the water and had the wind over the deck, which generates some airspeed that would help the parachute canopy deploy.

The camera followed him as the seat went up. He separated from the seat. His chute popped off his back and began to stream out behind him. It was just starting to open when it snagged on the port deck edge. Out at the end of the shroud lines, Ed became the weight on the end of a fast-moving pendulum. He swung down out of sight below the flight deck and slammed into the ship's hull.

Sailors handlined Ed up by the shroud lines. Put him in a Stokes litter and hurried below to sick bay. He was dead. The impact with the ship's hull broke his neck.

If Ed had been a few feet farther left, his chute would have missed the deck edge, and would have at least partially opened in the sixty feet between the flight deck and the ocean, breaking his fall.

The carrier has a bridle arrester at the business end of each catapult. The bridle arrester is housed in a fifteen-foot ramp that extends out and down off the front edge of the flight deck. The F-8 has a long nose with the nose landing gear set way back under the cockpit.

When Ed's nose gear dropped off the flight deck, the chin mounted air intake fell onto the bridle arrester. The F-8 ground to a stop with its nose gear dangling in the gap between the bow and the bridle arrester.

The main landing gear stayed the flight deck. There it sat—with an empty cockpit. They got out Tilley, the crane, and lifted the aircraft back on deck.

Watching the video, I think, *He did what they told us to do—he ejected. But he died. If he hadn't ejected, he'd be alive.* Within a couple of weeks, I will have cause to regret this thought.

A Board of Inquiry is convened to discover the causes of the accident. The board found that the valve that releases the steam to propel the catapult shuttle had been reinstalled backward after routine maintenance during the in-port period. The valve is designed to release the steam over two seconds, so the aircraft accelerates down the full length of the catapult. Installed backward, the full force of the steam is released all at once. The difference is that between a hard shove and a kick.[18]

Our air wing does well through the end of November. Everyone is blowing and going—except me. I am still off the flight schedule except as a spare. Eventually someone's aircraft goes down for a maintenance gripe, and I am launched on a road recce. "Yeee Haa!" But after that, nothing.

Roger "Ramjet" Duter and Don "Inky" Purdy.

340

AN OFFICIAL NAVY MESSAGE arrives addressed to Ensign Don Purdy. Naval messages are for official business only. They are not normally sent to ensigns. The message reads something like,

```
Congratulations. You are the
father of a 6½ pound son. Mother
and figment are doing well.
```

We congratulate the King of Denial. Don tells us they will name him Eric. Duter instantly christens the baby "Little Orphan Eric." Don breaks out some cigars, and the ready room goes to instrument flight rules for low visibility due to smoke.

Meanwhile, my sit-down is not fun. I get tired of briefing, manning up, starting up, taxiing to the bow, shutting down, trudging back to the ready room, taking off my gear, and then doing it again for the next launch. I am also tired of being the SDO for twenty-four hours every third day or so. I am beginning to feel disconnected from the fight and my squadron brothers.

After yet another fruitless brief as the spare on an Alfa Strike, I decide to go into the air intelligence spaces and listen to the mission on their speaker. The AIs listen to the strike frequency, to help develop a chronology they use when they try to piece together the pilots' accounts. It won't put me back in the game, but it will keep me connected.

I am nervous sitting at the table listening to the scratchy gray speaker bolted to the overhead. I get more anxious when the strike group goes feet-dry.

The first flak call
the first warbler
a missile launch called
then another
"Magic One, BREAK NOW!"
I have to get out of here

I walk out. Sitting at a table listening, visualizing the mission live is more than I can take. I leave and never go back. Years later, I will learn that YDK also had to leave the room at least once. I feel a little better, especially when he tells me it was when someone mistakenly reported it was my aircraft that had been shot down.

Finally, on December 1, my time in limbo is over. Not only am I no longer ahead in the mission count, I am now behind. Fly two missions on the first and then two more on the second and third. I am back in the game and happy to find I haven't lost my edge.

We have a good run with no losses after Ed Van Orden's cold cat, but our run of luck ends five days into December.

Lt. H.G. Meadows of VF-111 is flying escort for a photo-reconnaissance aircraft when his F-8 is hit by automatic weapons fire. He loses one of his two hydraulic flight control systems. The leaking hydraulic fluid catches fire inside the fuselage. Not good. He stays with it and gets feet-wet. As he reaches the southern SAR destroyer, he loses his flight controls and ejects. If you have to get out, being over a SAR destroyer is not a bad place to pick. Meadows survives and is back on *Oriskany* within a couple of hours. Such things are now routine in my life.

"GROUND EFFECT" occurs when an airfoil such as a wing comes close (nominally within half a wingspan) to a fixed surface such as the ground, carrier deck, or surface of the sea. The "effect" is an increase in the lift generated by the wings. The physics are elegant, but the pilot experiences it as a cushioning effect. Light aircraft—think Piper Cub—may experience it as floating when landing.

I am scheduled for a daytime armed recce. I go through the well-worn rituals. I start the engine and go through the post-start checklist with the plane captain. Following his signals, we cycle the speed-brakes, leaving them closed, wipe the cockpit with the stick to make sure all the control surfaces are responding appropriately, run the flaps down and up and back down again to half flaps for the takeoff, cycle the tailhook down and up, etc. The plane captain pulls the landing gear pins and shows them to me. He gives me a thumbs-up and wishes me luck.

The yellow shirt puts me on the brakes and orders the blue shirt to unchain the bird. He brings me off the deck edge, turns me forward toward the cats, and passes me to his counterpart up the deck. I am shuffled off into the line for the port cat. When I am behind the JBD a guy from the catapult crew holds up a chalk board with the gross weight I wrote on the nose to make sure it is right before he passes it to the cat officer and those who dial in the steam for the cat shot. I look at him and give a thumbs up. The ordinance man pulls the bomb and rack pins and shows them to me. Thumbs up. Our squadron's checker is also there, scanning my aircraft. He gives me a thumbs-up as the blast deflector drops in front of me.

The nose tiller is in, and the last yellow shirt taxis me up and over the shuttle. "Stop." The hold-back fitting is put in. The yellow shirt gives me off the brakes. I drop my heels onto the deck and the bird rocks forward against the restraint like a car in park on a hill. The yellow shirt passes me to the cat officer. He sweeps his arm forward below the waist. The deck edge shooters bleed in a little steam, and the plane lurches, leaning forward, squatting down on the landing gear as the bridle is pulled taught. The cat officer gives me the overhead twirling signal (full power). Throttle against the stop. Friction lock tight. Fingers over the throttle and the holdfast bar. I watch the engine RPM build to 100 percent. The engine pressure ratio is good. Exhaust gas temp is normal. Oil and hydraulics are normal, the artificial horizon is set, the clips are on the radar-screen housing and shoulder harness locked.

I wipe the cockpit one more time
one last check of the cockpit gauges
back straight
head up
pressed against the seat
all good
all set
salute the cat officer
right elbow in my gut
hand open to catch the stick
eyes on the horizon

the cat officer touches the deck
WHOOSH
down the track
off the bow
rotate: six degrees nose up
horizon rising?
I'm sinking!
SHIT!
vertical speed indicator needle settles
it is below level
eyes on angle of attack indicator
pull nose up to V max—fuck, six degrees
Eject—Too late!
holding my breath
the aircraft starts wallowing
on the edge of a stall
she stops sinking
Ground effect!
big breath
still wallowing
Hold it still
Don't try to climb
You'll stall it
I hold it still

The airspeed begins to creep up
Wait . . .
finally, she starts to climb
Gingerly, I lower the nose a bit
to get off the razor's edge of a stall
Wait to pull up the gear
raising it momentarily increases the drag
Okay. Now—gear up
flaps up
nose up
a gentle roll right

I clear to starboard

What the hell was that?
Engine is good
cat shot felt normal

Damn that was close.

I don't know what happened
but the ground effect saved my young ass
That ain't much of a margin for a fully loaded A-4 off the cat

Should have ejected . . . Why didn't I?
Never mind.
Fly the mission.
Think about it later.

As I wait for signal Charlie after the mission, I realize that half the A-4's wingspan is thirteen feet. The drop tank and bombs hang three feet below the wing. That means the ground effect starts when there is only ten feet clearance above the water. *Holy shit!*

In the ready room, they tell me that, on the closed-circuit videotape, it is clear the flaps were only down about two inches. At half flaps, the trailing edges of the flaps are about seven inches below the wing.

"*I put the flaps down before I taxied. I know I did. . . . They must have bled up. . . . Why didn't the checker catch it as I went on the cat?*"

I am incensed, no—mad, no—angry about my near miss. I go find the checker.

"What the fuck were you doing! You nearly killed my sorry ass! Pay fucking attention!" I am loud and angry, and he can do nothing but take it. I am an officer and he is enlisted.

"Yes, sir. Sorry, sir."

"Sorry doesn't cut it."

I stomp off. Not one of my better moments.

I watch the video. The flaps are barely below the trailing edge of the wing. The plane goes down the cat and disappears below the deck. A pause, and I come back into view, wallowing along, so low that my exhaust leaves a rooster tail on the water. One of my buddies who was behind me in the line for the catapult says, "When you sank out of sight, I thought you were dead."

I didn't. I was too busy flying it to think about dying. That came later—when I was safe from that threat. Thank you, Major Cowboy, USMC at Barron Field. Your safety brief saved another pilot.

Later that evening, Doug Mow, our skipper, comes to me in the ready room. He takes me aside.

"They checked the flaps out. They stay where they are put. They do not bleed up. The cockpit indicator is accurate. It shows where the flaps are. You set the flaps there. If you had checked the indicator on the cat, you would have seen they were set less than a quarter down, not half down." The Skipper pauses to let this info sink in. Then he says, "The checker feels bad. He's a good man and takes his job seriously. He wants to be reassigned. He didn't deserve a chewing out, at least not from you. You should go apologize."

"Aye, aye, sir."

I find him and apologize.

Writing this a half century later, I still feel bad about what I did, and how I treated him. I *am* sorry. I nearly killed myself and was angry at me. I spilled my anger on you and should not have. Find me and I'll buy you dinner and a beer—maybe two.

By the next launch cycle, our checkers have a little stick about seven inches long. Their ritual now requires they physically put the stick in the gap between the flap and the wing's trailing edge.

I screwed up when I set the flaps. I screwed up again by not checking them on the cat. I also screwed up when I didn't immediately eject—but, why?

I don't know. I know the rule: If you don't climb off the cat—EJECT! NOW! Every time. No questions. No exceptions. I have practiced dropping my left hand onto the alternate ejection handle between my legs dozens of times. I have rehearsed doing it in my mind countless times—obviously not enough. Then I remember thinking after Ed Van Orden died: *He ejected and he died.* Maybe that is why I didn't eject when I still had time.

My three mistakes in a row are the closest I come to accidently killing myself—that I know of. Pure, dumb luck.

ON DECEMBER 12, I fly a flak suppression mission. I put six Mk 82s on a five-gun 57mm flak site. All five guns are within the fifty-foot kill radius of at least one of my five-hundred-pound bombs. The site goes quiet. I feel only elation. Bombing flak sites is a fair fight. I win this time. I respect the gunners' courage and skill but will never grieve their deaths.

THE F-8'S CHIN mounted intake is like the maw of a shark. It can suck a bucket full of water chained to the nose gear dry. The next day Aviation Machinist's Mate (Jet Engine Mechanic) Airman (ADJAN) Wayne Michalak of the VF-162 Hunters, a jet engine mechanic who works on their flight deck troubleshooting crew, gets a step too close. Wayne is bodily lifted of the ground and sucked down the intake in a flash.

His body wedges deep in the intake just short of the engine's compressor blades. I watch the video. The pilot shuts down the engine. It takes an engine seven or eight seconds to run down to zero, but a sailor immediately dives down the intake after Michalak. *A brave man.* A second sailor goes in up to his waist to grab the first sailor's ankles. Others on the deck pull the three men out like linked sausages. Michalak has *numerous* fractures and internal injuries that include two collapsed lungs.

The doctors work on him all through the rest of the day and all night while the carrier steams south to close on USS *Repose*, a navy hospital ship stationed off South Vietnam. I watch the helo take him south. I ask our haggard flight surgeon if he'll make it. He says "Maybe," but he shakes his head.

Wayne Michalak turned 22 on February 2, 1968. On February 4, 1968, he died.

CHUCK NELSON was a year ahead of me in the pipeline. He joined the squadron fresh out of the training command before the '66 cruise. He is a quiet man. A good pilot. Steady as a rock. He is what is known as a "Good stick" and hard to best in a mock dog fight.

Chuck flies with an expensive camera around his neck. The focus is set on infinity, so he can pick it up with one hand, point, and shoot. He misses some of the shots, but many are spectacular.

On December 14, we are tasked with a seed mission. A "seed" is a bomb, usually a Mk 82 fitted with a magnetic-mine fuse. The mine fuses are delicate, so the bomb must be delivered with snake-eye fins that open like speed-brakes to slow its fall. Snake eyes are designed for very low altitude deliveries. But low-altitude deliveries are too risky over defended targets. We deliver the seeds from our standard forty-five-degree dive, releasing them at five-thousand feet to keep us clear of small arms. With the snake eye fins open, the seeds fall slowly, drifting like milkweed seeds in the wind. They can generally be relied on to go anywhere but where they are aimed.

Chuck Nelson

We are going to plant our seeds in a waterway just south of Haiphong. Because the target is well within the Hanoi-Haiphong web of SAM sites, the Ghost Riders are scheduled to provide two Iron Hand birds in support of the strike group. Wuff flies one, Chuck Nelson the other.

The Sundowners of VF-111 will provide their fighter escorts. Dick Schaffert, a good man to have your back in a fight, is Chuck's escort. Chuck and Schaffert are on the extreme left of the main body of the strike group. Wuff and his escort are on the right flank. The strike group itself is protected from MiGs by a TARCAP of two F-8s.

Chuck and Wuff carry a Shrike on each of their outboard wing-stations and two Mk 82 bombs on both the inboard wing-stations. They also have our paltry forty rounds of ammo for each of the two 20mm cannons, which fire a thousand rounds a minute. That means the guns are empty after 2.4 seconds of firing.

As the strike approaches the target, Chuck and Wuff accelerate ahead of the strike group to engage any missile sites that light up their guidance radars. Chuck and his escort are at eighteen-thousand feet when Red Crown reports four MiGs airborne out of Phuc Yen— headed their way. Because they are approaching the target from the south, Chuck's section is between the strike group and the MiGs coming down from the northwest. Chuck and Schaffert are vectored to intercept the MiGs. Chuck passes the lead of his section to Schaffert.

They spot two Bandits. Both MiG-17 Frescos, an afterburner-equipped version of the MiG-15 of the Korean War. Every aircraft design is the result of a myriad of compromises that result in relative strengths and weaknesses. The MiG-17 can turn tighter than the A-4 at almost all speeds and altitudes. Because the MiG-17 has an afterburner, which is like a car's turbocharger on steroids, it has a higher top speed, can accelerate more quickly, and has a higher rate of climb than the A-4. Against our two 20mm cannons, the MiG-17s are armed with Atoll heat-seeking air-to-air missiles, a credible Soviet copy of the Side-winders carried by our F-8s, a 37mm cannon, and two 23mm cannons, all with ample ammunition. Although the MiG 17's cannons have slower rates of fire than our 20mm guns, they pack a heavier punch. The A-4 is rugged, but even a single hit by a 37mm shell is likely to bring it down.

The only tactical advantages the A-4 has over the MiG-17 are its higher roll rate and the fact that the MiG-17 does not have hydraulically boosted flight controls. Because of this, it is very difficult to physically move the MiG-17 control stick at low altitudes and high speeds. American pilots who fly MiG-17s "donated" by defecting pilots report they have to put their feet on the dashboard and use both hands to pull out of high-speed dives at low altitudes. In short, although capable of turning at higher Gs and therefore in a tighter circle than the A-4, the MiG pilot cannot apply the Gs as quickly an A-4—if we can force the MiG to fight at low altitudes and speeds above 300 kts.

The cannons of fighter and attack aircraft fire straight ahead from fixed mounts in the nose or wings. You aim the guns by aiming the airplane. Therefore, each pilot in a fight wants to maneuver behind his opponent where he can bring his guns to bear on the enemy and where the enemy cannot shoot at him. When two aircraft are trying to get behind each other, the one with the tightest turn radius has the advantage. But, high-G turns increase drag dramatically and will quickly slow an A-4 below three-hundred knots. To maintain speed, we have to constantly resist the effort to turn as tightly as we can to stay out from in front of the attacking MiG. We have to be patient and rely on our faster roll rate and hydraulic flight controls to make faster reversals as we pass head on in a scissors to gain the advantage.

Another advantage the MiG-17 has in a dogfight with an A-4 is its lead-computing gunsight, which automatically calculates the lead necessary to hit the target. The A-4s are equipped with a bombsight good enough for strafing attacks against a fixed target on the ground. But, lacking a lead-computing gunsight, when trying to hit a maneuvering aircraft the A-4 pilot has to aim by guess and by golly.

The F-8 Crusader is a different story. It is armed with a pair of Sidewinder air-to-air missiles and four 20mm cannons, each having two-hundred rounds of ammunition. It is equipped with a lead-computing gunsight, has an afterburner, and hydraulic flight controls.

The F-8 is superior to the MiG-17 in all but turn radius at some speeds and altitudes.

Whatever you are flying, the trick in aerial combat is to force the enemy pilot into a fight that pits his aircraft's weaknesses against the strengths of your aircraft while avoiding the opposite. This is easier to say than to do on the fly in three dimensions when your life hangs in the balance.

A DOG FIGHT pitting a F-8 and A-4 against a pair of MiG-17s might be seen as something approximating an even match, but Chuck cannot possibly stay with Schaffert when he maneuvers his F-8 at the edges of its performance envelope. Whatever the odds, Chuck and Dick Schaffert engage the two MiGs. Moments later, the odds are tipped heavily against them when a second pair of MiG-17s join the fight. It is now four against two, and one of the two, Chuck, is at a distinct disadvantage.

Chuck says, 'The fight quickly becomes a confusing melee. My F-8 fires his Sidewinder missiles and misses. The MiGs fire their Atolls and miss. I lose sight of Dick."[19]

The MiG pilots understand the equation of comparative strengths and weaknesses among their MiGs, Schaffert's F-8, and Chuck's A-4. Three of the MiGs engage Schaffert, leaving the fourth to gobble up the A-4. Single-handed against three enemy fighters, Dick Schaffert has given the MiGs more than they can handle.

Chuck says, 'Three of the MiGs break away and dive away from me toward their airfield. If only I had a Sidewinder."

Schaffert tells Chuck he is low on fuel and must head for a tanker. Chuck has gas and stays.

"But the fight isn't over." Chuck continues, "I am able to locate the fourth MiG, and we start a good old-fashioned dogfight. We start at eighteen-thousand feet and are soon down to around a thousand feet. I have forty rounds of 20mm in my strafing guns. I fire and miss.

I occurs to me that I still carry a Shrike, which (lacking a lock on a transmitting radar) will behave like a rocket and fly straight. If I am lucky, I can hit the MiG with it. By that time, I have gained the 'advantage'—in other words, I am now behind and above the MiG and know that he is not be able to shoot me down."

The MiG-17 passing underneath Chuck in a head-on pass.

What Chuck doesn't say in his account is that the fight starts with a series of head-on passes known as a "scissors" maneuver in which both pilots try to gain an advantage. We know this because Chuck is taking pictures *"to show that I really did see a MiG!"* He takes several photos as he and the MiG pass each other head-on.

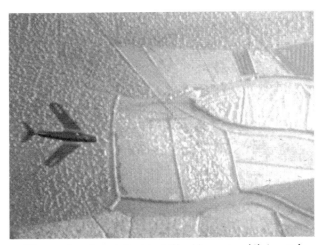

Picture taken through the top of Chuck's canopy while inverted.

Notwithstanding the MiG's superior dogfighting capabilities, by using his skills to exploit the A-4's superior roll rate and ability to quickly put G-forces into a turn, Chuck forces the fight down to low altitudes. He resists the temptation to apply heavy G's and is able to keep the speeds up where the MiG pilot is wrestling with a stick that feels like it is mounted in setting concrete. But, even after Chuck gains the advantage, the MiG pilot stays in the fight.

Chuck continues to snap pictures of the MiG trying to kill him. In one pass, the MiG flies directly underneath Chuck going the opposite direction. Chuck rolls inverted and snaps a picture through the top of his canopy looking down on the MiG. The MiG pilot is looking up at Chuck. You have to wonder what the MiG pilot is thinking while this is going on.[20]

Each time I pull in behind, he turns hard." Chuck says, "He does not know that I have no ammunition left. I start a short count on the radio so that other F-8s in the area can home in on my radio and join the fight. 'This is Magic Stone 410—1–2–3–4–5—5–4–3–2–1—just to the South of the Hourglass rivers at five thousand feet.' Then, maybe thirty seconds or so later, I repeat the call. Our radios have ADF (automatic direction finding), and a needle on the F-8's electronic compass will point in the direction of [my] radio signal.

"Another section of F-8s calls that they have us in sight. I respond that I am pulling off, up, and away so that I will not get shot down by my own shipmates. The first F-8 in fires a Sidewinder. It misses.

"The F-8 is closing so fast on the MiG that he overshoots and flies past it. With the F-8 in front of the MiG, it is impossible for the F-8 to shoot another missile or engage the MiG with his four 20mm cannon. Worse, it exposes the F-8 to the MiG. The MiG pilot pulls up and fires his cannons at the F-8 but also misses."

"Another F-8 (flown by Lt. Richard Wyman) rolls in, fires a sidewinder. . . ."

Chuck's last picture tells the end of the story.

The first Sidewinder's smoke trail crosses at the bottom of the photo. Wyman's Sidewinder enters from the bottom right and ends with its detonation hitting the MiG. Just beyond the detonation is the cloud of smoke marking the MiG's impact on a rice paddy. The MiG pilot did not eject.

As cool as Chuck is throughout the engagement, he is clearly wound up tight.

"[A]fter the shoot-down, while I was headed back feet-wet, I tried to drop a five-hundred-pound bomb on a bridge. When I hit the bomb pickle—SWOOSH—off goes the Shrike! In the heat of the action, I forgot that the Shrike is fired by the bomb pickle and not the trigger that is used for the cannon and rockets.

"The whole fight lasts quite a long time, possibly fifteen or twenty minutes. I would think it is one of the longest dogfights of the war. Adrenaline plus!"

AFTER THIS, the MiGs go back to pretty much ignoring us in favor of trying their luck against the Air Force strikes—or at least strikes not escorted by F-8s. However, a senior pilot from one of the F-8 squadrons comes back from one mission excited because he got a shot off at a MiG-21 with a Sidewinder. He missed but is still pumped.

His target was not a MiG-21, it was an A-4 flown by C-10.

C-10 was furious.

He is still hot when he lands and gets back to the ready room. He tells his story before heading to AI for the debrief. Cmdr. Bob Arnold, our ops officer, says he will go with C-10 to the debrief. In the AI spaces, the shooter is telling his story.

C-10 interrupts, "No MiG, just me."

Things become incandescent. C-10 is considerably outranked by the would-be MiG killer but is becoming less deferential by the second. Bob puts his arm around C-10 and steers him out of the room.

THE WING SHAPES of an A-4 and a MiG-21 are similar. I have no doubt the F-8 pilot thought he saw and shot at a MiG. But I have lived in Maine.

Every fall, a deer hunter or two will shoot at a deer that turns out to be a cow, dog, other hunter, or someone silly enough to walk in the woods during deer season, all of which look less like a deer than an A-4 looks like a MiG-21. Also, it seems to me that the target who has a Sidewinder streak past his cockpit is less likely to be mistaken about being shot at than the shooter is to be mistaken about the target. However, to this day neither party has changed his story.

On December 16, 1967, the fourth line period is over.

CHAPTER 23

R&R

Hong Kong, circa *1967. Kowloon is on far side of the harbor.*

WE LEAVE the line for a double in-port period. The first stop is Cubi Point, for the normal resupply and maintenance. The second is Hong Kong for our R&R (rest and recuperation) break. We arrive at Cubi Point on December 18 for a five-day stay.

There is an informal officers' bar perched on the ridge overlooking the Cubi airfield. During happy hour every night, they offer the special of the day at ten cents each. Even the most impecunious of pilots can get well and truly drunk for less than a dollar, and we often start our festivities at the bar. On one of those nights, the drink du jour is the stinger, an awful concoction of crème de menthe, orange bitters, and cognac.

A pilot who has just flown in from Yankee Station walks in still dressed in flight gear. He shoulders his way to the rail holding a $10 bill aloft. He slams the tenner on the bar top, shouting, "Innkeeper! One hundred stingers for my friends!" A grand gesture. My kind of man.

On another vaguely memorable evening, we have a squadron party at the Subic Bay Officers' Club. Subic is the surface navy side of the base, and its club is more formal than that at Cubi. It is the last night of the in-port period. The ship will depart Cubi for Hong Kong mid-morning the next day.

About 2:00 or 3:00 a.m., we reluctantly agree to leave the club. We call for a bus to transport us to the ship. We are ushered outside to wait at the curb. Finally, a bus comes. The driver parks it, gets out, and disappears through the doors of the now closed O Club. We all get on, but the driver does not reappear. Our ops officer, Bob Arnold, says, "I can drive this damn bus." He climbs in the driver's seat, fiddles under the dash, magically starts the engine, and we are off.

About halfway to the carrier pier, we are intercepted by the shore patrol, the navy's version of the military police. Bob Arnold is drunk but not stupid. He opens the passenger door and abandons the driver's seat to become a passenger sitting inconspicuously among his fellow Ghost Riders. The shore patrol boards the bus demanding to know who was driving.

Bob's voice is heard, "Boomy Spuddivecki."

"Where is he?"

A chorus of helpful voices: "We don't know." "He left." "He ran into the jungle."

The bus driver is produced, and we head for carrier pier followed by the Shore Patrol. When we pull up on the quay, the shore patrol stands at the front door of the bus taking everybody's name as they get off. A quick-thinking Navy combat pilot leads a group in the back of the bus out the emergency-exit door, where they scamper as best their alcohol-impaired legs will allow around the other side of the bus and up the gangway to the ship's quarterdeck.

The next day, the Shore Patrol's search for a pilot named "Spuddivecki" proves fruitless. The admiral of our carrier group is contacted. He is not amused. The list of names taken by the Shore Patrol all happen to be Ghost Riders. Doug Mow, who was not present, takes the hit, but refuses to throw Bob under the navy bus. The matter is resolved with a profuse apology to the commanding officer of the Subic Bay Navy Base, including a sincere promise that it will not happen again.

When the dust settles, Bob Arnold confesses that Boomy Spuddivecki was his best friend growing up in Philadelphia. For his sins, Bob is affectionately known as "Boomy" from that day forward.

Boomy's leadership qualities and initiative will be recognized and rewarded. He goes on to command his own squadron and retires as a captain. The quick-thinking leader of the rear exit exodus goes on to make admiral. Doug Mow's career survives the hit. He goes on to command an air wing, leading the Navy air support during the raid on the Son Tay POW camp. He retires as a two-star admiral after thirty years of service.

WE HEAD for Hong Kong on December 21, 1967. About half of the pilots are allowed to fly ahead to meet their wives and girlfriends. Having told my wife not to come, I am one of those who stays aboard and rides the ship.

As we cross the South China Sea, we sail into the tail end of a typhoon. As the we approach the storm, every aircraft that will fit is moved into the hanger bay. Every tie-down chain on the ship is used hold the aircraft in place.

The seas grow quickly. Soon, we have sixty-foot swells throwing green water down the flight deck. The *O Boat* pitches and rolls like a drunken Brama bull. People walk down the passageways with arms out to either side to keep from being thrown against a bulkhead. We learn to stop and time our trips up and down ladders to the pitch and roll of the ship. On the closed-circuit television, we watch as our escorting destroyer turns intermittent submarine. Don Purdy has the SDO desk and creates an inclinometer to measure the ships angle of roll with thread and a paper clip on the light board. He draws an arc matching the swing of the paperclip. The bottom of the arc is labeled "0°." He puts tick marks on either side and labels them, "10°," "20°," and "Abandon ship!" After three days of trying to stay upright, we sail into Hong Kong harbor.

BECAUSE MY WIFE will not be coming, I volunteer for shore patrol duty on Christmas Day. Not as bad as you might think. My duty station is the lobby of the Hong Kong Hilton.

On Christmas morn, I am standing around in the lobby in my whites, wearing an "SP" armband. A young American about my age walks up. Turns out that he is the far-east representative for Levi Strauss out of San Francisco. He asks if I am from one of the ships in harbor. I admit to it. He wonders if it would be possible for him to provide a Christmas dinner for some sailors at the Hilton that afternoon.

"How many?"

"Could you get about thirty?"

"I could get thirty-five hundred."

He laughs. "Thirty will do."

He goes off to make the arrangements, then comes back and tells me when the hotel will be ready. It will be in a long banquet room off the lobby. I call Chief Mac.

About thirty minutes before the appointed time, thirty sailors arrive turned out in their inspection whites and best behavior. At the appointed time, the doors are opened. There is a long table draped in snow-white table linen, silver plate flatware, napkins, with a water and two wine glasses by each china plate. There are five-big roasted turkeys spread along its length. A sideboard is loaded with all the trimmings waiting for the eight servers who stand at attention before seating the guests. The room smells like home.

God bless Levi Strauss and its far-east Rep. I remember his name long enough to have the skipper and CAG write to Levi Strauss thanking them for his thoughtfulness.

Today, I wish I could remember his name. Thank you, whoever you are. You did a good thing.

We leave Hong Kong on December 30, 1967, for our fifth and last line period.

CHAPTER 24

DUTHIE'S CHOICE

Larry Duthie

*There are no extraordinary men . . . just extraordinary
circumstances that ordinary men are forced to deal with.*
—*Admiral William Halsey*

I WANT to tell you about something that will not happen until fifteen years after I am sent home from my war. By then, I will have become a lawyer and be representing an electric company in a lawsuit involving a steam plant that powers a large electric-generation station. The steam plant and generators were located in a small town in northern Arizona. The boiler is huge—eight or nine stories tall. Although coal-fired, the boiler uses fuel-oil to preheat the boiler and ignite the coal. The oil system is kept charged in case the coal fire goes out.

The steam plant operates 24/7. The night-operating crew is only a half-dozen men. All but one of the crew works in the control room. One man is out walking the sides of the boiler checking things that can't be monitored from the control room. On this winter night, the outside man is someone in his mid-thirties. He has a wife and a couple of kids. Just an ordinary guy doing his job.

A filter on the fuel-oil-feed line springs a leak high on the outside of the boiler. The oil pump kicks in to maintain the pressure. The leaking oil runs down the side of the boiler. Eventually, the oil fumes find an electrical arc in an automatic switch. *Whoosh*. The flames shoot up.

At that moment, the outside man is on about level six, halfway up on the far side of the boiler. He sees a glow reflected on a nearby building and realizes there is a fire on the other side of the boiler. He runs, boots clanging on the grating of the aluminum catwalk, toward the fire. As he rounds the curve of the boiler, he sees the entire side above and below him engulfed in flame.

He can smell the oil burning and knows there must be a leak somewhere above him. He also knows that if the fire heats the side of the boiler, softening its steel, the boiler will not be able to hold the pressure of the superheated steam and will explode, killing him, all the members of his crew in the control room, and maybe even some of those over on the electricity-generation side of the plant. Every one of them is a neighbor in the small town founded by Mormon pioneers. Most attend the same LDS Ward he does. He knows there is no hope of his putting the fire out, but he can get water on the boiler side to cool the metal. He drops the clipboard and runs to a fire hose hung on the walkway a few feet from the edge of the flames.

The hose is accordion folded into a storage rack. Every second counts, but he has the presence of mind to stop and pull the entire hose clear of the rack, flaking its entire length out on the catwalk before he charges it with water. If he doesn't do this, the water will swell the hose, wedging itself tight in the rack, choking off the flow like a kinked garden hose useless. It takes precious time when every second may be one too many, but it must be done. When he finishes laying out the hose, he takes the nozzle and pins it as tight as he can under an arm so he can use both hands to turn the wheel, charging the line. He takes the nozzle in both hands just as the surging water reaches it. Leaning forward against the thrust of the water, he staggers forward, playing the water stream on the side of the boiler. As he walks to the edge of the flames, he thinks:

The fire is too big. It's going to blow.

He doesn't drop the hose. He doesn't run for his life. He keeps walking forward, concentrating the water on the boiler side above him where the fire appears hottest. Drops of melting aluminum from the catwalks above him fall onto his helmet, shoulders, and arms, burning through his heavy jacket, searing his flesh. He takes another step— *BANG!* As he flies backward through the air he thinks—*I'm dead!*

He finds himself sitting on the deck, still clutching the hose, six feet from where he was. It wasn't the boiler. It was a pressurized air tank a few feet in front of him that got too hot. A small-scale example of what the boiler is going to do.

He gets up, takes a deep breath, and goes forward again, back toward the heart of the flames.

As I sit across the table from him while he tells me what happened, I think, *This is one of the bravest men I have ever met.*

Going into the fire the first time is an act of immense courage and selflessness. He goes in alone with the faint hope of saving his friends—knowing he will be the first to die. At best, he will die instantly in the explosion. At worst, he will be engulfed in fire and blown off the boiler to fall in flames six stories to the concrete below.

But, thinking it exploded. Thinking you are dead. Then getting up and going back into the fire a second time takes a kind of courage few are called on to find and fewer have. I wish I could tell you his name. It's gone, but the memory of him is not. He'll be retired now. A man living in a small town in northern Arizona, who on one cold night saved the lives of his coworkers and neighbors. I hope that his kids and grandchildren know.

I tell you this story because it is linked to something that happened near the end of our first cruise, but which I would only learn about in the next century.

WHEN LARRY DUTHIE and Dick Hartman were shot down in early July on day five of combat operations, Duthie ejected and was rescued, but his back was injured, and his knee destroyed in the process. Duthie was eventually flown to the States for treatment and rehabilitation.

During the next seven months of the cruise, he pushed through the long and physically painful rehabilitation. The months were also emotionally painful. Throughout the process, Duthie received letters from the squadron that kept him abreast of our losses. He was forced to be a spectator on the side lines. He knew that other air wings had begun to refer to us as the Bloody Sixteen.

During his long sojourn at Oak Knoll. Duthie was unable to ignore the young men that surrounded him at the rehab center. Many were young marines with catastrophic wounds—some with shattered psyches and souls.

Being a thinker is one of Duthie's curses. He thought about our losses, the mutilated young men he saw each day, and the war. Duthie read about Daniel Berrigan, a former Jesuit priest turned antiwar activist who poured blood on draft records, and about a young Quaker boy who set himself on fire and died a horrible and painful death to protest the war. However heartfelt, Duthie did not find these credible sources or persuasive arguments.

Then Duthie happened across the text of a speech at a small California college. The speaker was General David M. Shoup, USMC. David Shoup was awarded the Medal of Honor during World War II.

He went on to become Commandant of the U.S. Marine Corps and sit on the Joint Chiefs of Staff. General Shoup *was* a credible source. He argued the war was not worth the cost—in blood or treasure. Duthie found his arguments hard to ignore.

If Duthie wasn't convinced the war was fruitless and futile, he certainly had some unanswered questions. At the turn of the year, Duthie's rehab was about complete. The doctors said he will soon be medically fit to return to flight duty.

AGAINST THIS backdrop, something unusual happens during our fifth line period. In California, an officer arrives unheralded to talk to Larry Duthie. The officer is from BuPers (the navy's Bureau of Personnel, rhymes with "view-purrs") in Washington, DC. He asks Duthie what he would like as his next assignment. Not a choice JOs usually get to make.

The normal routine is for the junior officer to fill out a form known as the "dream sheet" and list their top-three choices for their next assignment, in order of preference. The form is sent off to their "detailer," an officer in BuPers charged with seeing that all the slots are filled with those best suited to do the jobs. The first criteria are, of course, the immediate needs of the Navy. After that it is who is most likely to do the best job based on training, experience, and past performance Finally, the preference lists on the officers' dream sheets are considered and, occasionally, among a pool of equals, who is most deserving. Sending someone across the country to ask a junior officer where he wants to go next is way out of the ordinary course of Navy business.

Duthie has already showed up for two cruises, all that any of us are asked to do. He survived the fire that ended his first cruise. On his second cruise, he was shot down, seriously injured, and rescued only by the grace of God, great good luck, and the incomparable heroism of two helicopter crews, all at the cost of another brave man's life. His flight leader was shot down, abandoned, and captured after the loss of a Big Mother and her entire crew.

Duthie has done his part and more.

Now he is well out of it—sitting in a hospital room in Oakland. He is acutely aware of *Oriskany's* continuing losses. He is not twenty feet from the fire and a long way from safety. He is the most part of eight-thousand miles away from his danger. Duthie is safe as houses. And he is being offered a lot of safe choices, including many that will let him fly the airplanes he loves.

Duthie chooses to go back into the fire a third time. He tells the detailer he wants to rejoin our squadron and once again try to fly a complete combat cruise.

CHAPTER 25

HAPPY NEW YEAR

USS Oriskany *launching aircraft on Yankee Station.*

THE NEW YEAR and our fifth line period arrive with a splash. S-10, who shares the other end of our stateroom with C-10, is quieter than some, certainly quieter than C-10, but he is always there when you need him. Physically slight, he is quick and up to anything asked of him.

George "S-10" Schindelar

S-10 celebrates New Year's Day 1968 by flying a night armed recce in the panhandle just above the DMZ. For no apparent reason, he has a complete electrical failure and his ailerons jam. Because the flight controls are hydraulic and manual, not electric, it is hard to think of how this could happen without the intervention of enemy fire, but, if S-10 was hit, he failed to notice.

The ailerons control roll. With no aileron control, you can only change direction by skidding the nose to one side or the other with the rudder. Eventually, the aircraft will follow its nose. However, steering with the rudder can cause a spin at landing speeds

S-10 is flying above a low overcast when whatever happened to his aircraft happened. He skids the nose around to the east and heads toward the water. Once he is feet-wet, S-10 decides to eject rather than attempt a landing with no ailerons. He gingerly lowers himself below the overcast and sets off to find the southern SAR destroyer.

When S-10 sees the destroyer under the overcast, he notices they have already launched its helo. As he reaches the ship, he pulls up into the overcast, to put some more airspace under him in case something malfunctions with the seat or parachute. He slows to a crawl, pulls the throttle to idle, and ejects. The seat works as advertised. So does the chute. S-10 finds himself safely dangling under the canopy in the clouds. So far, so good.

Then, in the sudden silence under the parachute canopy, S-10 hears a helicopter. Close. Below him. He looks down as he emerges from the cloud base. He is descending directly onto the blades of the hovering helo. *Oh, shit.* He is about to be sliced and diced by a flying Vegematic.

S-10 scrambles to get his survival radio out to tell the helo to shear off. Someone on the ship beats him to it. The helo skitters off to the side. Seconds later, S-10 goes for a New Year's Day swim, becoming the first Ghost Rider to join the Tonkin Gulf Polar Bear Club.

The pickup is routine. Instead of taking him to the SAR destroyer, they fly him directly to a navy hospital ship stationed off Danang. The hospital ship is like a slice of home, complete with medicinal brandy and women nurses. I am glad he survives. S-10 is one of those I bonded with before Dick Perry was killed. His death would have hurt.

S-10 will survive our second cruise—but will die too young in 2011.

With S-10's swim in the gulf, the original inhabitants of our four-man stateroom have racked up four ejections. Barry Wood and S-10 have one each, and C-10 has two. I am the only one of the four who never uses a parachute except as a backrest. Initially, I am smug about my Irish luck. Then, I begin to feel like I am the only guy not invited to the high school party, or that maybe I am not carrying my share of the load. I can remember thinking, *It's not that I didn't try. I did my best to join the group by flying into the beam spray of a missile and taking off with quarter flaps.* When I remember that C-10 makes up for my lack of participation by ejecting twice, I feel a little better, but still like the odd man out. Looking back, I wonder how all of this seemed to make perfect sense in 1968.

THE NEXT DAY, Lt.j.g. Craig Taylor of VF-111 dances with Brother Death. He is the fighter escort for an unarmed photo-reconnaissance RF-8. He has a partial engine failure and a total electrical failure. The remaining thrust from the engine is not enough to sustain level flight. Craig puts the bird in a powered glide toward the water, crossing feet-wet at about twelve-hundred feet. About seven miles out to sea, he runs out of altitude and airspeed, ejects, and is recovered. I barely notice.

Two days later, the bell tolls again. Rich Minnich of VF-162 is flying TARCAP protecting a strike against a railroad bridge about ten miles north of Haiphong. He is hit by a SAM. His F-8 catches fire, pitches nose down, and enters a flat spin. No one sees Rich eject. There is no call on the survival radio. We assume he is killed by the SAM warhead, but no one saw him in the cockpit on impact, and so he is listed as MIA. I know Rich, but I walk past his death without a pause. Stuffing the loss away with all the others as I go.

His remains will be returned to the United States on December 4, 1985.

On January 5, I launch a Shrike at an active site and follow it in to use my bombs. My F-8 escort and I have three SAMs shot at us by other sites as we follow the Shrike in. We dodge the incoming missiles and find the original site. I give them four Mk 82s, just to remind them they aren't duck hunting. I damage the site but miss the trailer.

Late that afternoon, Skip Foulks, the JO in VA-163 who had been shot down and rescued in October, despite his premonition he would not survive the cruise, is flying a road recce. He and his leader find and attack some trucks. The leader is in first, but when he pulls off his run, he can't see Skip. He calls on the radio. No answer. Unlike C-10 on day one, Skip does not show up in *Oriskany's* landing pattern—or anywhere else. There is no emergency beeper, even after he would have run out of fuel.

I notice Skip's death, remembering his smile—but only for a moment. I refuse to hurt.

Skip's remains are repatriated in December 1988.

Decades later, I will think about his loss and wonder whether I made myself into a sociopath or was a sociopath from the get-go. I am told by a competent professional that neither is true, but . . . .

I AM BUSY not thinking about the end of our last line period. Thinking about home will get me killed. I stay in my bubble.

One morning, Skipper Mow tells me I will become the squadron schedules officer when we get back to the States. It is an important job, and I am flattered. I am being told now so I can write the training schedule for the four-month workup period to prepare for the next cruise. The skipper, the XO (the presumptive next CO), and the ops officer all want to review the plan when I have a draft.

There is a problem, now all my spare time must be devoted to thinking about what we will do when the cruise is over. I worry about my bubble. I decide to see the job as a puzzle or game with no connection to any reality I will experience.

I get to work on it, but a four-month schedule that will meet all the Navy's requirements, our needs, and get us through the inspections and exercises at dates not yet set, is like trying to organize a bowl of spaghetti. Too many variables and far too many unknowns. In January 1968, we have no desktop computers, no word processors, no automated spreadsheets, no scheduling software, no internet. We are at sea on the far side of a very big ocean, which means no telephone. Mail has to get off the ship and then across the Pacific to the Fleet Post Office in San Francisco, then to the addressee—and back again—to answer the simplest question.

Finally, I face the fact that I cannot get it done before we leave the ship to fly back to the States and the start of our thirty-day post-combat leave. "Post-combat leave?" my soap bubble winks out of existence. *Arghh!* The schedule must be in place on the day the leave period ends. If I can't finish it by the time we get back to Lemoore, the only time left is the leave period. So . . . I write my wife and family, telling them we will have to cancel the leave plans. I go to find Doug Mow.

When I find him, I say, "Skipper, I won't have the schedule done by the time we get back to the States, but I'll stay at the squadron, and it will be ready when everyone comes off their combat leave."

Doug looks at me for a moment, "Mike, the Navy doesn't treat you like you are indispensable and, Lord knows, it doesn't pay you like you are indispensable. So why do you think you are indispensable? The Navy got along for almost two-hundred years without you. If, God forbid, you are killed this afternoon, the Navy will sail on with barely a ripple. . . . Now, how much will you be able to get done before we get to Japan?"

"A couple of days. Maybe a week, sir."

"Good. Go on leave. When you get back, you can write the next week's schedule while we are flying the first week."

"Aye, aye, sir."

Doug's point goes home. Not only do I not much care if I die, but no one else will much notice either. The Navy's structure, traditions, and culture are all built to absorb losses without a pause in its day-to-day operations. The living step up, fill in the gap, and press on. My death will be like pulling your hand out of bucket of water—a small ripple, but no hole. During the years ahead, Doug's reminder that I am not indispensable will help me stay grounded.

I go back to my stateroom to write letters telling my wife and family, "Forget my last letter."

JANUARY 11, 1968 is the last day of combat operations for *Oriskany* on this cruise. Twelve more hours of flight ops, and we are done for five months. I am on the flight schedule for an armed recce. It will be my 114th combat mission. I spend the whole morning repeating my mantra,

Don't let down. There is no tomorrow.

My log tells me I fly a CCA instrument approach, even though it is a day hop, so I know the weather was bad. Other than that, I remember nothing about the mission.

Done!

A-4 on a wave off (landing gear, flaps, and hook down; speed-brakes closed).

Back aboard, I am safe for five months. Five months is an eternity.

Meanwhile, my squadron brothers are finishing the rest of the flight schedule. Deny Weichman launches on an armed recce well out of the high-threat area. Tom Lamay, a seasoned veteran and our rock-steady LSO, is flying his wing instead of C-10. They are both flying the last combat mission of their second cruise. Both will be combat-limited and assigned shore duty on our return. This will be Wuff's 400th combat mission. Four hundred missions! I have flown barely a quarter of that number and think I have climbed Everest. Wuff is amazing.

As always, Wuff presses his bomb runs lower than most for better accuracy. Low threat or no, Wuff is hit by small arms fire. The bird is hurt bad, and Wuff is a long way from the water. He turns east toward the gulf, nursing the aircraft as gently as he can. Before he reaches the beach, his aircraft catches fire. Lamay calls for Wuff to eject—but Wuff stays with it.

As Lamay watches, Wuff's aircraft begins a long slow barrel roll, a climbing, rolling turn of ninety degrees to an inverted position flying south then continues the roll into a descending turn of another ninety degrees back to right side up on the original heading. The flight controls are gone. Both hydraulic systems and the backup cables have burned through. Wuff has no control of the aircraft. He is a passenger in a single-seat airplane.

The aircraft completes the barrel roll, ending up pointed back at the water and starts another barrel roll. To Wuff, the important fact is that, burning or not, uncontrollable or not, one more barrel roll will get him past the water's edge. He stays put. At the end of the second barrel roll, he is feet-wet. Time to get out.

I never talk to Wuff about it, but he must have had his doubts about ejecting. At six feet, six inches, Wuff is the tallest pilot on the ship. He is also taller than the ejection seat's design limits. The story is when Wuff first tried to get in the flight program, he flunked the physical. Too tall. He finagled a second test a week or so later. In the interim, he carried around heavy bags of sand or cement to compress his spine. It worked; he just squeezed under the maximum height limit.

It is always amazing to watch Wuff fold and unfold himself in and out of the A-4's little cockpit, a slow process both ways. But the ejection seat leaves no time for unfolding. Wuff's leg is broken when it does not clear the instrument panel as the seat rockets out of the cockpit. The impact doesn't slow the seat, and everything else works as advertised. Broken leg or no, Deny is in the water.

Enemy boats began to gather but were held at bay by Tom Lamay and others who arrived to support the SAR until a helo got to him.

Wuff had another reason for not ejecting sooner. After he was recovered, he told Tom Lamay, "I wasn't going to eject over land. They know me down there."

The amazing thing is that I will forget all of this. Totally forget—until YDK mentions it fifty-one years later while we are discussing a draft of this book. I am astounded. I think about it for days and finally convince myself that I do remember—vaguely—a little bit.

Eventually, I realize that my lack of memory is the final proof that I had succeeded in becoming a warrior. Why should I remember? First, we got him back. Second, there was no lesson for me to learn—he had the bad luck to occupy the same space at the same time as several rounds of heavy machine gun bullets. Third, although he broke his leg because he is too tall for the damn cockpit, that is not a problem I have. Fourth, he will leave the squadron when we get back stateside, but I have another cruise to go. My bubble and I move on. None of us, not even Wuff, are indispensable.

Deny Weichman may have drifted out of my bubble, but he was not done serving—nor done with combat. Four years later, the combat limitation policy of "two and done" will, of necessity, have been dropped. Wuff returned to combat in 1972 as executive officer of VA-153, the Blue Tail Flies, flying the A-7B Corsair II, the replacement for the A-4. In February 1973 Wuff flew his 625th combat mission over Laos,[21] the most of any Navy pilot during the Vietnam War. Through it all he stays sane and never loses his sense of play. He is the quintessential combat pilot. I can think of no higher praise. C-10 and Wuff remained friends and stayed in contact through the decades.

Eventually, brother Death ambushes Wuff. He died on his birthday in 1995 at the age of sixty. When C-10 tells me Wuff is gone I want to weep. But cannot.

We had been on the line for 122 days, the Air wing flew over 9,500 missions, including 181 Alfa strikes, most into the Hanoi-Haiphong defense complex. A third of our pilots were casualties, and we lost more than half our aircraft. God only knows what the next cruise will be like.[22]

AS WE TURN SOUTH and sail away from the line, I tell myself, *When I get back home, I cannot let down. I need to keep my edge.* I still have another cruise to go.

But for now, we are headed home. I am a month away from my twenty-fifth birthday. I feel like I am seventy-five. I have outlived my life expectancy.

Part VI

ENDGAME

USS Oriskany sails home under the Golden Gate Bridge
after the 1967–68 cruise.

CHAPTER 26

ESTRANGEMENT

Oriskany ghosting under a broken cloud deck

(Looking in) the mirror. I feel as if I am looking at a dead
friend, hoping he will come alive.
—John Le Carré

WHEN WE RECOVER the last aircraft from the final launch of the cruise we leave the Tonkin Gulf. That night we hang the "Secret Briefing – No Entry" signs on the ready room doors and have a medicinal brandy party.

We sail to Cubi Point for a brief in-port period. The combat aircrew disembark. When the ship sails, we are flown up to Japan. There, we wait for the ship to cross the mid-Pacific chop line and then board a chartered Continental Airline's 707 that will get us home a week before the ship sails under the Golden Gate Bridge.

IT IS WINTER in Japan, an upper-Midwest kind of winter. I get sick. Then sicker. I will not go to the hospital for fear they will admit me, and I'll miss the flight back to the States. By the time I board the airliner that will take us home, I am sicker than I have ever been. I am spiking a fever and nodding in and out through the long flight over the pole to Travis AFB in northern California.

When we arrive on the far side of the Pacific, word comes back from the cockpit, "Travis is fogged in." We suggest landing at NAS Lemoore. Nope. It, too, is fogged in. We stooge around in a holding pattern waiting for something to open up, but we don't have that much fuel to spare before we will have to divert to Portland, Oregon. At the last minute, we manage to sneak into Oakland. We land about 10:00 p.m. California time. No one is expecting us. After an hour or so, a Greyhound bus arrives. The only available driver has just arrived in Oakland from somewhere else and is looking forward to a good night's sleep. Needs as must. Off he and we go.

The fog clears a little as we climb the coastal range, but, as we descend into the San Joaquin Valley on the other side, we dive back into pea soup. The going is slow. The driver is nodding off.

He says, "I can't do it. I have to stop."

"Nonsense."

The heavies sitting in the front row tell him to keep going.

"We'll keep you awake."

They talk, cajole, threaten, encourage, poke, and prod. Several hours later, he says we are coming up on a scheduled rest stop. He has to piss and needs more coffee. His thermos is empty. We stop. He goes to a pay phone. Comes back and says another driver is on the way. He refuses to get back on the bus.

This is not the first time the Ghost Riders have been short a bus driver. However, we promised never again. We wait. Somewhere in fog-shrouded California, we sit in a diner, watching the fog and waiting for what seems like hours, in the middle of a night I think will never end. Eventually, a relief driver arrives. We board the bus and disappear into the fog.

Sometime about 10:00 a.m., we roll up on the main gate at NAS Lemoore. A young Marine sentry comes on board and tells the driver to pull over and park on the side. He has orders to hold the bus until "they" can muster the band, platform party, and press for the homecoming ceremony.

Magnolia, the Saints' skipper, is sitting behind the driver. He asks the Marine in his best Alabama drawl,

"Son, is your side arm loaded?"

"Yes, sir."

"Good, because the only way you are going to stop this bus is to shoot me as I drive it through your goddamned gate."

Our relief Greyhound driver shows signs of distress. We are wearing civilian clothes, but the young Marine knows the voice of command when he hears it. The sentry steps down off the bus and waves it, and the crazy Navy officer, through his gate with a smart salute. As we drive past, he is in the guard shack on the telephone.

Magnolia directs the bus driver to the flight line at the airfield. We begin to straggle off the bus. It doesn't take long for the word to spread across the wives' network. Within minutes they begin to speed up in their cars, many with children in tow. I stagger off the bus and stand in the thinning crowd. I see my wife arrive and hurry across the tarmac carrying my daughter as she scans the crowd. I stand there and watch as she walks right past me, still looking. Apparently, I have changed a bit. I turn and call her back.

The next morning, every breath hurts so bad that I tell my wife I have to see a doctor. I drive to the base hallucinating from a fever.

Driving is a mistake. I should just pull over and hope someone stops.

383

But I keep going. I will fly it into the ground or whatever else gets in front of me.

The doctor is appalled. I have full-blown, bilateral pneumonia. He shoots me full of antibiotics. He says I will be hospitalized for several days until the antibiotics kick in. I resist. Being in the hospital here is not much better than being in the hospital there. I tell him I am *just* back off cruise and would rather sleep in my own bed. He thinks a moment and says:

"Okay, but you go home, get in bed, and stay in bed and get lots of sleep."

I assure him I am in no mood to do anything but sleep.

He loads me up with meds, tells me to "drink lots of liquids, but no alcohol, take the meds, and come back in three days."

I go home and get in bed, thinking: *This is as sick as I ever want to be.*

The antibiotics work.

MY DAUGHTER, wife and I go on our post-combat leave. We spend a week with my family then go to Indiana and spend two weeks with my wife's family. For me, it is a three-week out-of-body experience. I know I have to go back. I want, I need, to keep my combat edge. That means I keep everything and everybody at arm's length so I will not miss them when I go back.

I try to teach my daughter any life lessons a fifteen-month-old can learn while I can. It's only necessary that she understand what she should and should not do. She can figure out why later.

MY WIFE and I talk about who she might marry should I be killed. She talks about "if you don't come back," I talk about "when I am killed." But we are the same page. Turns out we had the same guy in mind. He was a neighbor who was a Naval Aviator in another air wing.

In 'Nam, guys referred to the States as the "real world." For me, the "real world" is no longer real. It is all illusion and delusion. Real is behind the curtain. Real is Yankee Station.

In addition to the exaggerated startle reflex, flashbacks, and nightmares, I am intolerant, impatient, and angry at odd moments. They seem to let up some when we return to Lemoore a week early so I can work on the training schedule and flight schedule. The next week, we start flying again. I get even better.

Chapter 27

Back In the Bubble

Back at it.

Ghost Rider A-4 off the starboard catapult of USS Hancock (CVA 19) in 1968. The catapult bridle has fallen free onto the bridle arrester. When we move from CVW-16 to CVW-21, our tail letters change from Alpha Hotel to November Pappa. The aircraft is on a flak suppression mission armed with six four-packs of Zuni high-velocity rockets.

WORD COMES down that the Ghost Riders and our sister squadron the Saints of VA-163 are being assigned to Carrier Air Wing 21. We will deploy aboard USS Hancock (CVA 19) for the next cruise. VA-152 will leave the air wing to transition from A-1s to A-4s. That leaves only one squadron, VA-25, still flying Spads. It too will lose its A-1s at the end of its current cruise in April 1969. *Sic transit gloria mundi (Thus passes worldly glory).*

VA-152's place in the air wing will be filled by a third A-4 squadron, the Warhorses of VA-55.

ON JULY 18, 1968, we depart the carrier pier at NAS Alameda. As I watch my wife walk away down the pier, I see her receding, disappearing into the past—outside my bubble.

We sail west under the Golden Gate again with one long blast on the ship's horn. It is different than the first time. I am different. I am not worried about my ability to handle what will come, nor am I excited. But am glad to be going back.

I am going home.

Roger "Ramjet" Duter
Entertaining the plane captain

UNLIKE our trip out on the first cruise, we are not allowed to fly after we leave Hawaii and head west. We are told that, because there

388

are no nearby airfields in case of a problem on the ship, "it is too dangerous." I don't know whether to laugh or cry.

Although it is not clear to me at the time, our political masters are looking for a way out that will save political face. For starters, they have us stop here and there on the way over. It takes over a month to get to Yankee Station. When we finally arrive, we have fewer Alfa Strikes against Hanoi and Haiphong. We do more armed recces.

Our political masters decide to reduce the heat in the hopes it will encourage the North Vietnamese, who are still sitting around a table in Paris, discussing a peace treaty. The result is that we are told to conduct combat operations for twelve out of every thirty-six hours, instead of twelve hours out of twenty-four. That means we fly midnight to noon, then noon to midnight: day after night, night after day. A biorhythm killer. After a few weeks of this the pilots, aircrews, and flight deck personnel are all zombies. Eventually Washington gets the message and we go back to twelve out of twenty-four.

Milestone flight
Mike "Willy" Williams (150th mission), Roger "Ramjet" Duter (200th mission), Mike "Mule" Mullane (200th mission), and Larry "C-10" Cunningham (200th mission).

Then Washington imposes a "bombing pause" above a geographic parallel, cutting us off from all the high-value (and highly dangerous) targets in the north; then, a bombing pause covering all of North Vietnam. We find ourselves over the jungles of Laos bombing the Ho Chi Minh Trail as it winds its way south under the jungle canopy. Roger Duter quips that the most lasting effect of these missions will be generations of neurotic, paranoid monkeys. The day will come when I wonder if monkeys get PTSD (post-traumatic stress disorder).

We will end up with only 107 days of combat for the cruise, against the 122 days on our first cruise.

I soon realize my death is possible, but no longer certain. I don't feel any sense of relief. Whether I live or die is no longer of much interest to me, nor am I going to be lured into thinking that it is.

If it can get better, it can get worse.

Plans A and B are still operative. Flying combat missions is still shooting dice with Death. The North Vietnamese are still doing their best to kill us whenever and wherever we show up, and we still damage and destroy things and people. Flying off and on the boat is still dangerous. We fly more night missions on the second cruise. Always a stress fest.

On October 12, 1968, the optical landing system goes down while I am flying a mission. I fly an OK-3 pass with only a little help from the LSO. A proud moment.

THE GHOST RIDERS lose Cmdr. Don Erwin, our new executive officer. He is hit by AAA. He is only a quarter of mile off the beach when he has to eject. The local coastal defenses can reach out to where he entered the water. They send out a small boat to try and snatch him up or kill him before we can get a helo to him. There is one man on a sculling oar in the stern. A second is lying prone with an AK-47 in the bow. He is shooting. I can't see what he is shooting at, but fire my last rocket at them and miss. Strafe and miss. They keep coming. Brave men.

I end up as his SAR commander. I see this as a chance to make up for not being there when Dick Perry ejected.

I find Don's parachute floating just under the surface like a gigantic jellyfish. They are holding the helo a couple of miles off shore until I can get eyes on Don. Minutes later, I see the glint of sun off reflective tape. It is his helmet.

I am elated. I report to Red Crown that I have him in sight and ask them to release the helo.

While the helo is inbound, I do a low pass. The helmet is empty, buoyed up by its foam liner. I report my mistake. They send in the helo anyway. It arrives and kills the two men in the small boat. I get some Spads and A-4s and have them work the tree line on the beach. Nevertheless, the helo soon has to abandon the search in the face of increasingly accurate fire from the beach. Don Erwin joins Dick Perry and Rich Woynarski in my survivor-guilt closet. It is only later that I am told Don was limp while descending in his parachute.

On the last day of the second cruise, I complete a full circle. I have the SDO desk. Lt.Cmdr. Roger Meyers, our maintenance officer, is on the last launch for a night armed recce. When the cat is fired, the nose gear on his A-4 collapses. It dives off the cat straight into the water. He does not survive. That morning, Roger had mentioned he was anxious to get home and meet the child he had never seen.

Brother Death is a heartless bastard.

The two men we lost were both good men and good officers. I regret both of their deaths, but do not grieve either of them—I don't do grief.

THE CRUISE ENDS. I don't want to leave the game. Flying combat is what I do. I am good at it. I am where I belong. Why replace me with a combat virgin? Nevertheless, my request to recycle for another combat cruise is denied. "Everyone gets two. No one gets three. We want to spread the combat experience as widely as possible for the next war."

I don't want to spend twenty years in the peace-time navy practicing for the next war. My contract is up in September. I am out, but have no idea what is next. My father the business executive writes, "Law school is better than an MBA." My father the plumber's son adds, "And you'll have a trade."

Okay. I can do with three years of quiet.

When the second cruise is over, I feel like I have outlived my purpose.

IN 1969, I returned to a country that has changed its mind. I come back thinking, *I am a combat veteran.* It won't be long before my countrymen teach me, I am a *Vietnam* veteran. Even those who do not think it right to hate us are embarrassed by our service. It is not something that should be discussed in polite company.

The discomfort and disconnection I experienced between the cruises is back in spades, plus some new tricks. Anger, lack of tolerance, isolation, nightmares, insomnia, hypervigilance, exaggerated startle reflex, constantly ambushed by unsuspected triggers, flashbacks, long bouts of depression, and a year-long flirtation with suicide—I have them all.

LOOKING BACK from the next century, the second cruise will seem like trying to avoid the hangover by taking a couple of stiff drinks the morning after. It only postpones and exacerbates the day of reckoning. But in 1969, I lack fifty years of hindsight.

My problems will go away. It will just take some time to readjust.

They don't.

A year later, I tell myself: *It's okay. It is who I am. I am just different. I am tough enough.*

I stuff them all in the emotional trunk. I am a combat-seasoned Naval Aviator. I have survived 212 combat missions. I am hard, resilient, disciplined, focused, and I don't quit.

Valedictory

I come back alive
euphoric I have survived

passed the test
I will live

There is nothing
I cannot face

nothing I cannot do
The world is mine

Ha! I have no idea.
I cannot imagine
that the days are coming
when my life will hang
by threads of love spun
by first one
and then a second
dog

not yet
born.

A DECADE will pass before the American Psychiatric Association will include post-traumatic stress disorder in the 1980 revision to the *Diagnostic and Statistical Manual of Mental Disorders*. The VA will then capitulate and recognize PTSD as a service-connected injury.

In the mid-1980s, the wheels are coming off my life. I see a private psychologist. She says, "You have PTSD." I pay cash and walk out.

I'm not signing up to be mentally ill.

I can hack it.

AFTERWORD

Squadron Requiem

Do not blame us.

Like our fathers before us,
we did not choose the war.
Nor did we choose how it would end.

We did not choose to live.
Nor did our brothers choose to die.
We chose only to keep faith
with each other.

If you ever knew us,
if ever you cared,

if ever you knew
a name on
the wall

We ask only that you remember,
some gave what they had,
and some still pay
to this day

for keeping you far
from the abyss

from that day
to this.

November 11, the date of the Armistice of the Great War, had become one of the few . . . occasions, when . . . faded medal ribbons, and thinning ranks of aging warriors were momentarily honored for what they had done in an increasingly dim past.

—*James L. Stokesbury*

Dear Reader,

Thank you for reading this book. I have another favor to ask of you. Please, read the following list of the Ghost Rider casualties during the three cruises between May 1966 and March 1969.

I do not ask that you remember their names or their individual stories. It is enough if you remember we were there. Remember we kept faith with one another. Remember that some of us died. Remember that strangers came to save us and that many died in the attempts. Remember that some of us were prisoners of a ruthless enemy for long years and that some died at their hands.

And, if you will, remember to look for those of us who survived, who still live, and struggle still with who and what we became. And, when you see us, old men brushing past you today on the fringe of the crowd, give a thought for what we cannot forget.

—Mule

Pencil rubbing of Dick Perry's name on the Wall. (Vietnam Memorial, Washington, D.C.)

1966 Cruise (May 26, 1966–November 16, 1966)

- Ens. George P McSwain, Montrose, CA: Prisoner of War July 26, 1966 (age 26) (repatriated March 4, 1973, after 2,411 days in captivity).
- Lt.j.g. Donavon L Ewoldt, MN: Died in operational accident July 29, 1966 (age 24).
- Lt.j.g. William H Bullard, Elsinore, CA: Killed in Action, August 25, 1966 (age 24).

- Lt. Frank C Elkins, Bladenboro, NC: Killed in Action, October 12, 1966 (age 27).
- Cmdr. Clyde R Welch, Sommerville, TX: Died in USS *Oriskany* fire, October 26, 1966 (age 38).
- Lt.Cmdr. Daniel L Strong, Big Bear City, CA: Died in USS *Oriskany* fire, October 26, 1966 (age 29).
- Lt.j.g. William A Johnson, Charlotte, NC: Died in USS *Oriskany* fire, October 26, 1966 (age 25).
- Lt.j.g. J L Brewer, Memphis, TN: Died in USS *Oriskany* fire, October 26, 1966 (age 24).

1967–1968 Cruise (June 16, 1967–Jan 31, 1968)

- Lt.Cmdr. Richard D Hartman, Clark, NJ: Shot down July 18, 1967; Taken prisoner July 22, 1967. Died while a POW (place and cause of death not disclosed) (age 32).
- Lt.j.g. Larry Duthie, El Paso, TX: Wounded in Action July 18, 1967 (age 24).
- AX2 David R Chatterton (Helicopter crew, HC-2 Det USS *Constellation*), Twin Falls, ID: Killed in Action July 18, 1967 during the first attempt to rescue Lt.j.g. Duthie (age 29).
- Ens Donald P Frye (Helicopter copilot, HC-2 Det, USS *Constellation*), Los Angeles, CA: Killed in Action July 19, 1967 during the second attempt to rescue Lt.Cmdr. Hartman (age 23).
- AX2 William B Jackson (Helicopter crew, HC-2 Det, USS *Constellation*), Stockdale, TX: Killed in Action July 19, 1967 during the second attempt to rescue Lt.Cmdr. Hartman (age 32).
- AX2 Donald P McGrane (Helicopter crew, HC-2 Det, USS *Constellation*), Waverly, IA: Killed in Action July 19, 1967 during the second attempt to rescue Lt.Cmdr. Hartman (age 24).
- Lt. Dennis W Peterson (Helicopter pilot, HC-2 Det, USS *Constellation*), Huntington Park, CA: Killed in Action July 19, 1967 during the second attempt to rescue Lt.Cmdr. Hartman (age 28).
- Lt.Cmdr. Richard C Perry, Carlin, NV: Killed in Action August 31, 1967 (age 35).
- Lt. David L Hodges, Chevy Chase, MD: Killed in Action October 7, 1969 (age 29).
- Lt.Cmdr. John F Barr, Hope, AR – Killed in Action October 18, 1967 (age 33).
- AMS3 Richard M Woynarski, Barker, NY: Died in operational accident (age 21).
- Lt.j.g. Fredric W Knapp, Huntington, NY: Killed in Action November 2, 1967 (age 24).

- Cmdr. Denis Weichman, Chattanooga, TN: Injured during ejection due to enemy action, January 11, 1968 (age 33).

1968–1969 CRUISE (JULY 18, 1968–MARCH 3, 1969)

- Cmdr. Donald E. Erwin, Hobart, IN: Killed in Action October 2, 1968 (age 39).
- Lt.Cmdr. Roger A Meyers, Chicago, IL: Died in operational accident February 8, 1968 (age 35).

ACKNOWLEDGMENTS

The days I keep my gratitude
greater than my expectations are really good days.
—Ray Wylie Hubbard

MY PARENTS are the source of my resilience and whatever good I have done. My mother filled my childhood with simple magics and the awe of the commonplace. It is from her that I got my love of dogs and reading and optimism—all the things that somehow carry me through the days and nights. In my fifties, she told me, "Michael, remember you are still a work in progress," which was and is a message of hope. Mom always said, "You have a book in you." I am only sorry she is not here to read it.

My father taught me duty, loyalty, service, and what it is to be a man and a naval officer—all by example. Wayne taught me to find solutions—not blame. He gave me my love of flying and of naval aviation. He was always there to help me find a way. He died too young.

They never abandoned me when I crashed my life into one wall after another.

MY SISTERS: Beth who made it her business to become my friend and anchor to windward, especially in these last difficult years;

Ginger who has never let her own pain stand in the way of helping others. Both read early drafts and were generous with their time and insights.

DOROTHY, MY AUNT and loving godmother, who has never let me forget it. She read a draft and, as always, gave me her honest, unvarnished opinions.

401

MY COUSINS. Jim Eckes and Suz Eckes-Wahl of Dos Eckes Productions, who helped us tell the story of *Lady Jessie*, Jessie Beck, and Dick Perry. In the process, I found the courage to remember and walk out of the shadows to tell their stories.

Mary Eckes, author and teacher, who also was good enough to read an early draft. She gave me thoughtful advice and encouragement. I shudder to think how difficult that read must have been.

ROSEMARY CULVER AND HUGH KELLEY who took me in as their client at the Vet Centers when I finally sought help. I never would have survived and kept on without them. They both encouraged me to remember and write.

I owe a similar and ongoing debt to the veterans of the groups that I have sheltered in over the last decade. They have my back and trust me with theirs. I can think of no higher compliment or tighter bond.

I found Rosemary, Hugh, and the groups in Vet Centers in Maine and Maryland. If you are a veteran who lives with the aftermath of combat or sexual trauma, I encourage you to find your local Vet Center. They exist to help you find an easier way to live in the world. Neither the DOD nor the rest of the VA will ever know you are there unless you tell them. Give it a try. You are always free to do an about-face and walk out.

If you are someone who loves a veteran struggling with the aftermath of combat or sexual trauma, encourage them to walk through the door of a Vet Center.

MY FELLOW GHOST RIDERS. There is no end to my love or the debts I owe them. My greatest boast is that they count me among them. They are the demi-gods of myth and legend that fill my life. I list them in alphabetical order.

Larry Cunningham, "C-10," with whom I bunked on both cruises. A man whose joy of life was undented by all we went through. I am especially indebted to him for allowing me to share his account of his first combat mission and his treasure-trove of stories and photographs.

John Davis, who joined the Ghost Riders as a must pump replacement during the 1965 cruise. He went back in 1966 and lived through the fire, and then flew the entire '67 cruise. He became a sturdy bridge between the heavies and the nugget JOs. John and I both knew and loved Dick Perry; we both found and find our own ways to cope with his loss.

Larry Duthie, a gentle soul with a warrior's heart, whose courage was exceptional even among those who stayed the course of our war. My life is enriched by the friendship he has extended over the ensuing decades. This book is immeasurably better than it would have been but for his efforts.

Leon "Bud" Edney, one of the lions at the heart of our squadron. Budney is a man of extraordinary talent and serious purpose who never lost the ability to laugh at his own foibles.

Sam Holmes, an extraordinary combat pilot who led me in and out of deep shit with grace and style. I'm sorry he never got his MiG.

Chuck Nelson, a quiet, gentle, humble man of ferocious bravery. A good man in any fight. I am especially grateful to him for allowing me to use his firsthand account of his MiG engagement. I am also deeply indebted to him for his permission to include some of the stunning photographs he took in the midst of combat.

Don "Inky" Purdy, a man who has led an extraordinary life, survived more waltzes with Brother Death than most, and whose empathy survived it all. He is a man of many parts. His poetry, art, whimsy, and sense of the ridiculous are unerring. I thank him for allowing me to use some of his writings, and for applying both his eye for detail and his encyclopedic knowledge of all things nautical, naval, aerial, and digital to proofing multiple manuscripts. Most of all, I thank him for being my friend even after decades of my neglect.

Jim "YDK" Waldron, whose extraordinary memory and uncanny ability to understand us all have been a source of solace, laughter, and recovered memories buried deep under the detritus of my life. I am proud to say he is my friend.

MY FRIENDS, starting with my former partner Michael Addis Beale. Mike has read several drafts from which *Dead Men Flying* has emerged. A former paratrooper, trial lawyer, and sometime rugby player, Mike was also an English major who never forgot what he learned. His expertise, enthusiasm, and encouragement kept me going when I might otherwise have given it up as a bad job.

Rob Kuhn grew up in an Army Air Corps family and served in the Air Force during Vietnam. A skilled lawyer and college dean, Rob has shared many Friday afternoons with me in Paddy Murphy's pub talking, arguing, and laughing about the world in all its craziness. A good friend who made life easier when I needed it.

Dan Robinson, another friend who walked into my life late. A Vietnam veteran, pharmacist, educator, and healer of souls, Dan helped me through the rough times of this century. He has inspired, read, and contributed to much that I have written.

MY EDITORS: Norm Chimsky of Portland, Maine. Norm is an extraordinary talent and has taught me much of what I know about writing for others and has become a friend in the process. Finding him is another proof that it is good to be Irish.

I also wish to thank Katherine Pickett of POP Editorial Services and Mary Eckes for their wide-ranging insights and detailed editing of the manuscript at a critical time.

Roz Duthie for her life-long campaign to keep Larry sane and healthy and for taking my "final," "clean" draft and expending a box full of number two-pencils correcting, suggesting, and asking simple questions with long tails.

Max Edwards at Service Scape who provided a sorely needed copy edit. Thanks Max!

PETER FEY, AUTHOR of *Bloody Sixteen*, the definitive history of CVW-16. He offered both encouragement and advice. His book also proved a valuable resource when I needed a view from outside the world of the Ghost Riders, CVW-16, and USS *Oriskany*. My remembrances of "facts" have benefited from his prodigious research.

I also relied heavily on *The Tonkin Gulf Yacht Club, U.S. Carrier Operations Off Vietnam* by René Francillon, and on Chris Hobson's *Vietnam Air Losses, United States Air Force, Navy and Marine Corps Fixed-Wing Aircraft Losses in Southeast Asia 1961-1973*. Both books helped immensely sorting out dates, places and names.

I AM GRATEFUL TO OK-3 Publishing who brought the book to life, especially its art, development, and editing departments, and to Steve Chiasson and Forrest Audio of Belfast, Maine who brought the audio book to life.

LINDLEE, my wife, friend, confidante, and backstop. We did not meet until the dawn of this century, thirty years after I left the Ghost Riders. She fell in love with who I pretended to be and loves who I am even more. She has blended seamlessly, if slightly incredulously, into the world of geriatric Naval Aviators. A world I could re-enter only because she is there covering my six o'clock. Without her, neither I nor this book would be.

—Mule

ABOUT THE AUTHOR

After leaving the Navy in August 1969, Mike Mullane attended law school. He practiced as a trial lawyer for fifteen years in Phoenix. In 1987 he moved to Portland, Maine and joined the faculty at the University of Maine School of Law. Twelve years later he moved to Fayetteville, Arkansas to join the faculty of the University of Arkansas School of Law. In 2009 he moved to Bangor, Maine to become a dean at Husson University, retiring in 2012. His poem, *Squadron Requiem* was awarded second place in the 2018 National Veterans Poetry Contest.

During all these years he struggled with the aftermath of combat, surrounding himself with dogs, two of whom kept him alive through the darkest years. At the turn of the century, he met Lindlee. With her in his life he began the long struggle to reverse the downward spiral of his life. It was not until 2010, almost forty years after he left combat, that he walked into the Vet Center in Bangor and asked for help.

He is the author of *Medicating with Dogs*, a memoir of his life with Post Traumatic Stress Disorder (PTSD). He and Lindlee married in 2019.

Lindlee, Mike, and his last dog, Rose, live in Encinitas, California, and continue to summer at their camp in Maine.

DEAD MEN FLYING, A REMEMBRANCE is available at Amazon.com, and, beginning in early 2022, at independent booksellers.

You may contact the author by writing to:
OK-3 Publishing at 262 C, #124
Annapolis, MD 21401

or by email at: mwmullane@yahoo.com subject: "DMF."

Also from
Okay-3 Publishing
AVAILABLE AT AMAZON.COM/BOOKS

MEDICATING WITH DOGS
BY MIKE "MULE" MULLANE

Coming home after 212 combat missions, Mike Mullane discovered he had brought the war with him. He found himself battered by guilt, isolation, anger, flashbacks, hypervigilance, nightmares, insomnia, and an exaggerated startle reflex. For the next four decades, he waged a losing battle to fake being normal.

Deep in denial he struggled alone what eventually came to be recognized as Post Traumatic Stress Disorder (PTSD). He tried several forms of self-medication, all of them self-destructive, except the dogs who shared his life. They saved him from depression and the siren call of suicide.

Medicating with Dogs is an honest portrait from inside the mind and soul of someone living with PTSD. It is written for others like him and those in their lives who try to understand and help them.

After leaving the Navy, the author was by turns a student, lawyer, and professor. He and his wife live north of San Diego and in Maine.

PRAISE FOR *MEDICATING WITH DOGS*

<u>**To think I thought His first book was over the top.**</u> An outstanding story of the price so many of our combat veterans pay ,,, and continue to pay for their service to our country. I can think of a dozen people right off the bat, who could benefit from the revelation of the author's experiences. God bless you, Mule!

Marc A. Reider

A chilling yet heart-warming story of courage and recovery. My brother-in-law, ... recommended that I read "Medicating with Dogs". He knew I would be fascinated with the story because of my life passion for rescuing dogs and my experiences with human and animal trauma and recovery. ...

In my work, I have carried out in-depth interviews with soldiers who were deployed in the Iraq war, and I listened to many of their close family members, whose heart-wrenching stories revealed how the person they loved and knew before the war, came home a troubled, distant stranger. ... The most compelling part of their stories for me, however, was the incredible bond they formed with the Iraqi dogs that adopted them and that often saved their lives. Caring for these dogs was often the only sane and loving part of their war. ...

The stories of Meg, Kate, Emma, Bo and all the [author's] other dogs made me laugh. Threads of sanity and open-hearted love were richly woven into the author's life by each precious dog, holding him and this story beautifully together.

I appreciated reading the thoughts and motivations of a pilot who went to war and would have done it all over again, as many of them swear they would do. You see, I was one of the flower children of the 60's who joined peace rallies and carried posters that said "War Is Unhealthy for Children and Other Living Things." I did not - could not - understand at that time how anyone could choose to join up, go to war and drop bombs. Having read this book however, with its frank honesty on so many levels, I totally get it. I now understand and respect the choices these airmen made and the difficulties they dealt with every day. I am truly grateful for their service and I hope people who read this will become more sensitive to what our brave warriors go through.

I'm so grateful that "Mule" Mullane had the guts to share his story, and to shine a light for those still walking in the dark.

CJH

Fighting the black dog of Post Traumatic Stress Disorder (PTSD). Many books cover the subject of PTSD either directly, or indirectly. All of them has a special place in my collection. But Mike " Mule" Mullane's story, Medicating With Dogs, touched me deeply. ... Scarred by war and weighed down by guilt, Mike continued to fight his inner war for the next 50 years.

He still fights that fight to this day.

And when the predatory eyes of the black dog that is PTSD glints in the firelight, his pack of dogs draw close to help him stave off this beast of nightmares and deep depressions. ...

And that's what makes Mule's story unique...the dogs.

He's not the only veteran who benefits from dogs' unadulterated love and loyalty. At times, Mike's story is heartbreaking. Especially when it's time...

Mike's correct when he writes: "When god gave us dogs, he got only one thing wrong—their life expectancy."

It's far too short.

Christoph Lombard

What the hell happened?. Mike "Mule" Mullane tells a compelling first- person account of living the challenges of PTSD. ...

[H]e writes of the many companion dogs woven into his life. All together, a remarkably honest and loving story of survival after war.

Those living with PTSD, and those who know them, will find this book unforgettable.

Anonymous

Where the High Winds Sing
BY DON PURDY

Awarded the Military Writers' Society of America's Gold Medal

A vivid tapestry of flight from the experiences of a naval aviator who lived through the bloody brawl that was the air war over North Vietnam. Its compelling verse soars beyond the limits of prose to draw the reader into a visceral appreciation of the sights, sounds, and passions of aerial combat. The poetry ranges from the pure celebration of flight to the always demanding, sometimes humorous, often tragic drama of wartime carrier operations. But it also presents evocative images of transformative interludes at sea and reflections on the effects of combat, especially the loss of friends.

Don Purdy's poetry is accessible to all. It is reminiscent of an earlier era when such poets as Wilfred Owens, John Gillespie Magee Jr., and Rudyard Kipling elevated "war poetry" to a unique literary genre. Many of the poems are illustrated with the author's own evocative artwork.

Praise for *WHERE THE HIGH WINDS SING*

Few of us are willing to write as Don Purdy has so eloquently done what was in our hearts, minds and gut during the times we flew off a carrier into combat in Vietnam. '... Thank you Don Purdy.

Rod Magner

[A] tight and beautifully written collection of poetry, prose and art. Don Purdy will convince you that you're in the hands of a master. I couldn't put this book down.

I loved this book. ... [T]his is a must-read. ... No matter where you are coming from, do be prepared to be moved. And be ready to own a book you will return to often

Wingwalker

Best description of what it like to come back to a carrier at night and get aboard, living on the edge of one's emotions.

F. Navoff

Don is an accomplished artist, and now has shown that he is a very insightful poet. He adds context to "been there, done that" Bravo Zulu Don!

Mark4

Thank you for the book. It is incredible. "Night Carrier Landing", "Songs of War", and perhaps most of all "The Debt" were gripping, moving, and provide deep insight into the humanity, learning, and thoughtful reflection of what it means to serve. Fear, struggle, pain stand alongside perseverance, duty, and honor. A powerful reflection and ode to comrades not to be missed

David W.

RETURN TO SAIGON
A MEMOIR
BY LARRY DUTHIE

The author ejects from his burning Navy jet onto a karst ridge near Hanoi, and what follows is one of the most implausible and heroic rescues of the air war of North Vietnam. The events immediately following carry him to a secret base in Laos and then to a makeshift hospital in Saigon. The larger story, however, is of a man's complex relationship with Vietnam.

It begins in Saigon, where he completes high school and comes to love the Vietnamese people. When he departs for college, he believes he is done with the country. But becoming a Navy Pilot, is a direct line back.

After he leaves the Navy, Vietnam tightens its grip. Three decades later, he climbs the karst ridge where he and his flight leader were shot down. He learns his guide's brother was one of the gunners—then she leads him deep into a cave. Later that day, seated at a table in her thatched home, he begins to find reconciliation.

PRAISE FOR *RETURN TO SAIGON*

This memoir mirrors a generation's involvement with a war that in some way affected all Americans ... This is a unique book in a crowded field of war stories.

F. Conn

"Return" is the tale of one man's odyssey through the dark night of the soul towards the light of hard-won wisdom. ...Just try not to be moved.

Mike Dillon

Read it! Larry Duthie's memoir Return to Saigon is a love story. ... [T]he author vividly describes ... his lifelong bond with fellow flyers ..., and a deep love of both the landscape and people of Vietnam. ... Return to Saigon represents a major contribution to the literature of America's venture into Southeast Asian affairs in the 1960's. It easily belongs on the bookshelf alongside Caputo's Rumor of War. Read it!

Dick Kirkpatrick

I am not into "war books" but my husband suggested I would like this story in particular. I did! Very much! ... Duthie made me feel as though I was there with him. I recommend this book to everyone!

Cheryl Walker

A gripping and moving story, extremely well told. This book is amazing. Heartbreaking in places. And inspiring.... I didn't want this book to end. I highly recommend it.

Scott Sparling

Great book. Spellbinding.

Jeff Kaufman

A compelling drama that you won't want to end. I could not put this book down and read it in one sitting. ... This could be a great novel, but its entirety is all true and very real. .., Kudos and my highest recommendation for an excellent read.

JH

As someone who flew combat missions off the Hancock in 1972, I found the author captured the action and emotions accurately. Thank you! Great book!

Arne P. Soderman

This is the real thing not just a story, I know I was there for part of it. An incredible true story with such vivid detail. It makes you feel like you are there. ... It will make you cry several times.

Jelloman

Well Written Perhaps, along with "With the Old Breed" among the best personal combat memoirs I've read.

Robert Merrell

Awesome. Outstanding! Surprising! In depth. Could not put it down.

Thomas Brown

Wonderfully written book that puts you in the pilot seat. Return to Saigon is one of the finest air combat books I've read. ... [P]rovides insight and context not found elsewhere. Great writing. A real page turner.

Phillip Warman

A gripping and honest window into the world of a Vietnam naval combat aviator.

Smedley Freeberger

Fighter Pilot Panache & Deep Humility Duthie presents a remarkable view of his evolution from no-account teenager to cocky fighter pilot to deeply thoughtful human. ... in an exciting and sometimes almost heart breaking way and leaves one understanding how good life is.

Education John

What a story! Before I picked up "Return to Saigon" I knew almost nothing about the life of a Navy pilot in Vietnam. ... This book perfectly balances its necessarily compelling human elements ... War makes heroes of regular people, and this memoir shows how that happened to one guy, ... makes clear that he never did, and likely never will, see himself as anyone's hero. But you'll never be able to think of him as anything else.

John Shore

ENDNOTES

1   There were five earlier ships christened *Lexington*, the first being a brigantine commissioned in 1776.

2   What I describe is *so* last century. Now everyone uses the catapult first time, every time. Takeoff and landings are "Look, Ma, no hands." The computer does both. I might be jealous if I had to get her aboard on a dark and stormy night, but those days are behind me now. Besides, being a dinosaur wasn't all bad. We got to do dinosaur things, and were good at them.

3   Cmdr. Albert D. Pollack, USN, was known as "Dave." He flew fighters in the Pacific during World War II. During the Korean War, he was the commanding officer of VF-51, the Screaming Eagles, flying the F-9 Panther from the USS *Valley Forge* (CV-45) against the vastly superior MiG-15s.

4   I have read that subsequent testing revealed that a sharp blow could trigger the ignition sequence on one out of a thousand flares, and that this may have triggered the first flare. But I tell the story as I heard it in 1966 and 1967.

5   The three legs of the United States nuclear deterrence strategy are ballistic missile submarines, land-based ICBMs, and aircraft.

6   More than fifty years later, I will hear an interview of a former Soviet navy officer on National Public Radio. He describes an anticipated nuclear attack on another Soviet naval base by a single American aircraft "that somehow has escaped all of our air defenses." He goes on to describe how the weapon would be put in the harbor so that the blast would throw the water up on "the hill above us where a big wave will roll down to flood" the base. I smiled, thinking, *Wrong base, but that airplane would have been me.*

7   James B. Stockdale was shot down while flying an A-4 in September 1965. Captured, he became an acknowledged leader of POW resistance against their captors. He intentionally sliced his scalp to disfigure himself in an attempt to make him unusable in propaganda films. When the North Vietnamese put a hat on his head, he beat his face with a wooden stool. When discovered with material that

indicated he knew the names of others engaged in the resistance leadership of the POWs, he cut his wrists to commit suicide to prevent himself from revealing these and other secrets he carried in his head. He survived seven and half years of captivity and was awarded the Medal of Honor for his courage and leadership while a POW. Retiring as a vice admiral, he went on to be president of the Citadel. H. Ross Perot picked him to be his vice-presidential candidate in their run for the U.S. presidency in 1994.

8   The spelling of "Alfa strike" is correct in the context of this book. My friend Larry Duthie spent time researching command reports and other historic documents about CVA 16's combat cruises during the Vietnam war. He discovered that somewhere in the unrecorded past, someone in the VA-164 command structure used the "Alfa" spelling in official documents. The spelling was adopted by other squadrons and the Airwing 16 staff. Meanwhile the rest of the Navy and Pentagon failed to get the word and used the "Alpha" spelling.

9   Barton Meyers, *Vietnamese Defense Against Aerial Attack*. Paper presented at the 1996 Vietnam Symposium, Center for the Study of the Vietnam Conflict, Lubbock, Texas, April 19, 1996.

10   The Negritos are an indigenous people thought to have migrated to the Philippine islands from Southeast Asia twenty-five-thousand years ago. Today they are a tiny minority in the Philippines. There is a history of considerable animosity between them and dominant ethnic and cultural majority. The U.S. Navy also employed the Negritos as highly effective security guards at the Cubi Point airfield.

11   The fog of war and the erosion of memory over decades inevitably intrudes. I have told the story of the attempts to rescue Dick Hartman as I heard them at the time, subject to my conversations with Larry Duthie over the intervening years. A more detailed and compelling account of these events can be found in Larry Duthie's memoir, *Return to Saigon*.

While writing this book, I heard that someone thought that Big Mother saw the smoke of a Zuni rocket fired at a flak sight on the valley floor and mistook it for smoke marking Dick Hartman's location. I have found an unattributed statement by a participant that there was smoke from a Zuni rocket impact on a nearby karst that may have led the crew of Big Mother 67 to believe they were on the wrong karst. I read an account by Lt. J.M. (Bud) Watson, an A-1 pilot from VA-152, that says a cluster bomb dropped on the valley floor to suppress a flak site failed to open and left a cloud of white smoke, which the Big Mother crew mistook for the smoke of a Zuni Bud Edney fired to mark Hartman's location on the karst.

Watson also states that a Clementine was inbound to attempt to rescue Hartman after Big Mother was lost when the mission was aborted due to the risk. Watson's account can be found online at http://lfeldhaus.tripod.com/cmdrjackfeldhaususn/id3.html. (Accessed October 23, 2020.)

I think none of these other versions are likely. Bud Edney had eyes on Dick Hartman before Big Mother arrived. Dennis Peterson, the Big Mother's pilot, was in radio contact with Bud. He knew Hartman was on that karst, not the valley floor. As Big Mother flew down the Karst, Bud told him he had just overflown Hartman. Under these circumstances, I find it hard to conclude Peterson left the ridge because he thought Hartman was on the valley floor or another karst ridge. I also think it is unlikely that Bud Edney would have used a Zuni rocket to mark Hartman's position when he told Hartman to "pop smoke" as Big Mother approached.

Their natural reaction to being told they had just overflown the downed pilot, would be to instantly circle back in their standard right-hand orbit.

I have no doubt that there was a lot of ordnance going off on the valley floor, anyone of which might have been seized upon in the chaos of the moment as an explanation of why the helo came off the karst.

Of course, we will never know what Dennis Peterson and his crew knew, saw, or thought.

Whatever happened, nothing diminishes the enormity of their courage and sacrifice. Every man who flew in the Big Mothers, Clementines, and Jolly Greens is a hero in every sense of the word.

12   Dick Hartman was not the only American POW to "die while in captivity." North Vietnam ratified the Geneva Convention in 1957. But it refused to treat the American prisoners as prisoners of war, claiming they were political criminals. Torture, malnutrition, denial of medical treatment, and other abuses were ubiquitous.

The United States government has determined that six-hundred-eighty-seven prisoners were returned by North Vietnam, and that sixty-two POWs died during captivity. This is a loss rate of just under 9.02 percent. Excluding the POWs, Americans who served in Vietnam had a loss rate of 2.15 percent, including those killed in operational accidents. (I am aware there are sources stating that more POWs died while held prisoner, but find the government study more persuasive.)

13   See "Donald Vance Davis," Arlington National Cemetery website, http://www.arlingtoncemetery.net/dvdavis.htm (accessed February 12, 2019). The remarks accompanying this entry state that pilots were not allowed to attack SAM sites prior to the 1967 cruise. This is not accurate. The SAM sites were first hit on October 17, 1965, and never went off the target list. Search "Iron Hand" at https://www.nationalmuseum.af.mil, National Museum of the United States Air Force (accessed May 1, 2020).

14   The Hukbalahap or Huk bo ng Bayan Laban sa Hapon (People's Army Against the Japanese) was a communist guerilla force that resisted the Japanese occupation. The Philippine people achieved independence in 1946. Some of the former Huk soldiers rose against the new government. The rebellion ended in 1954.

15   Dave is now a noted motivational speaker and author of *The Ways We Choose: Lessons for Life from a POW's Experience.*

16   When researching this book, I stumbled across a blog post by June Collins. See Woodrow Wilson Knapp (Lt. J. G.), *Jodi's Antiques Plus*, July 15, 2018, https://www.jodisantiquesplus.com/2018/07/15/ (accessed July 2, 2020).

Ms. Collins says she met "Woodrow Wilson Knapp" and had dinner at the Otani Hotel. YDK remembers meeting her with Woody over dinner at the Sanno Club, which was our squadron's unofficial HQ in Tokyo. She accurately relates other facts about Woody that makes it a certainty her Woody Knapp is our Woody Knapp. This section is based on their mutual recollections. Although no one in the squadron that I have spoken with was aware of his proposal, it seems to fit.

17   Photocopies of the telegram are available at the Library of Congress.

18   Peter Fey reports in *Bloody Sixteen: USS Oriskany and Air Wing 16 during the Vietnam War* that the keel pin on the F-8 failed and that it had not been replaced after 500 catapult launches as required by the maintenance specifications. Ed's launch was the 505th catapult launch for that keel pin. Accidents usually have more than one cause, so we may both be right. Fey also says that this accident happened on the first cat shot of the launch. My memory is that I was maybe the third or fourth A-4 off that catapult, and that Ed was next off behind me. I believe he was the first F-8 to launch off that catapult.

19   This and the following quotations are from an undated note from Chuck Nelson to the author received in early November 2018. Used with permission.

20   This happens almost twenty years before an exaggerated version of the incident is incorporated into the 1986 movie *Top Gun*.

21   See VA-153 Blue Tail Flies Attack Squadron U.S. Navy Skyhawk Corsair (seaforces.org) (accessed February 10, 2021).

22   See Peter Fey, *The Effects of Leadership on Carrier Air Wing Sixteen's Loss Rates During Operation Rolling Thunder, 1965-1968*, *https://apps.dtic.mil/sti/citations/ADA451820 (accessed 12/08/2020;* and the Wikipedia article about USS *Oriskany* (Return to Service) https://en.wikipedia.org/wiki/USS_Oriskany_(CV-34)#Return_to_service (accessed 12/08/2020).

Made in the USA
Middletown, DE
10 May 2022

65597294R00243